24/0   NOV 1 2 2001

923.142
M39w

W9-DCU-869

Mary Queen of Scots

Susan Watkins

photographs by Mark Fiennes

Mary Queen of Scots

With 194 illustrations in color

ELISHA D. SMITH PUBLIC LIBRARY
MENASHA, WISCONSIN

Thames & Hudson

**For Earl Jaeck, my father,
who filled my young imagination with
the mythical adventures of Achilles,
with love.**

Endpapers Cushion cover, probably worked by Mary Queen
of Scots, with the Scottish thistle, the English rose and the white
lily of France. Hardwick Hall, Derbyshire.
Page 1 Tapestry, probably worked by the Queen of Scots,
showing a marigold turning towards the sun, and her motto
'Non inferiora secutus' ('Not following lower things'). From
Oxburgh Hall, Norfolk, on loan from the Victoria and Albert
Museum, London.
Frontispiece Portrait of Mary Queen of Scots, detail from
the Curle Monument, *c.* 1620, Church of St Andrew, Antwerp.
Opposite *Mary Queen of Scots and David Rizzio*, by John Rogers
Herbert, 1830s. It appears to be a copy of *La Musique* by Jean-
Louis Ducis, exhibited at the Paris Salon in 1822, and now in
the Musée Municipal, Limoges.

The photographs on the pages below are by Mark Fiennes:
6 & 10, 8, 11, 12, 13, 14–15, 17, 18, 19, 22–23, 31, 32 (above),
33 (right) 34, 53, 55, 56, 57, 58–59, 60, 62 (right), 64, 65, 66, 67, 71
(right), 72–73, 74–75, 78, 90, 92, 93, 96, 109, 111, 112, 113, 114–15,
130, 132, 133, 134–35, 136, 139, 150–51, 154–55, 156, 158, 160
(background), 162, 163, 168, 174, 180 (foreground), 194 (background), 203, 204–5 (background).
All other illustration credits can be found on page 221.

Any copy of this book issued by the publisher as a paperback
is sold subject to the condition that it shall not by way of trade
or otherwise be lent, resold, hired out or otherwise circulated
without the publisher's prior consent in any form of binding
or cover other than that in which it is published and without
a similar condition including these words being imposed on
a subsequent purchaser.

© 2001 Susan Watkins

First published in hardcover in the United States of America in
2001 by Thames & Hudson Inc., 500 Fifth Avenue, New York,
New York 10110

Library of Congress Catalog Card Number 00-107615
ISBN 0-500-51038-5

All Rights Reserved. No part of this publication may be
reproduced or transmitted in any form or by any means, electronic
or mechanical, including photocopy, recording or any other
information storage and retrieval system, without prior permission
in writing from the publisher.

Printed and bound in Singapore by Star Standard Industries

Contents

Above and right Details from the *Double Portrait of James V and Mary of Guise*, artist unknown. In 1538 King James V of Scotland married a Frenchwoman, the widowed Duchess of Longueville, Mary of Guise. She was descended from the Princes of Anjou and King Louis IX of France. This portrait (a copy of the marriage portrait at Hardwick Hall, Derbyshire, *c.* 1540) was commissioned by Lord Bute in 1895, and hangs in the palace of Falkland.

1

Child Queen, Daughter of the Auld Alliance

'I assure your Majesty, it is as goodly a child as I have seen...and as like to live.'
Sir Ralph Sadler, English envoy to Scotland, reporting on the infant Queen of Scots, March 1543.

On 7 August 1548 a convoy of royal galleys set sail for France from Dumbarton on Scotland's west coast. The flagship contained a precious cargo – five-year-old Mary Stewart, Queen of Scots – accompanied by an entourage of playmates and protectors. As her craft reached open sea, the winds became 'wondrously wild' causing seasickness in Mary's companions, though the little Queen herself reportedly fared better and was well enough to poke fun at the others' discomfort. Yet the turbulence increased, and thrashed the vessel with wind and waves of such ferocity that one night, 'ten leagues from the Cape of Cornwall', the rudder of Mary's galley was broken. Fortunately, and much to the relief of the noble company on board, crewmen managed to replace the rudder, and seven days after her departure from Scotland the Queen of Scots at last safely disembarked on French soil.

But the torments at sea had been as nothing compared to the ravages of Scotland's lowlands, where English armies had put 'man, woman and child to fire and sword'. English soldiers – on Henry VIII's orders – relentlessly burned, looted and slaughtered their way through towns, villages and farmland, leaving behind a spectacle of such devastation that it was to remain 'a perpetual memory' like 'the vengeance of God' – events set in train by the birth of Mary Stewart on 8 December 1542.

At the time of her birth, Mary's father, King James V, was at Falkland Palace where he had retreated to wallow in melancholy over the humiliating defeat of his army and kinsmen against the English at Solway Moss. James and his wife had recently suffered the deaths of their two young sons, and it was hoped that the news

Above This painted genealogy of *c.* 1603 (Long Gallery at Parham, West Sussex) traces the Tudor ancestry of Mary Queen of Scots. She appears in the second row above her parents and those of her second husband Darnley. In the fourth row down is Margaret Tudor, sister of Henry VIII, wife of James IV of Scotland and grandmother of both Mary and Darnley.

of the birth of another child would rouse James from his anguish. But, learning that the new heir to Scotland's throne was a girl, he is said to have sighed, 'It cam wi a lass, and it'll gang wi a lass,' referring to the daughter of Robert the Bruce through whom the throne had come to the Stewarts in 1371. The Protestant reformer John Knox reported the King's words as: 'The Devil go with it! It will end as it began. It came from a woman and it will end in a woman.' James then lapsed into delirium, completely overcome both physically and mentally, and died six days later. Princess Mary, just six days old, became Mary Queen of Scots.

Henry VIII soon learned of James's death and he immediately determined to secure a peaceful union with Scotland, bringing it under his control through a marriage between his son Edward, then aged five, and the infant Queen of Scots. Children were commonly used as pawns in the royal game of marriage alliances, and there was a precedent for Henry's plan – his sister Margaret Tudor had married James IV of Scotland in 1503, resulting in a temporary peace between two countries that had long been traditional foes. Scottish antagonism towards the English was perhaps best expressed in 1320 in the valiant Declaration of Arbroath: 'For so long as there shall but one hundred of us remain alive, we will never give consent to subject ourselves to the dominion of England.'

Early Scottish historians reinforced nationalism by tracing the line of Scottish rulers back to Fergus MacFerquhard (330 BC), who was descended from Gathelus, a Greek prince, and Scota, daughter of an Egyptian Pharaoh. During the ensuing millennia, the historians claimed, Scotland had never been conquered, not even by the Romans. The apogee of these glory years, the golden age of Scottish 'fredome' from 1058 to 1296, was followed by the 'dark ages' of war with England when Scottish might alone could no longer repel English invasion. Thus in 1296 Scotland ratified an alliance with France, establishing a defensive and offensive league against England. The alliance, which came to be known as the 'Auld Alliance', was maintained intermittently, and in various forms, for the next 250 years; and the interrelations between Scotland, England and France were to play a vital part in the life and lifestyle of Mary Stewart.

Below *Henry VIII*, artist unknown, *c.* 1542. Henry initially sought a peaceful union with Scotland through the betrothal of the infant Queen of Scots to his five-year-old son Prince Edward.

With the marriage of Margaret Tudor of England and James IV of Scotland – the 'Union of the Thistle and the Rose' – a pro-English party entered the Stewart court. In 1512, however, the Franco-Scottish alliance was reconfirmed; France was at war with England, obliging Mary's grandfather, James IV, to distract Henry VIII's forces by invasion. The result was the disastrous Battle of Flodden in 1513, in which the King and nine thousand of Scotland's best men were slain. Scottish families escaping the loss of a father, son or brother were few; Flodden became, and to a certain extent still is, a scar on the nation's consciousness. Following Flodden, warfare along the border with England continued, but so did rivalry between the French and English factions in Scotland – an alliance that required a weak country to provide military support for its stronger, wealthier ally was losing appeal.

There was, however, another effect of the centuries of contact with France – the impact on Scots learning and culture. Monastic links with France in the twelfth century had created an important network of international exchanges from which Scotland gradually developed a broader political outlook. The Auld Alliance was a product of this wider view: Scotland was now part of Europe, politically as well as ecclesiastically, opening up communication and contact with a country that was one of the great centres of art and scholarship. Generation after generation of Scots went to France, especially to Paris, for training in law, medicine and theology. English universities rarely welcomed scholars from Scotland, and the founders and lecturers of Scottish universities, established from 1411, inevitably attended continental universities, particularly in France. Even after the foundation of their own universities, Scots continued to be educated in France, where they were also benefice-holders and ministers, and Scottish philosophical works were printed on French presses.

The French military also attracted Scotsmen. In the cathedral of Ste Croix in Orléans is the tomb

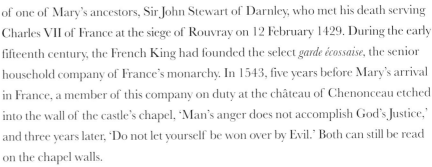

Below *Double Portrait of James V and Mary of Guise.* On 8 December 1542 Mary of Guise bore James a daughter, Mary Stewart.
Opposite One of the twelve oak panels depicting scenes from the life of Christ, Flemish, *c.* 1520, formerly in Bishop Lamb's chapel in Leith, where Mary of Guise worshipped, now at Traquair House.
Page 12 Linlithgow Palace, Mary's birthplace. The fountain with its early Renaissance elements was added by James V, *c.* 1538; behind it are three niches formerly holding statues of the three Estates – Clergy, Lords and Commons.
Page 13 Representations of James V's Orders over Linlithgow's main entrance, and St Michael's church beside the palace.

of one of Mary's ancestors, Sir John Stewart of Darnley, who met his death serving Charles VII of France at the siege of Rouvray on 12 February 1429. During the early fifteenth century, the French King had founded the select *garde écossaise*, the senior household company of France's monarchy. In 1543, five years before Mary's arrival in France, a member of this company on duty at the château of Chenonceau etched into the wall of the castle's chapel, 'Man's anger does not accomplish God's Justice,' and three years later, 'Do not let yourself be won over by Evil.' Both can still be read on the chapel walls.

During the epoch of the Auld Alliance, scholars, soldiers and other visitors to France took back to Scotland countless works of art and literature: paintings, furniture, manuscripts, books, and objects in silver, gold and enamelwork. They also imported language – a number of Scots words have been adopted from the French, and Scottish court verse was influenced by French writers. There were also translations of significant French works into Scots, including, in the fifteenth century, the anonymous *Lancelot of the Laik*, based on parts of the earlier French tale of chivalry, *Lancelot du Lac*. Similarly, the alliance saw French artists and craftsmen finding employment in Scotland in the construction of churches, public buildings and the residences of nobles. Mary's father and grandfather had engaged in a programme of royal building that was unparalleled in Scottish architectural history. They created Renaissance wonders from medieval castles; French masons were instrumental in the design and construction of these new palaces.

During the minority of Mary's father, James V (he was seventeen months old when his father was killed), the connection with France was again formally renewed. John, Duke of Albany, the French-born heir-presumptive, acted as governor of Scotland from 1515 to 1524; he negotiated the Treaty of Rouen in 1517 providing mutual military support against England, along with the prospect of a French bride for James V. After Albany, Archibald Douglas, 6th Earl of Angus, became James's guardian – he had married Margaret Tudor, widow of James IV, and was pro-English. But he virtually imprisoned the young King, while distributing important offices among members of the Douglas family. James eventually escaped and assumed his kingship in 1528. The Douglases were forced to flee into exile in England; this, too, would ultimately affect the life of Mary Stewart.

In the following years, James V was to enter into a series of marriage negotiations, playing one country against another. The triangle of England, Scotland and France had become squared by the Holy Roman

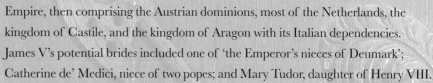

Empire, then comprising the Austrian dominions, most of the Netherlands, the kingdom of Castile, and the kingdom of Aragon with its Italian dependencies. James V's potential brides included one of 'the Emperor's nieces of Denmark'; Catherine de' Medici, niece of two popes; and Mary Tudor, daughter of Henry VIII.

While James negotiated for the hand of the Danish princess, Emperor Charles V sent military support to Scotland and bestowed upon James the coveted Order of the Golden Fleece, traditionally awarded for chivalry. James was later to claim that Charles V also promised to recognize him as heir-presumptive to the throne of England. Not to be outdone, Henry VIII in 1535 conferred on James England's highest order of chivalry, the Order of the Garter, though there was a contingency – Henry did not want the Scottish King to form a marriage alliance with the Empire. Nor did the French King, Francis I, who in 1536 invested James with another enamelled gold collar, his nation's highest honour, the Order of St Michael.

Eventually, in 1537 James married Madeleine of Valois, a daughter of Francis I, but she died six months after the wedding. Less than a year later he married the recently widowed Duchess of Longueville, Mary of Guise. Although not a royal princess, her lineage was nonetheless impressive. Her father, Claude Duke of Guise, had commanded France's armies in great victories, and her mother, Antoinette of Bourbon, Duchess of Guise, was descended from Louis IX (St Louis). Furthermore, her uncle, John, Cardinal of Lorraine, enjoyed great favour at the Valois court, and may have urged Francis I to choose her as James's bride. Mary of Guise was noted for her stature, being nearly six feet tall, and for a certain elegance and grace of manner. She also came with an attractive dowry, and, having given birth to two sons (though the youngest died within a few months), had proved herself capable of bearing a male heir to Scotland's throne. The couple were married by proxy on 9 May 1538 at Mary's castle of Châteaudun. Early in June, the bride made an emotional departure from her young son and members of her family. A second wedding, this time with James present, took place at St Andrews in Scotland.

The twenty-two-year-old Mary of Guise brought with her a new tide of French imports. She had been warned that Scotland was a barbarous country, and accordingly arranged for a French tailor and a constant supply of cloth to make the journey from France. And the Scots it seems came to admire Mary's French flair, for the Earl of Lennox's sisters had kirtles (petticoats) lined with 'French' red, and each received a gift of a 'French' hat, while the king himself ordered a saddle of the 'French' fashion. Mary's servants, like their mistress, wore garments made of 'French' and 'Paris' black, contrasting wonderfully with the brilliance of the crimson and yellow liveries worn by James's servants – in keeping with the royal

standard, 'a ruddy lion ramping in his field of treassured gold' – and with the King's magnificence dressed in crimson silk, purple satin, white or crimson velvet, or cloth of gold. The Stewart court was increased by the addition of the Queen's ladies-in-waiting, her secretary who assisted her in maintaining correspondence with France, her almoner, a dwarf, a fool, her master of household, and two French physicians. The ships that brought Mary to Scotland had also brought essential items, such as the Queen's great bed and her horse. Later came the luxuries: a carriage, gold 'works', dried fruits, cuttings from plum and pear trees, and 'a hundred cases of wine…from the Bordelais country where the wines are very good'. Her administration of the Guise properties and her husband's ducal estates, had made her a practical manager, shown by her sending for miners from Lorraine to quarry for gold in the hills of western Scotland, and for French masons to assist on the improvements of the royal palaces.

It was at Linlithgow Palace in a richly panelled and gilded room overlooking Linlithgow Loch that Mary of Guise gave birth to Mary Stewart on 8 December 1542. The palace with its 'princlie' comforts was favoured by Mary of Guise, and it was here that the young Queen of Scots was to spend the first seven months of her life. Situated to the west of Edinburgh, the distance from the capital to Linlithgow could be accomplished in a few hours on horseback. Mary's room in the north-west tower of the Palace (where Margaret Tudor had given birth to James V) was undoubtedly kept snug with a coal fire, while a team of women attended her. A Scotswoman was Mary's wetnurse, other ladies bathed and changed her, and still others rocked the royal cradle. From her cradle Mary could have gazed at the vaulted ceiling, coloured in blues and reds, with unicorns depicted on the ceiling bosses.

Rumours that Mary Stewart had been born prematurely and was therefore frail – even dead – were dismissed with some indignation by Mary of Guise. In March 1543 she ordered her daughter's swaddlings removed and the three-month-old made naked before Sir Ralph Sadler, envoy from England. The Dowager Queen was anxious that the new monarch's healthy plumpness be widely known, and Henry VIII was worried about his dynastic plans until Sadler was able to report that 'it is as goodly a child as I have seen of her age…and as like to live.'

Linlithgow had been transformed into a grand Italianate palace, begun in 1424 with James I's reconstruction of existing buildings,

and continuing under James III and James IV, Mary's grandfather. James IV's most spectacular addition was to the east front, creating a ceremonial approach to the quadrangular courtyard complex; he also built a chapel and a new west wing, linked to the Great Hall (which he had also improved) by a multi-tiered gallery. Mary's father, James V, moved the main entrance to the south, and beyond this he built an outer gate on which he set his laurels: the Golden Fleece of the Holy Roman Empire, the St Michael of France and the Garter of England. To these he added the Collar of Thistles, associated with the Royal Arms of Scotland since about 1502. Window surrounds were painted orange, and exterior walls tinted in various hues. But the centrepiece of James V's improvements to Linlithgow Palace was an elaborate courtyard fountain incorporating Renaissance elements in the treatment of its figures and medallion heads. The fountain, fed by a spring, supplied the court with fresh water; during festive celebrations it flowed with wine.

The date of Mary's christening is unknown, although it is recorded that the Lord Treasurer authorized payment of 54 shillings for white taffeta from Genoa 'to the Princess's baptism', which probably took place in the nearby Church of St Michael. A small door on the palace side of the church had been added for the court's convenience, and it was through this that Mary would have been carried. The font used to baptize the royal infant was destroyed by the Protestant Lords of the Congregation in 1559.

In July 1543 Cardinal David Beaton, then leader of the pro-French party in Scotland, assembled about seven thousand men to escort the young Queen and her mother from Linlithgow to Stirling Castle. It was feared that while the child remained at Linlithgow, a relatively unfortified palace, she was at risk of falling into English control. On 1 July 1543 the Treaties of Greenwich had been drawn up, providing for the marriage of 'the illustrious and noble Prince Edward, eldest son and nearest apparent and undoubted heir of the unconquered and most potent Prince, Henry VIII' to 'Mary, Queen of Scotland, now also a minor and not yet out of her first year'. There were pledges for peace and for Scotland's continued independence. Mary was to remain in Scotland until her tenth birthday, when she would be married by proxy and would move to England. But Henry demanded that the child be immediately given into his keeping, to be raised and educated in the Tudor court, 'a right high and right great inconvenience to the realm of Scotland'. England had entered into an alliance with Emperor Charles V against France, and the Scottish pro-French faction stood to weaken Henry VIII's concentration upon a continental campaign. Henry, therefore, impatiently insisted that some of the country's strategic castles be turned over to English occupation, and that all ties between Scotland and

Background Stirling Castle from the south west. Built atop a great ramp of volcanic rock, the castle is situated at the junction of several principal routes across Scotland – at the very heart of the country – a place, according to Scottish tradition, that had once been the domain of King Arthur and his Knights of the Round Table. It was to this stronghold that Mary was brought as a baby in 1543, and she lived at Stirling Castle for most of the next four-and-a-half years.

France be broken. Public outcry against the King of England's stance had been anticipated: 'There is not so little a boy but he will hurl stones against it, the wives will come out with their distaffs and the commons universally will rather die.' Stirling Castle, built atop a towering ramp of volcanic rock, would provide a more secure stronghold for Scotland's young Queen.

The move necessitated twenty-four horse-carts to transport Mary of Guise's bedding and that of her ladies-in-waiting. Men were appointed to carry the royal cradle, and others to stow the royal portraits, while the contents of the larder, wine cellars, bakehouse and an array of kitchen equipment were piled onto a further nineteen carts. On 27 July 1543, when all the furnishings were packed and ready, Mary of Guise and her seven-month-old baby – reportedly suffering with 'the breeding of teeth' – joined the cavalcade departing Linlithgow. With the exception of brief forays to avoid the encroaching grasp of English armies, Stirling Castle was to be the home of the young Queen of Scots for the next four-and-a-half years.

Henry's overlording tactics had begun even while the Treaties of Greenwich were being negotiated when he had seized Scottish ships. This, along with his other aggressions, including an offer to put five thousand English troops into Scotland, turned even some of Scotland's most powerful, pro-English nobles against the English marriage; and the mood of the country demanded a gesture that would unequivocally convey Scotland's intention to remain an independent nation with its own lawfully ordained monarch. Thus, on 9 September 1543 Mary Queen of Scots was crowned in the Chapel Royal at Stirling Castle. Sir Ralph Sadler, undoubtedly familiar with the lavish regalia of Tudor coronations, reported that the Scottish ceremony was conducted 'with such solemnitie as they do use in this country,

which is not very costlie'. Yet the imperial-style crown, made in France and used for Mary's coronation, was sumptuous. The crown was borne by James Hamilton, 2nd Earl of Arran, the sceptre by Matthew Stewart, Earl of Lennox, and the sword of state by Archibald Campbell, 4th Earl of Argyll; a vacillating trio of attendants. Arran, appointed Lord Governor, ruled Scotland in the minor Queen's stead, while taking every opportunity to add to his wealth. He was also head of the powerful house of Hamilton and heir to the throne in the event of Mary's untimely death. Mary of Guise described Arran as 'a simple and the most inconstant man in the world, for whatsoever he determineth today, he changeth tomorrow'. Lennox, Arran's eternal enemy, also had a claim to the throne, though immediately after the coronation he changed allegiance and sought his fortune in England. He even went so far in the service of his new sovereign as to make military raids into Scotland with the aim of abducting the young Queen. Argyll, a weak, indecisive man, though pro-French at the time of the coronation, later found new 'boldness' and became an ardent Protestant. 'I say poor Scotland!', wrote papal legate Marco Grimani, 'because it is so divided and disturbed that if God does not show his hand and inspire these nobles to unite together, public and private ruin is clearly foreseen.' It was a fair assessment of Mary's kingdom. Even the very date of her coronation – the thirtieth anniversary of the Battle of Flodden – must have added foreboding to the proceedings.

Above The crown used for the coronation of the nine-month-old Queen of Scots, although the bonnet was originally purple. This imperial-style crown had been completely remade in 1540; the circlet at the base was made from Scottish gold. The crown was set with 43 gems and 68 freshwater pearls from Scotland, incorporating a new orb and cross that had been specially purchased in France. James V had worn it for the coronation of his consort, Mary of Guise.

But the gloomy affairs of state would have been of little consequence to a young child, and there was so much to delight at Stirling. Court life, though no longer lavish, was, it seems, carried on with a certain degree of gaiety following the death of James V, 'sometimes in dancing, sometimes in shooting…and jousting and running of great horse at the lists with all the other games'. And there was music – the royal household and Chapels Royal resounded with fyne music' played on fiddles, harps, viols, citterns, recorders, tabors, rebecs, shawms and wind instruments. There were organists and singers, and a family group of 'Italian Minstrils', who were employed from 1502 until 1548 – the year of young Mary's departure for France. The arrival in Scotland of Mary of Guise in 1538 coincided approximately with the French import of gently polyphonic *chanson*. The previous year, the French poet, Pierre de Ronsard, for a time James V's page, brought fresh enthusiasm to another of the court's pleasures – poetry.

At Stirling, Mary Stewart was growing tall for her age, and showed a lively inquisitive nature. Castle folklore maintains that masons had been ordered to cut look-out windows into the walls of the parapet walk, for even a tall three- or four-year-old would have been unable to stretch above the parapet to view the panorama of marshland, plains and great hills – the Ochils to the north-east, Gargunnock to the west and Touch Hills to the south-west. West of the Ochils the tributaries of the River Teith flowed down to join the Forth.

Another of Mary's recreations was, allegedly, football. An aged ball, said to be 'Queen Mary's football', now takes pride of place in Stirling's Smith Art Gallery and Museum. Of sixteenth-century origins, according to experts, the ball was discovered in the rafters of the palace's ceiling during renovations in the 1980s.

James had fathered several illegitimate children (at least nine) and Mary's playmates at Stirling included three of her half-brothers: Robert Stewart who was ten when Mary first arrived there, John Stewart aged twelve, and James Stewart, already in his teens. Her half-sister, Jean Stewart was also a regular companion and was to become one of Mary's closest friends. A few years older than Mary, Jean shared in the love of Mary of Guise who cared for her as if she had been her own daughter. All four later accompanied Mary on the hazardous voyage to France.

James V's new quadrangular palace at Stirling was constructed at the summit of the castle within the existing battlements. Its ostentatious design was probably the work of a Frenchman, begun around 1538 and not quite completed at the time of the King's death in 1542; Mary of Guise had received the palace as part of her marriage jointure. The palace's astonishing exterior is a mixture of medieval and classical details: raised and recessed surfaces demarcated by horizontal string courses;

Below James V's ambitious project at Stirling – a quadrangular palace constructed at the summit of the castle's existing battlements. Perhaps the finest palace in Scotland, it is laid out around a central courtyard with a suite of rooms for the King and another for the Queen, involving a series of small rooms, an opulent hall where the monarch received special guests and a bedchamber. The exterior, probably of French design, combines medieval and classical details, with statues set on columns within arches. **Right** One of the statues at Stirling represents King James V himself.

arches containing statues set upon two-stage columns or pedestals beneath a crenellated parapet. On one wall St Michael spears a dragon, perhaps conferring added celebrity upon the palace's builder, a recipient of the Order of St Michael. On the opposite corner of the same wall is a statue of James V himself, with his right hand extended towards the saint. Between them are the now weathered planetary deities – Jupiter, Sol, Venus – who, with a laughing youth gazing heavenwards, appear conciliatory and welcoming; the main entrance to the palace was on this side. On all three sides of the palace are winged cherubs, and below are corbel heads portraying likenesses of such individuality that they are thought to have been members of James's court. One noble lady has a salamander on her shoulder, which some have claimed she is suckling. The salamander was the personal device of Francis I (*'Nutrisco et extingo,'* 'I feed and extinguish it'), ever present in the royal palaces that James had visited during a six-month stay in France in 1537. The south side of the palace looked towards England – the old enemy – and here statues of men-at-arms guard the roof's parapet, wielding sword, bow and arquebus, and poised for action.

Left A hermaphrodite devil on an exterior wall of James V's palace at Stirling. On the same wall a semi-nude girl tosses a ball of flowers above a toga-clad figure, while smiling pages bearing sun symbols attend the central figure – the devil. Englishmen at this time associated 'the devil at noontide' with sudden violence. Here as part of a composition dedicated to the sun and accompanied by armed figures on the palace's parapet, the devil sends out an unmistakable threat to England – Scotland's traditional enemy.

Opposite An oak roundel reproduced from one of the original 56 'Stirling Heads' on the ceiling of the Inner Hall, where honoured guests were received. Some of the heads represented historical, mythical or Biblical characters; others may have been members of the court.

Inside the palace, the former richness of the royal lodgings is suggested by one J. Macky whose observations were recorded in 1723:

In this Palace is one Apartment...the noblest I ever saw in Europe, both for Height, Length and Breadth: And for the Fineness of the Carv'd Work, in Wainscot and on the Ceiling, there's no Apartment in Windsor or Hampton Court that comes near it.... And in the Roof of the Presence-Chamber, are carv'd the Heads of the Kings and Queens of Scotland.

To this add colour, gilding, tapestries and stone fireplaces of French design. The 'heads' decorating the ceiling were mostly head-and-shoulder figures carved into oak roundels which originally amounted to fifty-six characters (now thirty-six) in various costumes and postures. One may have portrayed Margaret Tudor, others possibly the French Queens and ladies of the court, and there are two dancing putti, a court jester and a gentleman with laughter lines creasing the corners of his eyes.

An extra delight at Stirling, at least for the children, may have been the denizen of the palace's courtyard, sometimes referred to as the Lion's Den. A lion is known to have been purchased for James V in Flanders in 1537, and the creature may have been housed in the courtyard.

Stirling's royal garden was probably begun by James IV in 1501. It featured the King's Knot, which in the seventeenth century was expanded into a Renaissance-style parterre. Two centuries earlier, writer William of Worcester's romantic notion that Stirling was the home of the Order of the Knights of the Round Table was perpetuated by later historians who suggested that the royal garden was the authentic setting for King Arthur and his Round Table. James IV, a lover of chivalry, chose as a showpiece for the tournament he held in Edinburgh in 1508 a 'counterfuting of the round tabill of King Arthour'. In the same year poet Walter Kennedy referred to a hill overlooking the tournament as 'Arthuris Sete', and in 1530 Sir David Lyndsay, court poet to James V, referred to 'fair' Stirling with its high towers, 'Chapell Royall, Park, and tabyll rounde'.

But even an enchanted castle could not dispel for long the horrors being committed by England's armies. By December 1543 Henry VIII's confidence was such that he still refused to release the captured Scottish ships and failed to ratify the Treaties of Greenwich within the agreed two-month time limit. On 15 December the 'auld bands' between Scotland and France, 'so long and religiously kept', were once more confirmed, and the Scottish parliament repudiated the English betrothal. Francis I renewed his support for Scotland, and French envoys appeared at the Stewart court. Henry's fury now took the form of a programme of unprecedented devastation. In 1544 Edinburgh was burned, 'razed and defaced'. The following year

Above and opposite
Portrait of Edward VI (details),
artist unknown, *c.* 1547.
In 1547, at the age of nine,
Edward became King of
England upon the death of
his father Henry VIII, who
had betrothed Edward to
the infant Queen of Scots,
and had attacked Scotland
when the betrothal was
repudiated. After 1547 the
Rough Wooing continued,
with English forces now
seizing strategic fortresses
in southern Scotland.

the English employed a scorched-earth policy, ruining the autumn harvest so vital
to the Tweed Valley where the abbeys of Melrose, Jedburgh and Dryburgh were also
destroyed along with towns and villages. Later, Haddington, an important town
on the south-east trade route, was sacked and burned, and at the nearby seaport of
Dunbar, the inhabitants were encircled within the town before it was set ablaze. For two
years this chronicle of bloodshed continued; with wry Scottish understatement, it later
became known as the Rough Wooing. But it wasn't all woe for the Scots. In February
1545, at Ancrum Moor near the border town of Jedburgh they managed a rare victory,
and England grieved the loss of eight hundred men. It was only a brief reversal.

As the Rough Wooing proceeded, the Reformation was also advancing in
Scotland and throughout Europe. The Catholic Church in Scotland stood accused
of corruption and greed, and, although measures were being undertaken to correct
many of its abuses, it was now too late to curtail religious unrest. Henry VIII's
Reformation had begun ten years earlier when the Church of England was severed
from the authority of Rome. Protestant ideas and literature were already circulating
Scotland's coastal towns where the new doctrines were received by an ever increasing
audience. Even parliament had displayed a tendency towards religious reform when
in 1543, while negotiating the Treaties of Greenwich with Henry VIII, it authorized
the reading of the Scriptures in the vernacular. For Scottish Protestants Cardinal
Beaton was anathema; as Archbishop of St Andrews he was head of the Catholic
Church in Scotland, and as Chancellor since January 1543, he was also a powerful
political influence during the first administration of Mary's minority. Henry VIII
had approved several plots for the Cardinal's murder, but it was not until Beaton had
ordered the burning of George Wishart for heresy in the spring of 1546 that a plan
for the Cardinal's assassination succeeded. Wishart was a popular Scottish reformer
and his sermons were well attended, though his kindly manner belied the fact that
he was also an English spy. Two months later, in retaliation for Wishart's death,
Cardinal Beaton was stabbed by 'certain Fife gentlemen', and his mutilated body
hung naked from a tower window at St Andrews Castle.

Remarkably, these events were to pave the way for a second betrothal for the
Queen of Scots. On 31 March 1547 Francis I died, and was succeeded as King of
France by his son, Henry II, who appointed his close friend Francis, Duke of Aumale,
and the Duke's brother Charles, Cardinal of Guise, to positions of power. They were
Mary of Guise's brothers and, of course, Mary Stewart's uncles. In June 1545 French
troops had arrived to give the Scots temporary assistance, but since 1543 France
had been more occupied with its own interests. On 30 July 1547, however, under
instructions from Henry II, French forces arrived and recaptured St Andrews from

the Protestant rebels. John Knox, who had begun his career at St Andrews as a preacher of aggressive Protestantism, was taken prisoner and thrown into the French galleys, where he remained clapped in irons and at the mercy of the lash for at least nineteen months.

French aid in 1547 had also succeeded in raising serious support for a French marriage. The idea of marrying the Queen of Scots to a son of France's royal family, the Valois, had been raised as early as September 1543, although Mary of Guise, in touch with every morsel of gossip at the French court, may have considered the possibility earlier. The previous spring all the talk from France had been of Catherine de' Medici, who after ten years of marriage to Henry II, was, to everyone's amazement, pregnant. On 19 January 1544 she had given birth to a son, Francis. The child was said to be '*très vigoureux*', and the royal astrologers pronounced that the precise instant of Francis's birth was '*parfaite*'. Scotland now had a realistic alternative to the English union. By the end of 1544 the Earl of Arran (Governor of Scotland), Cardinal Beaton and Mary of Guise 'promised and made bond to the French ambassador, that the French King shall have the young Queen, to marry where he list…and also that they shall at the spring of the year, send both the young Queen and the old [Mary of Guise, Dowager Queen] into France'. The promise was soon put aside. There were others, Arran had been among them, who sought a marriage within Scotland. Arran's son was a possibility, and even the duplicitous Earl of Lennox, at twenty-six, had been considered as a bridegroom for the infant Queen. But it was to be the power of French armies and munitions, and – ultimately – bribes that won the hand of the young Queen of Scots.

On 28 January 1547 Henry VIII died, and was succeeded by his nine-year-old son, Edward VI. Henry's death did not, however, bring relief to the Scots, and the Rough Wooing continued. If there was a perceptible change in policy, it was that the English now focused on seizing and garrisoning Scotland's principal southern fortresses, attempting to control Scotland from a ring of strategic sites with a large concentration of troops at Haddington. Worse was to come. Led by the Earl of Arran, thirty thousand men from all parts of Scotland gathered at Musselburgh near Edinburgh, and on 10 September 1547, at the Battle of Pinkie Cleugh, ten thousand Scots were killed and a further fifteen hundred taken prisoner. It was another massacre to go down in the annals of Scottish history and in Scots' hearts. There was no longer any doubt, Scotland desperately needed the French – even at the price of handing over their young Queen.

While the Scots were counting their dead near Musselburgh, Mary was whisked away for greater safety to the secluded island Priory of Inchmahome, sixteen miles west of Stirling on the Lake of Menteith. Inchmahome was, and still is, a blissful setting well suited to the pursuit of spiritual perfection. The priory had been founded in 1238 for a community of Augustinian canons, a priestly order known as the Black Canons from the colour of their robes. At Inchmahome the canons followed the *Opus Dei*, a series of seven or eight services starting about half-past one in the morning and continuing through the day. The regular resonance of male voices chanting their psalms and prayers, and the sung Mass enhanced the haven-like atmosphere of

Inchmahome, worlds away from warfare. In the priory's church four-year-old Mary would have seen a tomb effigy of a Stewart knight carved in stone lying with his shield, and the charming double effigy of Walter Stewart, Earl of Menteith, who died in 1295, and his countess, Mary. The couple lie face to face, the countess's left arm tenderly caressing her husband – seven hundred years later she caresses him still.

Although the Queen of Scots was only four years old when she was sent to Inchmahome, and stayed only three weeks, legend claims that it was here that Mary began her studies – Latin, Greek, Italian, history and geography under the tutelage of the island's Commendator. In addition to schoolwork, she is said to have taken up gardening, and embroidery. On the island today Queen Mary's Garden,

Queen Mary's Bower and Queen Mary's Tree all honour the supposed activities of her three-week stay in 1547.

Towards the end of 1547 the Scots agreed to place Scottish strongholds in the hands of the French, and they discussed the young Queen's removal to France. Fifty French captains duly arrived in Scotland in advance of six thousand French soldiers, including mercenaries from Germany, Italy, Switzerland and Holland. In January 1548, Arran signed a contract with Henry II of France in which the Lord Governor agreed to summon the Scottish parliament and obtain their consent to the eventual marriage of the Queen of Scots to the Dauphin Francis. Mary was to depart for France, and Scotland was to hand over strategic castles. In return, Arran received a lucrative French duchy. The following June, French and Scottish troops laid siege to English-occupied Haddington, and on 7 July, in a nunnery outside the town, parliament met and confirmed with France's representatives that 'the ancient bond, confederation and amity' still held. The marriage was now formally agreed, and the five-year-old Queen became betrothed for the second time. The day after the treaty was signed Mary of Guise wrote to her brothers: 'Yesterday there was held here a Parliament of all the Estates, in which each consented to be subject to the said Lord [Henry II], because of the honour he is doing the Queen my daughter in wishing to marry her to his son. I start tomorrow to send her to him.'

In February 1548 Mary had been taken to Dumbarton Castle on Scotland's west coast, and in March, she fell ill with measles, severe enough for there to have been rumours that the young Queen was dead. Calamity! Scotland's rescue from English domination was bound to the life of this young child. Fortunately for all, the crisis passed, and during the spring Mary gained enough strength to allow preparations for her journey to France to go ahead. Indeed, Frenchman Jean de Beaugué found the little girl looking well enough to declare that she was 'one of the most perfect creatures that were ever seen', and 'there was reason to form as high hopes of her as of any princess on the earth'.

Mary of Guise bade her a tearful farewell, and, after some delay awaiting a fair wind, the convoy of galleys weighed anchor and set their course for France. For the young Queen of Scots there awaited the embrace of the family of Guise, obsessed with power and secret agendas, and the family of Valois whose court was to become renowned as one of the most sophisticated – and decadent – in history. John Knox said she had gone 'to the end that in her youth she should drink of that liquor, that should remain with her all her lifetime, for a plague to this realm and for her final destruction'.

Above Mary stayed for three weeks in the secluded Priory of Inchmahome. She was probably lodged in the Prior's living quarters in the west cloister. In this view of the cloister, the church's south wall and the Chapter House are on the left.
Overleaf Dumbarton Castle from John Slezer, *Theatrum Scotiae*, 1693. From here Mary sailed to France on 7 August 1548.

Becoming Queen of France

'We hold and esteem her for what she is, our daughter.'

Henry II of France writing to the Estates of Scotland, October 1548.

Left Detail of a portrait on vellum of Mary and Francis II, artist unknown. This double portrait of the young King and Queen of France comes from the Book of Hours belonging to Catherine de' Medici, now in the Bibliothèque Nationale in Paris. The Dowager Queen Catherine, Francis's mother, had the prayer book rebound to include 22 miniature portraits, including those of 'Francis II and Mary Stewart, Queen of Scotland, his wife'.

On the jagged coastline of northern France, the retreating tide revealed a beach at the foot of a great rock, and Mary Stewart touched her new homeland. She had been brought ashore at Roscoff, a small port near Brest on the coast of Brittany – one of the most perilous coastlines in Europe. From Roscoff the five-year-old Queen and her accompaniment of noblemen, ladies and children travelled four miles along a tidal river to the town of Morlaix. There, in the church of Notre Dame a joyous *Te Deum* was sung, thanking God for his mercy in preserving the Queen of Scots.

Mary stayed two days in Morlaix, lodging at a Dominican convent 'to refresh herself after the fatigue of the voyage', before embarking on the journey 'conducted by short stages' to Saint-Germain-en-Laye near Paris. Henry II wrote to the Estates of Scotland informing them of the Queen's safe arrival, and that, 'We are now causing her to be transported…to the place where our dearly loved son the Dauphin, her husband, is staying.' Their route took them overland to Nantes in the Loire Valley; from there they probably proceeded by river barge to Orléans, continuing by land to Saint-Germain-en-Laye. All along the way townspeople and villagers cheered *'Vive la Reinette!'* ('Long live the little Queen!') while crowding to catch a glimpse of her as she passed by. Henry II had commanded that Mary was to 'be received, treated and honoured…as if she were our dearly loved consort the Queen in person, having power and right to grant pardons and to set prisoners free'. Mary's grandparents, Duke Claude and Duchess Antoinette of Guise, soon joined the entourage making its way to Saint-Germain-en-Laye. The Duchess was in raptures at welcoming the Queen of Scots to France and into the Guise family fold; some six

uncles and three aunts were waiting to greet their niece. Mary of Guise's surviving son, the Duke of Longueville, was thirteen when Mary Stewart arrived in France, but duty had taken him to join the King campaigning in Italy, so the longed-for meeting between brother and sister was postponed. Mary's heroic uncle, Francis, Duke of Aumale, *le grand Guise*, was also away on military duty; he had gone to southern France to help subdue a rebellion against the King. The Duke's handsome face had been injured in 1545 during the battle of Boulogne against Henry VIII; to his soldiers the Duke of Aumale was *le balafré* (the Scarface), their idol.

During the journey with her granddaughter to Saint-Germain-en-Laye, the Duchess of Guise would have recounted with pride the glories of the Guises, descendants of Charlemagne. They were, in fact, a cadet branch of the House of Lorraine, with claims to the kingdoms of Naples, Sicily, Jerusalem, Aragon, Anjou, Guelders, Flanders and Bar; the Queen of Scots' great-grandfather, René, had styled himself King of Sicily. The independent duchy of Lorraine comprised vast territories close to the German border, and formed part of the Holy Roman Empire. Duke Claude and his sons Francis and Charles after him would occasionally call themselves princes of Anjou, a reason for a Frenchman, uncomfortable with the Guises' soaring power, to call them foreigners, although Claude had received lands in France from his father René and had become a naturalized Frenchman.

In 1515, Claude had been seriously injured in battle while trying to secure the duchy of Milan for Francis I. According to a Guise family tradition, it had been a Scottish gentleman, one James Scott, a member of the King's household guard, who had rescued the Duke – suffering twenty-two wounds – from the battlefield. A month later, when Francis I rode in triumph through Milan, Claude – bandaged, but still a mighty gallant bedecked in white velvet and cloth of gold – rode at the King's side. To Parisians he was 'the people's protector and strong bulwark when the Emperor came against us'. But Claude's pretensions and ambitions eventually fermented such distrust in Francis I that, from his deathbed, the King had allegedly warned his son Henry against giving too much power to the family of Guise, for they 'would strip us of our doublets, and our people to their shirts'.

The Duchess of Guise would also have delighted in informing Mary that her uncle, Charles, in his capacity as Bishop of Reims, had placed the crown on Henry II's head, and had been appointed Cardinal of Guise while still in his twenties. A man of intelligence and a superb orator, Charles, like his brother Francis, was an increasingly influential councillor of the King. Another brother, Louis, Bishop of Troyes, was also a member of the King's council. In April 1547, it had been reported

Opposite and right
Enamel portrait of
Antoinette, Duchess
of Guise, by Léonard
Limosin (now in the
Renaissance Museum
at Ecouen). In spite of her
occasional outbursts of
temper, Antoinette's
countenance appears
serene, perhaps because
of her faith, which was
paramount, along with her
sense of duty to her family
and to France. Mary had
a warm relationship with
her grandmother who was
instrumental in forming
the young Queen of Scots'
character.

to the English that among Henry II's advisers
Francis was 'in very great favour…but in the
greatest estimation and favour of all' was Charles.

In spite of her occasional bursts of temper,
Antoinette looks very appealing in her portraits –
it seems that kindness shone through her eyes,
and she had a gentle mouth that turned up at
the corners. Mary probably warmed – without
hesitation – to this woman who was to become
such an important figure in her life. And
the Duchess of Guise would have enjoyed
instructing her charge in the ways of the French
court, and on the glorious destiny that God had
chosen for her granddaughter – the future
Queen of France. In a letter to her son Francis,
she wrote of Mary:

*She is very pretty indeed, and as intelligent a child as you could
see. She is 'brune', with a clear complexion, and I think that
when she develops she will be…beautiful…for her complexion
is fine and clear, and her skin white. The lower part of the face
is very well formed, the eyes are small and rather deep set,
the face is rather long. She is graceful and self-assured.
To sum up, we may well be pleased with her.*

The Duchess, however, found little to please
in Mary's companions, 'the four Maries': Mary
Fleming, Mary Livingston, Mary Beaton and
Mary Seton. They were the daughters of nobles,
close in age to the Queen, and, apart from
Mary Fleming, each had a French mother or
stepmother. Antoinette found them unsociable
and unclean. Mary's governess Lady Fleming,
the illegitimate daughter of James V and Agnes
Stewart, Countess of Bothwell, managed to
charm her way into the Duchess's approval.
But even so, Antoinette considered that Lady
Fleming, like the 'Maries' needed to be washed.

Above and opposite
The grand Italianate façades of the château of Saint-Germain-en-Laye. Here, above the King's and Queen's apartments, lodgings had been furnished for the royal children. Mary Queen of Scots shared 'the best apartments' with the eldest royal daughter, Princess Elisabeth, who was two-and-a-half years old when the Queen of Scots, aged five, arrived in France. The companionship of the two girls soon turned into a close friendship – much to King Henry's pleasure.

On 9 October 1548 Antoinette was able to write to her son, 'I am bringing [Mary] by slow stages straight to Saint-Germain where I hope to arrive with her on Saturday next.' It had taken two months to make the journey from Roscoff. Mary joined the royal nursery at the château de Carrières near Saint-Germain-en-Laye, west of Paris, and it was here that she first met her future husband. The Duchess of Guise undoubtedly smoothed the way, explaining that the Dauphin Francis, then aged four, was rather frail; Mary must take care to play gently with him, while doing her very best to gain the little boy's affection. Court letters are full of the Dauphin's ailments, and many blamed the child's feeble constitution on the bizarre potions that his mother, Catherine de' Medici, had consumed in her desperation to become pregnant. Queen Catherine spent much of her time with astrolabes and magic mirrors, not daring to 'put one foot ahead of the other until she had consulted her astrologer'. The soothsayer Nostradamus was later appointed a royal councillor and the King's physician, and his duties included charting the horoscopes of the royal children. For now, the portents favoured the Dauphin, indicating that he would become a great King, although many believed this would only happen with the assistance of his future Queen.

The Duchess of Guise and the whole court waited with bated breath for a tender glance between Francis and Mary. The young Queen of Scots, who even then had a gift for winning hearts, made her first conquest, and Francis, coached by Jean d'Humières, governor to the royal children, showed great friendliness in welcoming her. The Duchess of Guise and d'Humières were able to inform the King that, from the very start, the children behaved like close friends. A few months later, Mary of Guise learned from the sentimental governor that the little Dauphin cared for her daughter 'and loves her like his sweetheart and his wife; and it [was] easy to see that God caused them to be born for each other'. The children's closeness touched most onlookers, and seems to have been genuine. They would go off into the corner of a room to be alone and share secrets, and the little boy was forever seeking out Mary's company.

Henry II wished Mary and the Dauphin to be brought up together, with their various attendants forming one household. Mary was to share 'the best apartments' with his elder daughter Princess Elisabeth, then aged two-and-a-half, in the hope that the two girls would become friends. The only other child then in the royal nursery was the Dauphin's younger sister, Princess Claude, still a baby. Catherine de' Medici had written to d'Humières: 'I hope that the number of my children may soon increase, and they may have with them the little Queen of Scotland…this gives me much pleasure.' From then on, the royal cradle was rarely empty. Charles, the future Charles IX, was born in 1550; the future Henry III in 1551; Francis, Duke

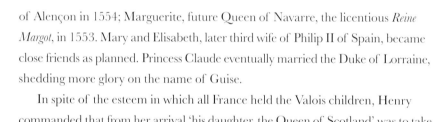

of Alençon in 1554; Marguerite, future Queen of Navarre, the licentious *Reine Margot*, in 1553. Mary and Elisabeth, later third wife of Philip II of Spain, became close friends as planned. Princess Claude eventually married the Duke of Lorraine, shedding more glory on the name of Guise.

In spite of the esteem in which all France held the Valois children, Henry commanded that from her arrival 'his daughter, the Queen of Scotland' was to take precedence and walk before the French princesses, 'For not only is the marriage to my son…fixed and settled, but she is a crowned Queen, and as such it is my wish that she should be honoured and served.'

At the château of Saint-Germain-en-Laye, lodgings above the King's and Queen's apartments were being specially prepared and furnished for Mary and the other royal children. Francis I had remodelled the château but kept much of the original medieval structure. He added two storeys, a terraced roof and completely renovated the inner façades, with external galleries running between turrets. Henry II then added a theatre (Château-Neiuf), a small, one-storey building consisting of clusters of rooms constructed around a court. Here the royal family and courtiers enjoyed a variety of festivities and dramatic performances. On the west side of the château there was an outer courtyard with a well and fountain; to the north lay gardens; and on the south and east sides, the park and forest. Three bridges linked the château to the park.

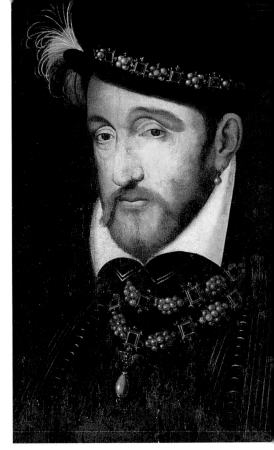

About a month after the children and their household settled at Saint-Germain, the King and the rest of the court joined them. Henry II had written to Francis, Duke of Aumale, to say that he was eager to form his own opinion of the Queen of Scots, 'since all who have come here, after seeing her, praise her as a wonder. This doubles the desire I have to see her, as I hope to do ere long.' In November 1548, when the King arrived in Saint-Germain-en-Laye he, like Jean de Beaugué who had been with Mary the previous August, judged the little

Queen to be 'the most perfect child that I have ever seen'. Henry II's usual melancholia vanished in the company of children, and he would enter into their amusements and concerns with playful humour. When Mary was but ten or eleven he would chat with her 'an hour at a time', and she was 'as well able to entertain him with good and sensible talk as if she were a woman of five-and-twenty'. This tall reserved man had succeeded to the throne at the age of twenty-eight. He was robust, a man of action, taking regular exercise in hunting, jousting and military games, and he was an expert swordsman. The King's favourite sport, however, was tennis: 'In the company of Monseigneur de Guise and other gentlemen, His Majesty played ball with a racquet. He was dressed in white, shod in white, and coiffed with a straw hat.' The young Queen of Scots also became fond of the game of tennis.

Henry's air of gloom may have resulted from his four years of imprisonment from the ages of seven to eleven; he had been harshly treated as a hostage of Emperor Charles V. Before coming to the throne, Henry had received little training in statecraft, and, as sovereign, he studied zealously to overcome this

Opposite below
The Queen of Scots, aged
twelve or thirteen, chalk-
and-watercolour drawing
attributed to François
Clouet, c. 1555. Mary's
gown and head-dress are
in the style worn by noble
ladies and children in
France at this time.
Opposite above
King Henry II of France,
probably by Primaticcio,
dressed in black and white,
the colours favoured by
Henry's mistress. The
usually melancholy King
delighted in his children
and in conversation with
the young Queen of Scots.
Above Catherine de'
Medici (by Clouet) and
Diane de Poitiers (by
Primaticcio) – wife and
mistress of Henry II. The
portraits of the King and
his mistress, his 'perfect
friend', hang at Anet, one
of Diane de Poitiers's
favourite châteaux.

inadequacy. He appointed the Constable of Montmorency as his chief minister, an experienced statesman of fifty-six, who also provided a useful counter-balance to the politics of the Guises. It is interesting that the Constable, although brutal on the battlefield and known as 'the Great Snubber', would write to M. d'Humières on nursery matters and the royal children's health. He sent them toys, and they gave him pet names.

In 1533 Henry's father had married him to Catherine de' Medici; the bride and groom were both fourteen. Francis I had hoped this political marriage would enhance his prospects in Italy, and the bride, whose family was in commerce, did indeed bring an impressive dowry. But as events transpired, Catherine lost her political significance. The Venetian ambassador reported that Catherine de' Medici could do nothing to win the French courtiers: 'If she gave them the whole of France, they would scarcely thank her, because she is a foreigner, and has neither credit nor authority, because she is not of royal birth.'

Instead, Henry II gave his love and loyalty to Diane de Poitiers, a strikingly youthful-looking widow, who had become the King's mistress when she was thirty-eight and he only nineteen. In October 1548 Henry conferred upon Diane the title Duchess of Valentinois, the highest distinction possible for a lady who was not a princess of the blood, enabling her to take her place among the princesses of France. The Italian envoy, Signor Ricasoli, remarked, 'Ink could not express the omnipotence at the French court of the lady Diane de Poitiers.' Henry would spend part of every day discussing matters of state with her and listening to her advice. His respect for her judgment was such that he gave her the right to distribute important offices. She had allied herself with the Guises and may have encouraged the King to appoint them as royal councillors; the Cardinal of Guise had become spiritual adviser to both the King and Diane de Poitiers, and her daughter Louise eventually married a Guise brother, the third son of Duke Claude – much to the young Queen of Scots' delight. In 1550, when Mary of Guise was planning a trip to France, she consulted Diane de Poitiers about her wardrobe. The Dowager Queen of Scotland needed to be correctly attired when appearing

at the Valois court after such a long absence, and she knew that Diane reigned as queen of France in all but title.

Diane de Poitiers merged with her alter ego, Diana, chaste goddess of the hunt, an image she encouraged and promoted, drawing a veil of mythology over the true nature of her relations with the King, seemingly above the ordinary level of royal mistress. The crescent moon, symbol of Diana the Huntress, was a favourite emblem of Henry II. He had a medal engraved with the figure of the goddess Diana and the motto, *'Nomen ad astra'*, ('Her name is immortal'). Crescents gleamed atop triumphal arches through which Henry passed in his formal entries into Lyon, Paris and Reims. He gave Diana gifts adorned with crescents, and the King eventually took three crescent moons with the motto *'Donec totem impleat orbem'* ('Till he fills the whole world') as his *impresa*. Henry further acknowledged for all the world the esteem in which he held Diane de Poitiers by wearing her colours of black and white, and everywhere emblazoning their interlocked initials.

Catherine de' Medici remained a faint shadow in the background, her placid face seeming to bear with equanimity her husband's relationship with Diane. She kept her true feelings towards the King's mistress concealed, while rumours circulated that she was planning to poison or somehow disfigure her. Poison had been suspected when Henry's elder brother had died after drinking a cup of water given to him by his Italian page; Catherine, the daughter of an Italian merchant, had suddenly become the future Queen of France. Diane de Poitiers took her fears of the Queen to Francis of Guise, who calmed her by implying that if Catherine ended Diane's life, she risked her own. Historian and poet Pierre de Bourdeille, better known as Brantôme, related the tale that the Queen had a number of holes pierced into the ceiling of Diane's bedchamber and used to spy on 'the game her husband and his lady should play together'. She would then sigh in her distress 'that her husband did never the like with her, nor ever went through suchlike amorous follies as ever she had seen him perform with his mistress.' To alleviate her fear, Diane doubled the number of her household and moved to the Hôtel de Graville which adjoined the royal Palace of the Tournelles and the Hôtel de Guise in Paris.

Even though the marriage between Catherine and Henry was not a love match, Diane de Poitiers knew that the King must have heirs to maintain the Valois dynasty, and she insisted that Henry occupy the Queen's bed. And it was Diane who first greeted the royal offspring upon their arrival into the world, steadfastly assisting Catherine during labour – which in one instance lasted forty hours. Henry thanked her for 'the service she had rendered the Queen and the kingdom', and entrusted to Diane the superintendence of the royal children, addressing his mistress as the

Opposite above Diane
de Poitiers as Diana the
goddess of the hunt, by
Primaticcio, 1556. In
promoting herself as the
chaste Diana, the King's
mistress perhaps sought
to draw a veil over the real
nature of her relationship
with Henry II. The
painting now hangs
at Chenonceau – given
to Diane by the King.
Opposite below
The entwined letters
H and D could be seen
in profusion decorating
the residences of Henry II
and the châteaux of his
beloved favourite. Here, the
initials decorate the wooden
door that once connected
the gallery at Anet to the
chapel; compartments in
the door could be opened
to reveal a grille through
which one could discreetly
hear Mass. The door can
now be seen at the Ecole
des Beaux-Arts, Paris.

'Tutelary Genius of the Royal Nursery'. The King's physician claimed that Diane 'secured for the princely children not only vigorous, healthy and well-complexioned nurses, but also wise and prudent governesses; while she caused them to be instructed by good and learned preceptors, as well in virtue and wise precepts, as in the love and fear of God.' It is not surprising, then, that the children, adored her, including Mary, preferring, it seems, Diane to the Queen.

Catherine, it must be said, also took a keen interest in every happening in the royal nursery and fretted over the children's health. Mary's relationship with Catherine de' Medici was, however, not ideal. Catherine eventually grew wary of the power of the Guises, which undoubtedly later coloured her attitude towards Mary. It has also been suggested that Mary, having seen the King so often in company with Diane, assumed her to be the Queen. It seems there was an awkward moment when Catherine first came into the nursery after Mary's arrival at Saint-Germain-en-Laye. She did so without ceremony, and stood back quietly watching the children at play. Mary took an instant dislike to this observer and demanded to know if she realized that she was in the presence of the Queen of Scotland! Catherine responded by asking Mary if she was aware that she was in the presence of the Queen of France. Another version claims that Mary one day lost her temper with Catherine and humiliated her by calling her a merchant's daughter. Catherine was more gracious. She wrote to Mary's mother that her child was all goodness and virtue – 'more so indeed than might be expected at her age…. You are wonderfully fortunate in having such a daughter, and I am more fortunate still because God has so disposed matters as to grant her to me, for I think it will be the strength of my old age to have her with me.' A few years later Catherine acknowledged that the Queen of Scots possessed what she herself lacked: '[Mary] has only to smile to turn every Frenchman's head.' Brantôme spoke of Mary's 'very sweet and true voice…she sang very well, accompanying her voice with the lute, which she touched so prettily with that fair white hand, and with those fair and shapely fingers which yielded in nothing to those of Aurora.' Her speaking voice was equally pleasing, for even when 'the little savage' (as she was occasionally called, not disparagingly but as a delightful curiosity) spoke the language of Scotland – harsh to French ears – it was said to have lost all its rudeness on Mary's lips. But the King of France ordered that Mary be immediately instructed in French, and her Scottish attendants removed. The four Maries were sent to be educated at the convent of Poissy, although Mary's vivacious governess, Lady Fleming, after some wrangling, was allowed to keep her post.

The object of Mary's education was to equip her with all the graces, learning and skills befitting a Queen of France, which meant removing every trace of the

M·SC·R· AVVNCVLO A

30.

LOTHARINGIA S·P·D

Carneades dicebat, spectatissime avuncu
le, liberos Regum nihil recte discere praeter
artem equitandi quia in omnibus ~~alijs~~
rebus vnusquisque illis assentatur.
Sed aegus ~~equitum~~ quia non inteligit
si sit pauper vel diues qui insidet
princeps an priuatus excutit a tergo
quicunque non bene insiderit ·
Nunc etiam hoc videmus fieri mul
tis in locis nam nec nutrices solu

Above and background
Two of Mary's Latin
exercises: one to her uncle
the Cardinal, telling him
that the art of horseriding
is the sport most befitting
kings; the other to the
Dauphin on learning.

child's Scottish inheritance. Mary Stewart not only mastered French but effectively became a Frenchwoman. The language of France became the language in which she spoke, wrote and thought. She would sign her letters with her given name 'Marie' for the rest of her days, and the French transformation now replaced 'Stewart' with the French spelling of 'Stuart' which she adopted. (For consistency 'Stewart' is used throughout.)

Pierre de Ronsard, the Prince of Poets, became Mary's tutor in literature. Jacques Amyot taught her Latin – Amyot had produced a French rendering of Plutarch's *Lives*, on which Sir Thomas North based his own English version used by Shakespeare. Mary studied Greek with the celebrated French Hellenist Pierre Danes, and her tutors, chosen by Catherine de' Medici, were Claude Millot and Antoine Fouquelin. Mary was a quick learner, and also acquired some Italian and Spanish. When she was twelve years old, she recited before the King and all the court a Latin discourse which she had composed herself. Her Latin compositions amounted to eighty-six set themes on the duties of princes and on fundamental virtues – bound in a small leather book now in the Bibliothèque Nationale, Paris. The exercises are written by a tutor in French on the page opposite Mary's translation – including mistakes. Most of the exercises are in the form of letters addressed largely to Elisabeth, her closest companion in the royal nursery, although sometimes to the Princesses Elisabeth and Claude together. There are two letters to the Dauphin, in one of which Mary advises: 'Love learning, most illustrious Prince!' There are references to Erasmus and to learned ladies of the Renaissance, such as Marguerite, Queen of Navarre and sister of Francis I, who died the year after Mary's arrival in France. This pious lady, who had a tendency to ridicule priests, wrote the *Heptaméron*, stories modelled on Boccaccio's *Decameron*, and religious poetry. Young ladies of noble birth, including Elizabeth Tudor, studied then imitated her works.

Two other letters written by Mary are addressed to her uncle, Cardinal Charles. One starts: 'Many people in these days, my uncle, fall into errors in the Holy Scriptures, because they do not read them with a pure and clean heart.' It was observed that Mary was very devout. Before receiving her first Communion at

Below A letter from Mary,
c. 1553, to her mother on
her going to Meudon with
her grandmother at Easter
to 'receive God'.
Right The 12th-century
Balfour Ciborium (a
Communion vessel), which
was probably Mary's.

Meudon, Mary wrote to her mother: 'Madame, my grandmother…and my uncle the Cardinal are of the opinion that I should receive God, whom I beseech to give me grace to start well.' Mary heard Mass daily, and travelled with her own Communion vessels. Guillaume de Laon was her chaplain, although the Prior of Inchmahome, who had made the voyage to France with her, also served as her chaplain.

Remarkably, one of Mary's letter-exercises was addressed to John Calvin. While the young Queen was working on her Latin themes, Henry II was tightening jurisdiction against heresy. Hundreds of French Protestants fled to Geneva where Calvin was attempting to create a city 'governed by God'. At the same time, Calvinism was spreading to many parts of France, distressing the King, Diane de Poitiers and the Guises. 'May Christ, the Son of God, recall thee Calvin!' Mary wrote.

Not only was Mary expected to converse like a future Queen of France, but her dress also had to convey her rank. When the Queen of Scots was nine years old, sixteen gowns were made for her in crimson, purple and yellow velvet, in white satin from Venice, and in taffeta in black, white, red and purple. There were gowns of golden damask and cloth of silver lined with silk and satin, and velvet muffs trimmed with sable. Pierre Danjou, the King's embroiderer, made a hat for her, three sets of sleeves (these were detachable garments in the sixteenth century) and several petticoats (often a highly decorated garment showing through an opening in the gown). The sleeves and petticoats were embedded with golden leaves and roses, and another pair of sleeves was made of quilted red taffeta. Danjou also made for her a cape of Florentine serge with a border embroidered in gold thread, and a satin head-dress trimmed with gold

The letter reads:

Ma Dame i'ai esté bien aise d'avoir le moien de vous pouvoir ecrire de mes nouvelles estant en bien grand peine d'estre si long temps sans en entendre des votres. Ma dame i'ai entendu que le Gouverneur s'est mis en votre volunté, et vous a remis entre mains les places principales du roiaume, de quoi ie suis tres aise et en loue tous les iours votre seigneurie et aussi dequoi tous les princes et grands seigneurs sont reformés a vous. Ie suis arrivée a meudon aupres de ma dame ma grand mere pour i faire la feste de pasques, pource qu'elle, et mon oncle monsieur le cardinal sont d'advis que ie recoive Dieu, auquel ie supplie tres hublement me donner la grace d'i bien commancer. Ie ne vueil oblier vous dire que ce present porteur a fait bon et agreable service au Roy. Ma dame en cest endroit ie vous presenterai mes tres humbles recommandations a votre bonne grace, suppliant le createur vous donner en santé tres heureuse vie.

Votre tres humble et tres obeissante fille
MARIE

Above Sixteenth-century engraving (French) of a young noblewoman playing a cittern, which resembled a lute, but with wire strings and a flat back. The Queen of Scots' courtly accomplishments included not only singing and accompanying herself on the lute, but also playing the harp, cittern and virginals. Poet/historian Brantôme admired Mary's slender white fingers caressing the strings of her lute, while Mary's favourite poet, Pierre de Ronsard, described Mary playing the lute for relaxation after the affairs of state.

and pearls. Sometimes she bound her hair with 'fine white silk braid', and there were hose in all colours, and, it seems, breeches, to be worn beneath the skirt for riding – a fashion introduced from Italy, possibly by Catherine de' Medici. In 1551 the accounts mention ten pairs of shoes – white, purple, black, red, yellow, with some in velvet. The royal goldsmith, Mathurin Lussault, furnished pins, combs and brushes, while another goldsmith, honouring the King and Diane de Poitiers, provided her with twelve dozen crescent-shaped buttons enamelled in black and white to trim a pair of sleeves and a head-dress. Three brass chests were necessary to house her jewels, which included a golden chain with green enamel set with pearls, a golden girdle enamelled in red and white, and a ruby ring. Mary gave the Dauphin a white silk garment which she had the embroiderer ornament with fifes and both their *imprese*. For novelty, the young Queen of Scots liked to adopt 'the outlandish garb of the wild people of her own realm', and thus, according to Brantôme, 'her mortal form assumed…the semblance of a perfect goddess.'

Lavish attire was in keeping with the pampered life-style of the royal children. Armies of attendants were on hand to answer their every need, their every whim. The household included a kitchen staff of fifty-seven. The food requirements of a single day, 1 December 1551, included: 2 calves, 16 sheep, 5 pigs, 7 geese; there were also choice cuts of beef, chickens, pigeons, hares, pheasant, partridges, larks and 36 pounds of cutlets and calves' feet. These were eaten with 72 dozen loaves of bread accompanied by wine provided by five different merchants. On 9 June 1553, 250 loaves of bread were consumed. Meat included 18 cuts of beef, 8 sheep, 4 calves, 20 capons, 120 chickens, pigeons, 3 deer, 6 geese and 4 hares. A dish associated with Mary and Chenonceau – one of the Loire châteaux she inhabited – is *dos de sandre Marie Stuart* (fillet of pike-perch of Mary Stewart). Fish only was the rule on fast days, as during Lent when, according to the royal accounts, not a single item of meat was purchased. Otherwise, meals were roughly divided into meat and fish courses and up to twenty dishes, including sweets were served. Fruit and vegetables were eaten sparingly in comparison to meat. Dried fruits were added to dishes for flavour, and sugar sprinkled as a spice in both savoury and sweet concoctions. Little cakes, pastries and sweetmeats were becoming more popular. During meals Mary sat on a great chair covered in green velvet, attended by two pages wearing cloaks 'banded' with yellow velvet and edged with red and yellow braiding.

The royal children were allowed to make sweets which they loved consuming, and comfits, aromatic seeds – coriander, aniseed, fennel and caraway – laboriously coated in sugar were enjoyed by all the court. The tradition that the word 'marmalade' came into usage after a royal chef stirred his boiling sugar and oranges while repeating again and again, '*Marie est malade*,' until the mixture became a golden confiture, makes a delightful story. The term 'marmalade', however, was in use a century earlier and derives from *marmelo*, the Portuguese for quince. From the fifteenth to the nineteenth centuries marmalade was a sliced sweetmeat made from oranges as well as other fruit, which Mary may have eaten. One fruit the young Queen devoured to the point of indigestion was melon. Indeed, her tendency to overeat made her uncle Charles anxious – nothing concerning the future Queen of France was too trifling for the Cardinal. But then, Mary's indulgence would sometimes bring on attacks of fainting, causing general alarm since poison – *le morceau italien* (a morsel of Italian poison) – was always a concern. A plot to poison her was uncovered in 1550, when an archer of the household guard named Robert Stuart had hoped to serve England by removing the Queen of Scots. He was imprisoned at Calais where, according to the Bishop of Ross, he was tortured into a confession, then hanged and quartered in 1551.

Mary's courtly accomplishments included not only singing and accompanying herself on the lute, but also playing the harp, cittern and virginals. She enjoyed dancing, performing each movement with a stately elegance, so pleasing to onlookers. She also became skilled in needlework. In 1551 worsteds (twisted woollen yarns) were purchased for the Queen of Scots to 'learn to make works' (needlework). Mary and the Valois princesses may have been urged to perfect their skills with the needle by Catherine de' Medici who had herself developed a talent for the craft as a student in the Convent of the Murate in Florence, where the nuns were renowned for the quality of their embroidery. Catherine would later be associated with the famous Valois tapestries depicting her spectacular pageants.

To amuse the royal children, there were thirty-seven playmates, the sons and daughters of the nobility. Further diversion was provided by a menagerie of pets, including four large 'well muzzled' bulldogs, twenty-two lap dogs, and several horses and ponies. Mary's favourite horses were Bravane and Madame la Réale. There were tame birds in cages, falcons and hawks, and, on one occasion, the children were treated to an exhibition of exotic animals and snakes from Africa. Wolves and boars were on show, and there were gifts of bears. Mary, who was always generous, sent to Scotland for ponies and 'erth-doggs' (terriers) to give to her playmates. In another show of magnanimity Mary begged her mother to raise the wages of her servants. 'Meanness is the thing she hates most in this world', wrote her uncle Charles to his sister Mary of Guise. 'Her spirit, I assure you Madame, is already so high and noble that she lets her annoyance be very plainly seen because she is thus unworthily treated.' Even dubious traits take on a lustre when wrapped in courtly language.

Below, opposite and background Celebrations for Henry II's formal entry into Rouen, from C'est, *La Déduction du somptueux ordre*, Rouen, 1551. Mary and her mother were together in Rouen in 1550 when the King was presented with a complete re-enactment of a Roman imperial triumph. Among the colourful tableaux that Mary and her mother would have seen were the elephants bearing blazing lamps; the host of creatures swimming in the Seine, including an artificial whale; and the display in which fifty 'Brazilians' engaged in realistic combat, routing their opponents.

The year 1550 saw both loss and reunion for the House of Guise. Mary's grandfather Claude, Duke of Guise, died in April at the family estate of Joinville in north-east France. Poison was suspected at the hand of some 'Anti-Christ and Minister of Satan'. Though this was never confirmed, suspicion of murder added a shade of gloom to the funeral ceremony, which was conducted with all the majesty due to a prince of Lorraine. Francis *le balafré*, Claude's eldest son and Mary's uncle, was now Duke of Guise and head of the family. A few months later, Mary Stewart's great-uncle, John Cardinal of Lorraine, died, and Charles Cardinal of Guise, another uncle, became the new Cardinal of Lorraine.

In September the Dowager Queen of Scotland, Mary of Guise, visited France, staying just over a year, marking a period of great joy for the nine-year-old Queen of Scots. Mary had written of the coming event to her grandmother:

Madame, I have been very glad to be able to send these present lines, for the purpose of telling you the joyful news I have received from the Queen my mother, who has promised me by her letter dated April 23rd that she will be here very soon to see you and me, which is to me the greatest happiness which I could wish for in this world, and indeed I am so overjoyed about it that all I am thinking about now is to do my whole duty in all things and to study to be very good, in order to satisfy her desire to see me all that you and she hoped for....

Mary of Guise's mission in coming to France was not only to see her beloved daughter and her son, the Duke of Longueville, but also to secure her accession to the Regency of Scotland in the place of Lord Arran, now Duke of Châtelherault. Mary had been 'dangerously ill' with dysentery, but had recovered sufficiently to greet her mother when she arrived at court on 25 September. The court was then at Rouen, ancient capital of Normandy, where the Queen Dowager and her train of nobles were received with great ceremony 'by all estates of the town'. For months past, the magistrates of Rouen had been busy with preparations for the King's state entry into their town on 1 October, and provided a series of public entertainments undoubtedly witnessed by both Queens of Scotland. For Mary, the highlight must have been a procession of six elephants: 'The first carried on its back a tray of lighted lamps, the second a church, the third a villa, the fourth a castle, the fifth a town and the sixth a ship.' A vast artificial whale swam in the river Seine as the King, clad in white velvet and cloth of silver, crossed a bridge to the town. He was saluted by a blast of artillery, and there was then a waterside theatrical display in which 'fifty Brazilian natives' landed to engage in combat between two ships. One of the ships was eventually given over to the 'savages' who ransacked and burned it, sending the ship's crew scampering to an island refuge. What marvels for a little girl to see! The following day Catherine de' Medici made her formal entry, accompanied by the King's sister and his mistress Diane de Poitiers.

The winter of 1550–51 was spent in the Loire Valley. At the château of Blois the round of festivities between Candlemas (2 February) and Shrove Tuesday included masques, tournaments and processions. Charles, now Cardinal of Lorraine, gave a magnificent banquet at which the King himself acted as a steward, overseeing the fun while his chief adviser, the Constable Montmorency, stood as clerk of the kitchen. The company was so beautifully attired that 'a man would have thought that all the jewels in Christendom had been assembled together, so gorgeously were the dames beset with great numbers of them, both their heads and their bodies.'

In June, the month of marriages, a committee of English ambassadors pursued with Henry II the possibility of a marriage between the Queen of Scots and her suitor of the 'Rough Wooing', Edward VI. Henry entertained the nobles with feasting and dancing in the company of 'the old and the young Scottish Queens'. A wrestling competition between Bretons and Englishmen was followed by a tennis match, more dancing and more eating, until Henry instructed Montmorency to offer the English representatives a reply:

By my troth, to be plain and frank with you, seeing you require us so to be, the matter hath cost us both much riches and no little blood, and so much doth the honour of France hang hereupon as we cannot tell how to talk with you therein, the marriage being already concluded between her and the Dauphin, and therefore we would be glad to hear no more thereof.

The English didn't press their suit, but instead made a proposal for the hand of Mary's friend, Elisabeth of Valois. After some negotiation, this prospect seemed at least possible, but came to nothing when two years later Edward VI died at the age of fifteen.

During Mary of Guise's stay in France, a scandal erupted at court. While Diane was at her château of Anet recuperating from an injury, the King had succumbed to the charms of Lady Fleming, Mary Stewart's vivacious governess, encouraged perhaps by Montmorency, his chief adviser, who took any opportunity to reduce the influence of Diane de Poitiers. The Guises allegedly told Diane about the King's affair, and Lady Fleming, according to Brantôme, brashly boasted to the whole court: 'God be thanked. I am with child by the King and very honoured and happy about it.' Diane de Poitiers and Catherine de' Medici, either separately or jointly, insisted that Lady Fleming should be sent back to Scotland. There she gave birth to a son whom Henry acknowledged as his own,

Above and opposite
Francis, 2nd Duke of
Guise, by François Clouet.
Mary's uncle, was known
as *le balafré* (the Scarface)
because of the scar from
an old battle injury. He was
a consummate leader of
men and a national hero.
His victory at Metz, won
with only 6,000 men against
Emperor Charles V's
60,000, was compared
to David's over Goliath.
Francis was also driven
by ambition for the family
of Guise, including the
Queen of Scots.

giving him the name of Henri d'Angoulême. The King committed other
indiscretions resulting in at least two other illegitimate children, but his affection
for and loyalty to Diane de Poitiers always endured.

This episode having done little to endear the Scots at court, the English envoy
Sir John Mason also noted:'The Dowager of Scotland maketh all this court weary
of her, from high to low, such an importunate beggar is she for herself and her chosen
friends. The King would fain be rid of her, and she, as she pretendeth, would fain
be gone.' Mary of Guise was becoming tiresome in her procurement of benefits
for her accompanying nobles. She was trying to secure their support in her bid for
the Regency, and was over-stressing the urgency of French military aid. But she was
indeed short of money, and had been reduced to borrowing from friends.

Then tragedy struck in her last few weeks in France. Her son, the Duke of
Longueville, had spent much of 1550 and 1551 becoming reacquainted with
his mother, whom he had not seen since her departure for Scotland in 1538. He
travelled with her as the court moved around and on visits to the family châteaux.
He also became better acquainted with his half-sister Mary, 'the most charming sister
in the world'. As his mother made preparations to return to Scotland, he suddenly
became ill. Mary of Guise nursed him, and he died in her arms. He was fifteen. She
wrote to her own mother, Duchess Antoinette, 'I think, Madame, as you are pleased
to write to me, that our Lord wills that I should be one of his own, since he has visited
me so often and so heavily.' Mary of Guise's grief was compounded by the agony of
parting from her only surviving child (whom she was never to see again). The young
Queen of Scots, who adored her mother, shared in this sorrow.

In 1552 tragedy was replaced by triumph for the family of Guise. The previous
year a federation of Protestant German princes applied to Henry II for aid against
Emperor Charles V. Henry complied, signing the Treaty of Chambord. In February
1552 the French King announced his intention of avenging the hardships inflicted
by the Emperor and restoring German liberties. In April Montmorency occupied
Toul, and then the imperial city of Metz was taken. The King visited Nancy, capital
of Lorraine, making himself Protector of the young Duke of Lorraine and installing
the Comte de Vaudémont as Regent of the duchy. From Nancy, Henry II pushed
on until, 'having watered his horses in the Rhine', he entered Verdun in June.
The King's relatively bloodless 'German voyage', securing three strategic fortresses
on France's north-east border and influence over Lorraine, has been described as
'one of the most successful military excursions in French history'.

This tide of victory was completed by Francis, Duke of Guise. It was inevitable
that Charles V would react, and in November, with 60,000 men, he laid siege to

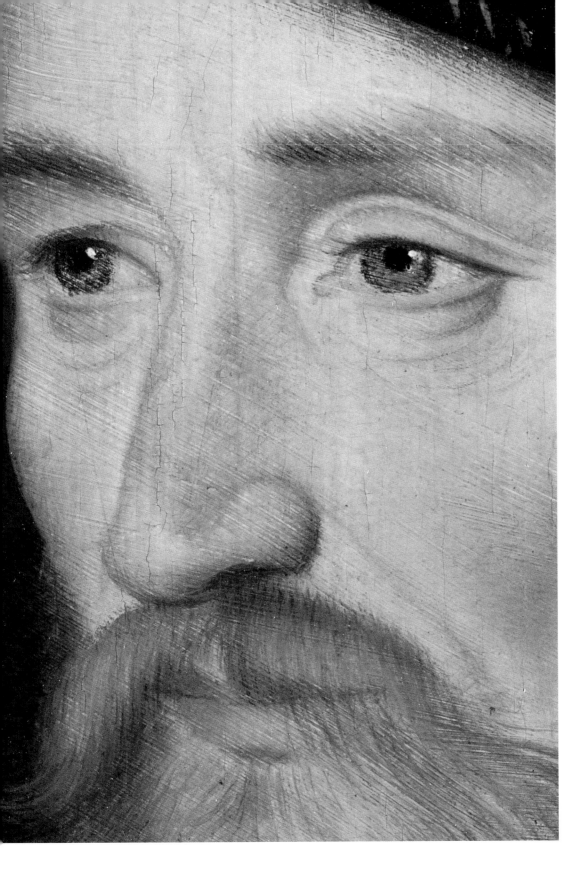

Metz where Francis, now Duke of Guise, was in command. The Emperor's forces bombarded the city for forty-five days, but Francis, with only 6,000 men and few arms, held out; his abilities as a leader of men came to the fore as he organized and encouraged his soldiers, fighting with them shoulder-to-shoulder. The Emperor was forced to withdraw on 2 January 1553, having lost 30,000 troops. Francis's victory was compared to David's over Goliath, and, while staying behind to tend both his own and the Emperor's wounded, *le balafré* became a national hero. Throughout France there were public rejoicings. English Ambassador Sir William Pickering wrote that, on 8 February, 'M. de Guise, accompanied by the princes and gentlemen who had been at Metz, came to the court, where there was such joy and feasting for the two days following as for that time almost nothing else was minded.' Henry greeted the hero with the words: 'You have conquered me as well as the Emperor by the obligation under which you have laid me'. One can imagine the pride that Mary must have felt for her uncle, as the news of his victory spread across Europe and beyond.

Around the time of her eleventh birthday Mary acquired her own household. This was a further drain on the Treasury of Scotland, and it had been necessary for Charles, Cardinal

Above Charles, Cardinal of Lorraine. A handsome intellectual and gifted orator, with a taste for luxury, this Guise uncle exerted a strong influence on Mary. He believed that noblewomen should read poetry, 'that a choice of the highest poetic thoughts might adorn the feminine mind'. His fellow student at the Collège de Navarre, Pierre de Ronsard, dedicated his *Hymne à la justice* to the Cardinal: Justice, driven from earth after the Golden Age, is sent by Jupiter to occupy the person of the Cardinal of Lorraine. But after the slaughter at Amboise in 1560, many questioned the Guise sense of justice.

of Lorraine, to write pleading letters to his sister, Mary of Guise, before final permission for the young Queen's household was agreed. On 1 January 1554 Mary Queen of Scots entertained Charles to dinner. All the Guises were exerting an increasingly strong influence on the young Queen, but particularly her uncle Charles. The Cardinal was handsome, attractive to women, and surrounded himself with luxury and literature. French writers dedicated their books to him, and scholars from all over Europe sent volumes of their works to his library. He believed that noblewomen should read a variety of classical and contemporary poetry so 'that a choice of the highest poetic thoughts might adorn the feminine mind'. Mary's favourite poets were Ronsard, Joachim du Bellay and Maisonfleur, all three of whom wrote verses praising her. Both Diane de Poitiers and Henry II had fallen under Charles's spell, and so, too, did Mary. The Cardinal of Lorraine, ruthless in politics, became the young Queen's mentor in statecraft and the 'one true religion'. In one of her Latin letters, Mary wrote to her cousin, Elizabeth Tudor, that the 'true grandeur and excellence of a prince is' in having 'nothing to do with foolish opinions of the vulgar'.

In her twelfth year, 'her perfect age', Mary asserted her authority over Scotland by choosing her mother as her Regent. The French parliament had decreed that the Queen of Scots had reached her majority at the beginning of her twelfth year, which accorded with Scots law. This transfer of power was something of a formality, as the Duke of Châtelherault (Arran), having received heavy financial inducements and other benefits, had already agreed to resign as Regent when the Queen of Scots reached the age of twelve.

There was also a change in Mary's immediate circle; after Lady Fleming's disgrace, the post of governess to the Queen of Scots was given to Mme de Parois, a sound Catholic. The Cardinal was initially pleased with this choice. 'I must not omit to tell you', he wrote to Mary's mother, 'that Madame de Parois is doing her duty as well as possible, and you may be sure that God is well served according to the ancient way.' Between Mary Stewart and the new governess, however, all was not well. The woman was irritable and petty, causing friction between Mary and Catherine de' Medici, and even upsetting Antoinette, the Dowager Duchess of Guise. Mary was so distressed over the governess's meddling that she began to fear that Mme de Parois would undermine the relationship between herself and her mother. Indeed, the domestic quarrels were making Mary ill, and she wrote to her mother that the governess's behaviour had nearly brought about her death, 'because I was afraid of falling under your displeasure and because I grieved at hearing through these false reports to many disputes and so much harm said of me.' Mme de Parois was at length replaced by Mme de Brêne, chosen by Diane de Poitiers.

Below Woodcut of the castle and town of Joinville, an early 17th-century imaginative view after *La Cosmographie Universelle de Belleforest* (1575). Franceso Primaticcio's designs decorated the castle's chapel. Also in the chapel and also designed by Primaticcio, was a monument to Mary's grandfather, Claude, Duke of Guise.

As an adolescent Mary began to take a keen interest in her appearance. She had on a previous occasion suffered the humiliation of appearing in silk while the Valois princesses wore cloth of silver. For a court wedding in the autumn of 1554, the young Queen was determined to outdress the sisters by appearing in a gown of cloth of gold, expensively embellished throughout with her royal cipher. The finishing touch was a necklace of pearls and rubies. When Mary's dresses became too small or out of fashion she gave them to her Guise aunts, Renée and Antoinette, who cut up the valuable cloth for altar coverings. Renée, only four years older than Mary, like many daughters of the nobility, sought a career in the church, eventually becoming Abbess of St-Pierre-les-Dames, Reims. Antoinette, eleven years older than Mary, was the respected Abbess of Faremoutiers. Mary formed a particularly close attachment to another aunt, Anne d'Este, wife of Duke Francis. When Mary obtained her own household, Anne served as her lady-in-waiting. The two would dance together before the court, sending the ever romantic Brantôme to his quill: Mary and Anne were like 'two suns' appearing 'together in the heavens to astonish the world'. Mary also enjoyed the company of her little cousins, the sons of Francis and Anne.

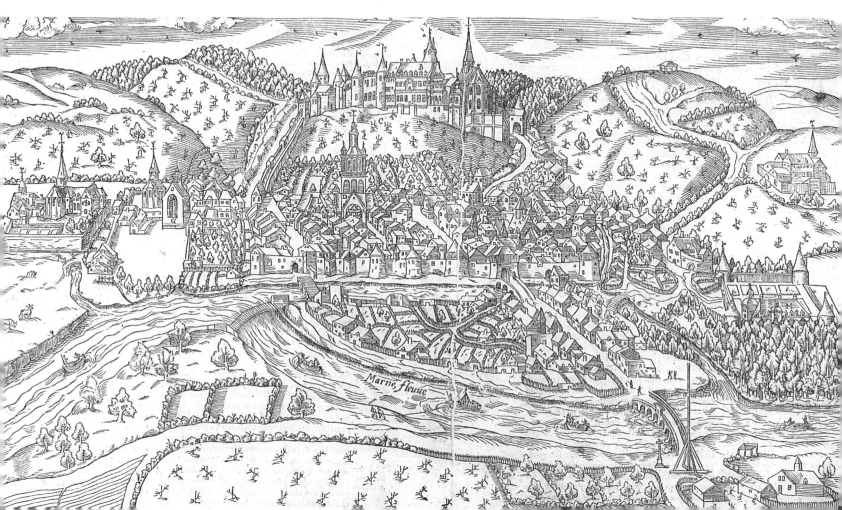

Marne fleuue

Above *God the Father,*
by Primaticcio, *c.* 1555.
A study for the central
tableau *The Adoration of
the Magi* for the chapel of
the Hôtel de Guise in Paris.
Here, in a style heavily
influenced by Michelangelo,
Primaticcio creates a
sensation of movement
and elevation.

Background An early
17th-century engraving of
the Cardinal of Lorraine's
château of Meudon, given
to him by Diane de Poitiers,
and often visited by Mary:
'Equal to the finest houses
in the kingdom, and just as
suitable for a great prince.'

In visits to her relatives Mary came to know as
second homes the principal Guise residences of
Joinville, Meudon and the Hôtel de Guise in Paris.
The eleventh-century castle of Joinville, about ninety
miles north-east of Paris, dominated a low hill
overlooking the town of Joinville and the River Marne.
It appeared to be swept up to the sky with more than
a dozen graceful spires, towers and pitched roofs.
Surrounding the castle were formal flower and kitchen
gardens, and in the orchard there was a diversity
of fruit trees – the usual apples and plums, but also
oranges, lemons and pomegranates grew in profusion.
Beyond the castle wall, vines covered the upper slope
of the hill, producing wine for the family and the
hundred-strong household. The Guises employed five
choristers for music at the daily services in the chapel.

In Paris it had been necessary to tear down or
incorporate four mansions to make space to build
the Hôtel de Guise, which was to become a centre for
political intrigue. Patrons of art, the Guises employed
Francesco Primaticcio and Niccolò dell' Abbate in
1555 to decorate the chapel on the first floor of their great house. Here, using
drawings by Primaticcio, Niccolò created a dreamlike fresco around the altar
representing the Star of the Magi supported by angels, probably modelled on Perino
del Vaga's central panel of the Sala dei Pontefici in the Vatican. Other rooms in
the mansion were gorgeously appointed, with series of tapestries on such themes
as the signs of the zodiac, animals, towns and landscapes.

Just outside Paris, near Sèvres, was the Cardinal of Lorraine's château of
Meudon. Here in April 1554 Mary attended the christening of Anne and Francis,
the Duke and Duchess of Guise's second son, Charles (the future General of the
Catholic League). Cardinal Charles and the Duke of Ferrara were godfathers, Diane
de Poitiers was godmother. Diane had given the ancient château to Cardinal Charles,
and he was altering and extending it during Mary's visits there. 'I can assure you',
he enthused, 'that when the house is finished…when we have added a few little
ideas that I have imagined, and our busts and marbles from Paris, it will be equal
to the finest houses in the kingdom, and just as suitable for a great prince.' Ronsard
glorified the château in verse, and it is tempting to imagine another great literary

figure, François Rabelais – who enjoyed the benefice of Meudon from 1550 to 1553 – dining there or spending hours in conversation with Charles. In 1549, Rabelais had dedicated *Sciomachie* to Charles, then still Cardinal of Guise. The book describes the celebrations in Rome for the birth of Henry II's second son. It has been suggested (but not proved) that Rabelais wrote his *Gargantua* and *Pantagruel* at Meudon; when Mary returned to Scotland in 1559, she took two copies with her.

In a letter to her mother, the Queen of Scots boasted of the Cardinal's great grotto at Meudon. It was a two-storey construction with rooms for relaxation and for taking refreshments, made to look as if it had been hewn from natural stone. To Ronsard the grotto was a place of enchantment that beckoned to 'the sylvans, the fawns and all the untamed creatures' of mythology.

In this world so conscious of form and beauty – the France in which Mary was nurtured and grew to womanhood – the aesthetic aspect of the Queen of Scots' education should not be underestimated. Francis I had made the Valois court a centre for art and learning comparable to papal Rome and Medici Florence. At the same time, he brought ceremony and spectacle to the monarchy in emulation of the Dukes of Burgundy – pageants, royal entrances and masques worthy to be called art. In Italy, Francis had been overwhelmed by all aspects of the High Renaissance; he scoured the country for works of antiquity and rare manuscripts as well as new paintings and sculptures, and brought these collections to his favourite château, Fontainebleau. He also brought artists – painters, sculptors, workers in mosaic, engravers, woodcarvers, goldsmiths, embroiderers – to create there an ideal world, a utopia for the aesthete. He wanted to bring Michelangelo to France, but instead managed to lure Leonardo da Vinci, appointing him 'First Painter, Engineer and Architect to the King'.

Above The château of Fontainebleau, showing what is today the main entrance. Philibert de L'Orme designed for Henry II an impressive horseshoe staircase, *c.* 1554, providing a direct entrance from the courtyard to the royal apartments. This staircase, destroyed in 1632, was replaced by the horseshoe staircase (above) designed by Jacques Androuet du Cerceau. Ambassadors from England, visiting the thirteen-year-old Queen of Scots at Fontainebleau in 1555, judged the château superior in 'outward beauty and uniformity' to England's Hampton Court.

The château of Fontainebleau is situated on the edge of a vast forest forty-five miles south-east of Paris. Francis I, after 1527 and throughout the rest of his life (he died in 1547, a year before Mary's arrival in France) began replacing the existing medieval structures with buildings more appropriate to his Renaissance court. He added a multiplicity of rooms, galleries, canals, courtyards, baths, gardens and a grotto. Yet, the architecture of Fontainebleau under Francis was marked overall by simplicity, leading the way towards classicism. Mary often visited Fontainebleau, which in the seventeenth century was still called 'a treasure house of marvels'. During her visits she would have entered through the Porte Dorée (the gilded door), and would have seen the Egyptian door (*c.* 1545), the first example of Egyptian art in French architecture. She would also have seen the two frescos painted by Primaticcio on the lateral walls of the entrance with scenes from the life of Hercules. But it was the beauty of Fontainebleau's interiors that made it legendary throughout Europe.

Rosso Fiorentino introduced France to Mannerism, a later Renaissance style or *maniera* that abandoned harmony for complexity, striving for artificiality and fantasy. From 1534 until 1537 he worked on the long hall called the Gallery of Francis I. Beneath a carved and gilded ceiling and above sculpted walnut panelling with gold letter Fs and crowned lilies, he created brilliantly coloured frescos with mysterious

Above Framed by elegant female figures, a scene from the life of Alexander the Great by Primaticcio, *c.* 1541–44. This fresco decorated the bedchamber of Francis I's mistress at Fontainebleau.
Right A copy of *Ariadne* from a bronze model cast by Primaticcio in 1543 for Fontainebleau.

themes, possibly expressing royal power or Francis's life in Homeric symbolism. Each of the frescos is surrounded by high-relief stucco decoration of caryatids, sphinxes, putti, masks, medallions, swags and garlands of fruit, like exquisite icing-sugar confections, and crowning each fresco is a golden salamander. In 1532 Rosso was joined by Francesco Primaticcio, another Mannerist from Italy, who decorated the bedchambers of the King, of the Queen and of Francis's mistress, and also the Gallery of Henry II (or the Ballroom).

The Gallery of Ulysses contained sixty frescos, designed by Primaticcio but painted by Niccolò dell' Abbate who came to France from Italy in the reign of Henry II. Mary must have seen the work in progress, just as at the Hôtel de Guise. In the following century the great painter Nicolas Poussin proclaimed the Gallery of Ulysses to be 'the place most proper for forming a painter and nourishing his genius'. It was sadly destroyed in the eighteenth century. Primaticcio's manner of figure drawing – elegant, elongated nudes – was copied by artists from all over the world, and established one of the most recognizable characteristics of French painting for the rest of the sixteenth century. Art historian Kenneth Clark said of 'the exquisite ladies of Fontainebleau' that 'in spite of their remoteness from ordinary experience, they are calculated to arouse desire; indeed their very strangeness of proportion seems to invite erotic fantasies.'

The Gallery of Henry II, for which architect Philibert de L'Orme designed a coffered wooden ceiling, was built between 1540 and 1550. Primaticcio

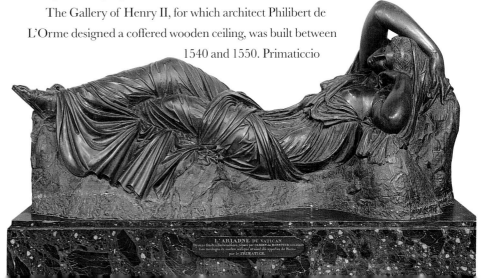

Left The Gallery of
Francis I at Fontainebleau.
Much altered over the
centuries, it remains the
most impressive interior
of Francis I's reign, and
was well known to the
Queen of Scots.
Background Henry II's
'Ballroom', Fontainebleau.
In 1552 Niccolò dell'
Abbate's first assignment
in France was to paint this
room with frescos based
on drawings by Primaticcio.
Mary would no doubt have
seen the work in progress.
Opposite top left *Portrait
of Francis I*, by Titian, sent
to the King by Pietro
Aretino from Venice in
1538, and possibly based
on a medal by Benvenuto
Cellini. **Top right** *Diana
and Callisto*, pen and ink
drawing, *c.* 1541–50, by
Primaticcio, a design used
for one of the murals in
the *chambres des bains* at
Fontainebleau. Diana
is discovering Callisto's
pregnancy for which
Jupiter was responsible.
Centre *Venus, Cupid, Folly
and Time*, by Bronzino,
c. 1544–55, and *St John
the Baptist*, by Leonardo
da Vinci, 1513–16.
Below This drawing by
Rubens has been identified
as Michelangelo's *Hercules*
(destroyed in 1714) which
came to Fontainebleau in
the reign of Henry II. The
gold salt-cellar was made
for Francis I by Cellini,
c. 1540–43 – a triumphal
arch holds the pepper and
a ship holds the salt.

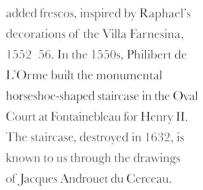

added frescos, inspired by Raphael's decorations of the Villa Farnesina, 1552–56. In the 1550s, Philibert de L'Orme built the monumental horseshoe-shaped staircase in the Oval Court at Fontainebleau for Henry II. The staircase, destroyed in 1632, is known to us through the drawings of Jacques Androuet du Cerceau.

Among the many extravagant pleasures at Fontainebleau were the *chambres des bains* or bathrooms installed beneath the Gallery of Francis I. The largest bath measured fourteen feet by ten and was three-and-a-half feet deep. Here one could languish in steamy scented water, listening to music and poetry while contemplating *Mona Lisa*'s smile, for Leonardo's painting and Michelangelo's deeply sensual *Leda and the Swan* were reputedly displayed in the bathing rooms. The bath chambers included six rooms for relaxation, decorated with mythological erotica designed by Primaticcio.

Other great works for Mary to contemplate from Francis I's collection were paintings by Raphael and his studio, including the *Belle Jardinière*; Leonardo's *Virgin of the Rocks*, his *Virgin and Child with St Anne* and the strangely compelling *St John*; Titian's portrait of Francis I; a Madonna by Andrea del Sarto; and Bronzino's *Venus, Cupid, Folly and Time*, perhaps the most famous of all Mannerist paintings. Lining the corridors of the château and in the privy garden were bronze statues made from casts which Primaticcio had brought from Rome in the 1540s so that French artists could study ancient sculpture – the *Laocoön*, the *Apollo Belvedere* and *Ariadne*, as well as reliefs from Trajan's Column. There were also Michelangelo's marble *Hercules*, casts of his *Pietà* (St Peter's, Rome) and his *Christ*, and 1550 saw the arrival of his *Rebellious Captive* and *Dying Captive*. It is small wonder, therefore, that sixteenth-century art historian Giorgio Vasari called Fontainebleau 'a second Rome' even though there were many works by French and Flemish artists also on display there.

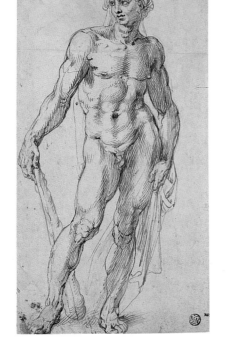

The great Florentine sculptor Benvenuto Cellini cast a bronze panel for the lunette of the Porte Dorée depicting the *Nymph of Fontainebleau*, a reclining Diana, which was later moved to Diane de Poitiers's château

of Anet. Cellini also designed a colossal figure of Mars for a fountain, and, to be cast in silver, twelve life-size candelabra of gods and goddesses commissioned by Francis I. Sadly, the only silver candelabrum to be completed was that of Jupiter. In 1543 Cellini presented Francis with the most famous of his works, a golden salt-cellar with a female figure representing Earth and a male figure holding a trident representing Sea. Mary may have been offered salt and pepper from this exquisite object; she certainly had plenty of opportunities to see it at one of the Paris palaces or other royal châteaux, as items of value moved with the court on the steady round from palace to palace. Even the frescos were, in a sense, transported. Towards the end of his life Francis had tapestries woven that reproduced the frescos and stucco work at Fontainebleau, and these too travelled with the court. Another outstanding feature of Fontainebleau was its library of three thousand books, which later provided the basis for France's national library, the Bibliothèque Nationale in Paris.

The court seldom stayed in one place for more than three months, endlessly moving among the châteaux relatively close to Paris, such as Saint-Germain-en-Laye, Villers-Cotterêts and Fontainebleau. In Paris the preferred residence was the Louvre, though the Palace of the Tournelles was also used. Then there were the delightful royal châteaux along the banks of the Loire, including Blois, Chambord, Chenonceau and Amboise. When the Valois court moved, as many as 18,000 people followed, with about 12,000 on horseback; ladies generally travelled in carts or litters, or by river on barges with luxurious cabins. This city on the move included a train of baggage carrying food, wine, plate and tapestries so that even en route, dining *al fresco* beneath the trees, 'the assembly were served as well as if one had been in Paris'.

Mary became well acquainted with the royal palaces of the Loire and each had unique charms. Blois, built on a sharp cliff, was the first monument of Francis I's reign. To the existing medieval structure he added a wing consisting of galleries and arcaded loggias, perhaps inspired by Bramante's Vatican. In the courtyard of the château, Francis's showpiece was an open, octagonal staircase, a hybrid of Renaissance and Gothic design composed of white stone exquisitely carved and fretted and further embellished with sculpted figures and ornaments. On each level of the staircase is a platform where the guard, resplendent in striped uniforms of blue, red and white, stood on parade to greet the King – by night

Opposite Francis I's showpiece at the château of Blois, an open octagonal staircase combining classical and Gothic decoration.
Above The double-spiral staircase at the centre of the château of Chambord. The staircase rises into a great lantern tower on the roof where Catherine de' Medici climbed with her astrologers to consult the stars. The design of the staircase may have been influenced posthumously by Leonardo da Vinci's sketches.
Right The loggias, *c.* 1520, of the château of Blois, overlooking the gardens. The balconies were decorated with heraldic bas-reliefs and mythological scenes showing Francis I as Hercules. The design of the loggias was probably inspired by that of Donato Bramante for the Vatican.

Above The château of Chambord, entrance to the main courtyard. Begun in 1518 and completed *c.* 1543, the château, consisting of 440 rooms, bears the hallmark of Italian style in its carvings, arched galleries and layout – the structure of the main building was designed to a plan identical to St Peter's in Rome. Henry II made several improvements to the château, and Dauphin Francis liked to hunt in the surrounding forests.

they held torches. The castle has Italian-style gardens on descending terraces, and when Mary lived at Blois there were numerous reflecting pools, fountains, pavilions and orangeries. Queen Claude, wife of Francis I, had introduced the rare greengage from Palestine to the gardens, still called the *Reine Claude*.

One's first glimpse of Chambord, in the distance through the trees, is quite magical. One nineteenth-century visitor to the château wrote that it appeared as if 'an eastern genie had kidnapped it during one of a thousand and one nights and removed it from the realm of the sun in order to conceal it in the realm of mist'. Indeed Chambord's extraordinary roofscape – a forest of sculpted chimneys – is the perfect expression of Renaissance theatricality, entirely appropriate for the Valois court, which had itself become a show of spectacle. Inside, the scene is all symmetry. All the rooms and apartments are laid out in the form of a Greek cross around a double-spiral staircase – a feat of engineering which allows two people, each climbing one of the two flights simultaneously, to see the other person without ever meeting. The staircase extends into the great lantern tower on the roof where Catherine de' Medici climbed with her astrologers 'in order to consult by night the sky and stars'. Leonardo da Vinci has been associated with the design of Chambord ever since Palladio wrongly described one of Leonardo's drawings as 'the Chambord staircase' in 1570. Leonardo, however, did play with a four-spiral

Below The flamboyant roofscape of Chambord, bristling with tall chimneys (365 of them), turrets, lantern turrets, huge ornate dormer windows and a vast central lantern tower – all seemingly conjured up from a tale of Arabian magic.

design, of which the Chambord staircase may be a variant. As for the rest of the château, the great master had drawn a similar scheme for a villa in Milan, and, although he carried out designs for Francis I, there is no certain connection with Chambord. Henry II continued to make improvements to the château, and the Dauphin, an enthusiastic huntsman, liked to spend short periods there.

Leonardo lived thirty miles down-river from Chambord in a comfortable manor house in the town of Amboise, and died there in 1519. The château of Amboise rises up from a rock spur above the town which lies on the south bank of the Loire. Its history stretches back into antiquity; Julius Caesar is said to have slept there and the château has belonged – in one form or another – to a series of French princes. The golden age of Amboise was in the fifteenth century, when the structure was

Below The château of Amboise on the Loire. The royal children, with the young Queen of Scots, frequently stayed there.
Opposite below The Gothic-style chapel of St Hubert at Amboise. The exterior is decorated with stone carvings of the chase. Inside rest the remains of Leonardo da Vinci.
Opposite above The château of Chenonceau straddling the River Cher.

enlarged by Louis XI and again by Charles VIII whose gardens lacked 'only Adam and Eve to make an earthly paradise'. Francis I spent much of his youth there and later added to a wing begun by Louis XII. At Amboise, Francis held magnificent festivities – balls, tournaments, masquerades – and fights between bulls and lions from the château's menagerie (which also included two leopards), and here in 1539 with great ceremony he received his old adversary the Emperor Charles V. Henry II reinforced the castle's defences, as did Mary's first husband upon becoming King Francis II. For Mary the château's particular attraction may have been its prominent position which still allows one to enjoy far-reaching views of the Loire meandering off into the distance.

A few miles from Amboise, set on piers over the River Cher, is a charming residence that used to belong to Diane de Poitiers, the château of Chenonceau. It was a gift from her lover, Henry II, and is, as it undoubtedly was then, one of

the most romantic-looking buildings in the Loire Valley. It was built in 1513,
basically, a square structure with pitched roofs and turrets at the four corners.
Francis I, who had always been fascinated by Chenonceau, acquired it for the
Crown, after making the château's owner bankrupt. In 1556, Diane asked Philibert
de L'Orme to design an extension consisting of a great gallery set on a bridge
spanning the river. The bridge was built between 1555 and 1559, but the gallery –
in fact two galleries – one above the other – were later completed under Catherine
de' Medici. From the bedchamber that Mary occupied she could open her
diamond-paned window to see the river flowing below, and, beside the river, Diana's
great garden. From 1551 to 1556 the labourers working on the garden were paid,
in all, for 14,000 days' work. Where a fountain gushed sparkling water, two paths
intersected diagonally to create four large triangles that were then subdivided into
geometric shapes; 13,000 hawthorns and hazels were uprooted from the woods
to form hedges lining the paths and leading to arbours, all designed for romantic
wandering walks, and there was that other essential of a great park, a labyrinthine

Opposite background
The garden of the château
of Chenonceau.
Above In 1556 Diane de
Poitiers asked Philibert
de L'Orme to design a
bridge suppoting a great
gallery, completed 1576.
Above right The room
occupied by Mary during
her visits to Chenonceau.
Her coat-of-arms is
displayed on the ceiling.
Right Diane's bedroom
at Chenonceau. The
chimneypiece by Jean
Goujon displays a portrait
of Catherine de' Medici
who took over the château
after Henry II's death.

Opposite A Flanders
tapestry from the château
of Anet, 16th century.
This is one of a series
of hunting tapestries
depicting falconry, bear-
hunting and duck-netting.
Diane de Poitiers is said
to have taught Mary to fly
falcons at Chenonceau.
Below *Lady at Her Toilet*,
School of Fontainebleau,
thought to be Diane de
Poitiers. Ronsard wrote
of this lady transforming
herself into Venus.
Below right *Lady at Her
Toilet, c.* 1558–60. The face
closely resembles Clouet's
authentic portraits of Mary.

maze. The beds were decorated with fruit trees, bushes and flowers, and included
6 peach-apricot trees (specially developed for Chenonceau), 300 banana trees,
currant bushes, 100 musk roses and lilies; 9,000 wild strawberry and violet plants
were gathered in the woods for Diane's garden, and 150 white mulberry trees were
planted to feed silkworms. Square plots contained the vegetable garden where
artichokes and melons grew alongside cucumbers, leeks, cabbages, peas, onions
and shallots.

It has been claimed that Diane de Poitiers taught Mary Stewart to fly falcons
at Chenonceau. Mary became a superb horsewoman and would ride into the woods
with her trained birds, despatching them to soar, then plunge at the quarry flushed
out by the royal hounds. The importance attached to hunting was such that the
Grand Huntsman of France was a great officer of state. The royal party was
generally accompanied by at least 25 couple of hounds and 60 whips, plus scores
of grooms and footmen. They stalked boar, deer, wolves and otters, moving towards

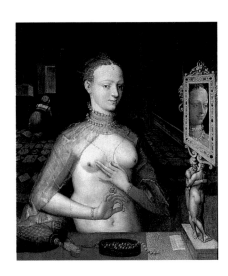

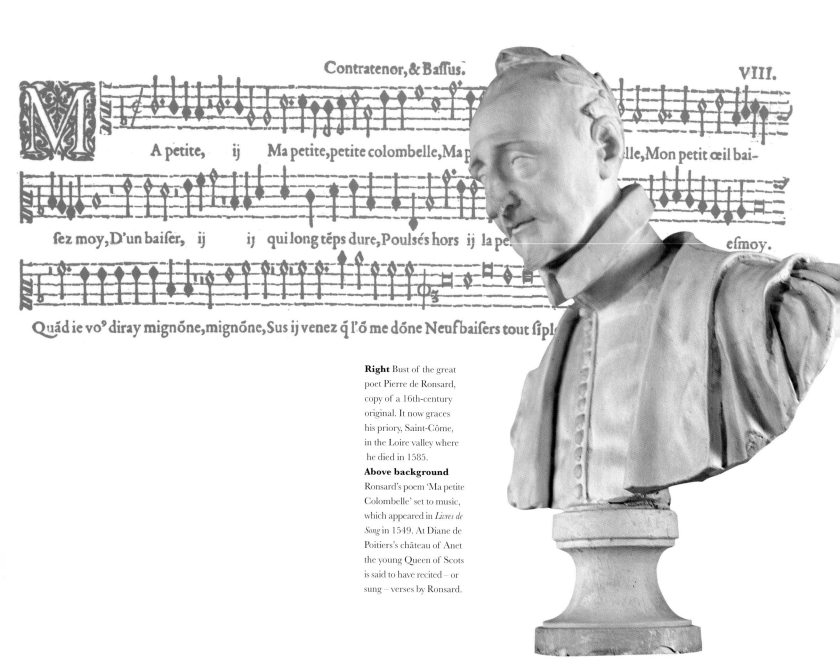

Contratenor, & Baſſus.   VIII.

M A petite,   ij   Ma petite, petite colombelle, Ma p[...]lle, Mon petit œil bai-

ſez moy, D'un baiſer,   ij   ij   qui long téps dure, Poulſés hors ij la pe[...]   eſmoy.

Quád ie vo⁹ diray mignône, mignône, Sus ij venez q̃ l'ô me dône Neufbaiſers tout ſipl[...]

Right Bust of the great
poet Pierre de Ronsard,
copy of a 16th-century
original. It now graces
his priory, Saint-Côme,
in the Loire valley where
he died in 1585.
Above background
Ronsard's poem 'Ma petite
Colombelle' set to music,
which appeared in *Livres de
Song* in 1549. At Diane de
Poitiers's château of Anet
the young Queen of Scots
is said to have recited – or
sung – verses by Ronsard.

the climax in stately procession, accompanied by the music of brass horns. The animals were slain by sword, crossbow, arquebus or boar-spear. These weapons were superbly crafted – often gilded and finely decorated. The return of the hunts involved further pageantry and yet more music.

Francis I's promotion of arts and literature continued to flourish in the mid-sixteenth century. French writers and artists, such as Pierre de Ronsard, Philibert de L'Orme and Jean Goujon, absorbed the best that Italy (and Greece) had to offer, and then went on to create works that were classical, but also deeply French. Under Henry II patronage and collecting continued, influenced by Diane de Poitiers, an intelligent connoisseur. At her château of Anet, Diane presided over literary gatherings attended by many distinguished men of arts and letters. There Mary is said to have recited poetry by Ronsard, a leading figure in a group of poets known as the Pléiade. They were passionate about the beauty and flexibility of the French language, shaping words that conveyed nuances of feeling never before expressed. Much of Ronsard's verse was intended for musical accompaniment, drawing on other senses to elevate what he regarded as a highly moral activity.

The Cardinal of Lorraine said, 'World travellers come to Anet and carry back to their countries fame of her beauty and knowledge of the arts.' The château was, and still is, one of France's architectural treasures. Once an immense complex of buildings and courtyards, what remains of the original château is still exquisite. Diane de Poitiers commissioned architect Philibert de L'Orme to build Anet between 1547 and about 1552. When Henry II ascended the throne, de L'Orme

Below The château of Anet as it appeared in the 16th century, from a drawing by Jacques Androuet du Cerceau. It was built between 1547 and 1552. Here Diane de Poitiers presided over gatherings of distinguished men of arts and letters. Mary's uncle, the Cardinal of Lorraine, said of Diane de Poitiers: 'World travellers come to Anet, and carry back to their countries fame of her beauty and knowledge of the arts.'

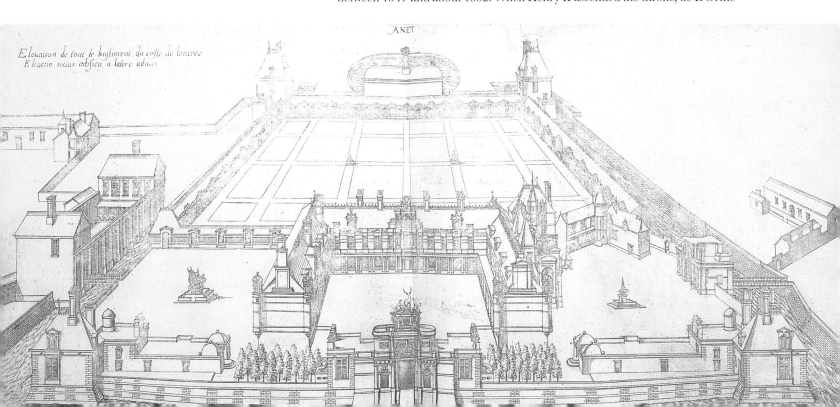

Left The entrance gate of the château of Anet. The triumphal arch is surmounted by a clockwork stag. In the tympanum is a plaster cast of Cellini's bronze relief of *Diana* (now in the Louvre). **Opposite** *Diana the Huntress* – a replica at the château of Anet of the marble and gilt bronze statue (now in the Louvre), which had been part of an impressive fountain in the courtyard of Anet.

was appointed Superintendent of Buildings, and throughout the King's reign he remained one of the most powerful figures in the French Renaissance, setting a standard that championed reason over blind conformity to classical models. Art historian Anthony Blunt said of him that his 'independence of mind makes him a worthy contemporary to the poets of the Pléiade, and a true representative of the first period in which France may be said to have produced her own classical style'.

Although the greater part of Anet was destroyed during the French Revolution, its essential features – the main entrance gate, the frontispiece from the main block and the chapel – have been preserved. The entrance gate has, according to Blunt, 'neither predecessor nor successor'. Its only classical components are Doric columns round the door, and, in concept, it is a sequence of masonry blocks building upward towards a central feature, a great clock. A work of ingenious mechanics, the clock consists of a bronze stag surrounded by hounds; the stag moves round with the striking of the hours, facing in opposite directions at midday and at midnight. Elaborate open-work balustrades extend round the whole of the structure. Cellini's bronze relief of Diana (now replaced by a plaster copy) had given an element of colour to the entrance gate. The frontispiece of the main block (today in the courtyard of the Ecole des Beaux-Arts in Paris) was developed from the medieval

château entrance which has been transformed by applying Orders one above the other in correct sequence, displaying a monumentality unprecedented in France. Even more remarkable is the chapel; here de L'Orme's genius must have been exalted by spirituality – the result is sublime. This is the first chapel in France to use the Renaissance principle that the circle is the perfect figure and therefore appropriate for the house of God. De L'Orme applies this principle with originality by creating not only a central circular domed space, but also creating side chapels that make a circle of the outer perimeter, interrupted only by the right angles of the two sacristies. The pattern of the black and white marble floor (Diane's favourite colours), composed of arcs of circles, reflects the coffering of the dome. Today a sign declares that Mary Stewart worshipped in the chapel.

The young Dauphin Francis wrote of Anet in 1550: 'I never slept better than in a big bed where I lay in the room of my King.' He then went on to praise the château's 'fine gardens, galleries, aviaries and many other good and pretty things'. During Mary's stays at Anet she would have enjoyed wandering in the gardens, bordered by *une galerie rustique*. The gardens surrounded a courtyard which boasted a vast fountain of high quality and individual style, with as its centrepiece *Diana*, the huntress with stag and hounds, sculpted in creamy marble and gilt bronze. It has long been regarded as Jean Goujon's most famous work although it has also been attributed to Benvenuto Cellini and to Germain Pilon.

There is no doubt, however, that Jean Goujon was responsible for the decorations in a room that was highly significant in Mary's life, the Great Hall (now called the Salle des Caryatides) of the Louvre in Paris, where Mary was officially betrothed to Francis. The Dauphin was not old enough to wed until his fourteenth birthday in 1558, a date that could not come soon enough for the Guises, whose opponents sought a French marriage for the Dauphin. At last, in October 1557, Henry II invited to France a group of Scottish commissioners, led by Mary's half-brother

Above and opposite
The chapel at the château of Anet, *c.* 1552, designed by Philibert de L'Orme. Its coffered dome ceiling, reflects the black-and-white pattern of the chapel's marble floor – the favourite colours of Diane de Poitiers and Henry II.

James Stewart, to enter into negotiations for the marriage contract between the Queen of Scots and the French Dauphin. The agreement that Mary eventually signed, witnessed by Diane de Poitiers among others, assured the Scots of their ancient freedoms and privileges; both Scots and French were given dual nationality; and in the event of Francis's death, Mary would have the choice of either staying in France or returning to Scotland. If Mary herself died without issue, the rights of the next legal heir to Scotland's throne would be upheld. But Mary was also persuaded to sign another agreement, a secret document that effectively nullified the contract with the Scottish commissioners. In this the Queen of Scots promised that if she died childless her kingdom would pass to Henry II, and that the French could draw payment from Scotland for expenses incurred in defending the Scots from the English. It was a sinister act, probably made under pressure from her Guise uncles, but then she was only fifteen and full of bright hopes for her future; Mary didn't intend to die, nor did she expect to leave France, so she signed away her country without any apparent qualms. On 19 April 1558 Mary and Francis were betrothed in the Great Hall of the Louvre, their hands ceremoniously joined by the Cardinal of Lorraine.

The ancient royal fortress of the Louvre had from 1546 been transformed into a palace by Francis I. Architect Pierre Lescot and sculptor Jean Goujon made it the first realization of Renaissance art in Paris, giving the façade of the building classical ordinance and larger windows. Under Henry II the western part of the palace was revamped, and in the Great Hall, Goujon – a Mannerist with his own personal style of classicism – designed a gallery supported by four caryatids, a monumental work that gives the Great Hall a commanding stateliness. The betrothal ceremony was celebrated with a ball in which Mary and Henry II led the dancing. Five days later, on 24 April, Mary and Francis were married.

It was the first time a Dauphin had been married in Paris in over two hundred years, and the Valois court, for whom spectacle was second nature, surpassed itself. All the city turned out to experience the colour, the sound, the richness of the show. According to medieval tradition, the wedding vows were exchanged outside the church doors and solemnized by Mass within the church. A pavilion twelve feet high, decorated with tapestries and fleurs-de-lis, was set up at the main entrance to the cathedral of Notre Dame. The pavilion was approached by an arched gallery covered with green boughs along which the state officials, clergy and the wedding

Opposite The Great Hall in the Louvre (the Salle des Caryatides) where Mary was betrothed to Dauphin Francis in 1558. It was in the gallery (designed by Goujon), supported by four caryatids, that the musicians played for the ball that followed the ceremony.
Above A painting of a wedding ball in the Louvre in 1581, attended by King Henry III and his mother, Catherine de' Medici (seated left), perhaps not unlike the ball given for Mary and Francis in 1558.

Below Enamelled copper cup, a wedding gift for Mary and Francis. The cup, dated 1556, is from the royal factory at Limoges. It displays *The Wedding of Psyche*, worked in *grisaille d'or* – subtle shades of grey picked out in gold – and the arms of Scotland are on the base.

party proceeded to the sound of a trumpet fanfare. First came the Swiss halberdiers, carrying their pikes, followed by the musicians of their regiment dressed in red and gold. Bishop du Bellay was accompanied by his cross-bearer and by choirboys carrying lighted candles. Francis, Duke of Guise, taking charge, endeared himself to the spectators by urging the lords and ladies not to crowd so much as to obstruct the view for onlookers. There were more musicians, followed by a hundred gentlemen of the royal household bedecked in their finest attire and the princes of the blood. In the procession there were also eighteen bishops and abbots, six cardinals; then came the fourteen-year-old Dauphin, led by the King of Navarre and accompanied by his brothers, Charles and Henry. Finally came the moment everyone had been waiting for – Mary, dazzling in white, the traditional mourning colour of French queens. It was the perfect choice for the slender fifteen-year-old bride, almost six feet tall, setting off her golden-brown hair, hazel eyes and fair complexion. On her head she wore a crown of gold, set with sapphires, rubies and pearls of inestimable worth, and, round her neck, diamonds and precious gemstones glittered, catching the sunlight. Two girls carried her exceptionally long train, and the crowd went mad with delight as this vision passed by, followed by Catherine de' Medici and the princesses. Brantôme wrote that Mary 'appeared a hundred times more beautiful than a goddess of heaven…even if she had neither sceptre nor crown, her person alone was worth a kingdom'.

The Archbishop of Rouen performed the wedding ceremony, and, when the couple had exchanged vows, Henry II removed a ring from his own hand and passed it to the Archbishop who blessed it, then the Dauphin placed it on his bride's finger; Mary was now Queen-Dauphiness, and the Auld Alliance became manifest. The royal party then went inside the cathedral to hear Mass, during which gold and silver coins were thrown to the crowds, exciting pandemonium on both banks of the Seine. Then the wedding celebrations began with a lavish banquet, followed by evening revels to which Mary and Catherine de' Medici rode in a golden litter. The highlight of the evening was a pageant of ships, which, with the undulation of the floor-cloth painted like the sea, appeared to dip in waves carrying the flotilla across the room. The ships, swathed in cloth of gold and crimson velvet, had silver sails gently billowing in an artificial breeze as the vessels proceeded to the place where the ladies of the wedding party were seated. Each ship was commanded by a masked nobleman, dressed in cloth of gold, who beckoned to a lady to accompany him; the King took Mary, and the Dauphin took Catherine, then away they sailed.

Above Miniature of Mary Queen of Scots, by an unknown artist. With her left hand Mary places a ring on the third finger of her right hand. Since the wedding ring was worn on the right hand, this was probably a reference to her marriage to Francis in 1558.

Right Cabinet given to Mary and Francis as a wedding gift, Italian, 16th century. It is inlaid with mother-of-pearl and engraved ivory, with gold plaques depicting mythological scenes.

Left Double portrait
on vellum of 'Francis II
and Mary Stewart, Queen
of Scotland, his wife',
from the Book of Hours
belonging to Catherine
de' Medici.
Right Château of Villers-
Cotterêts, as seen from the
Courtyard of Henry II.
Mary visited this château
fifty miles north-east of
Paris on several occasions,
and with Francis spent
the first few weeks of
married life there.

In the early hours of the morning the bride and groom in the age-old tradition
were put to bed by the royal family. There were undoubtedly the usual smirks and
ribaldry before the couple were left in peace. It seems that Francis was physically
unable to consummate the marriage, but the young people, always devoted
companions, were happy in their union. And Guise-inspired French poets wrote
of the gain to their country in, essentially, acquiring Scotland.

After a night in Paris at the Hôtel de Guise, the honeymoon was spent at the
château of Villers-Cotterêts, fifty miles north-east of the capital. The château was
built around two courtyards, one of which was used as a tennis court. Philibert
de L'Orme designed a chapel in the park for Henry II around 1550; it was built
in the form of a trefoil with a free-standing classical portico. Today it is gone,
and all that is left of the château is only a fragment of its former magnificence,
a haven for swallows darting through broken windows to build their nests in the
curves of decorative putti. The wing dividing the courtyards survives with its
classical exterior and Chapel Royal and two staircases within. The Stairway

Opposite Chapel Royal at Villers-Cotterêts. Though altered in the 18th century and now in ruins, the chapel still displays much of its original Italian-influenced decoration. The frieze in high-relief is composed of fleurs-de-lis, the collar of the Order of St Michael and the crowned salamander – symbol of Francis I.
Above Ceiling sculptures above the stairway at Villers-Cotterêts – Hercules strangling a lion and Venus disarming Love.

of Honour and the Stairway of the King, with their coffered vaults, are sculpted with mythological scenes representing a satyr ravishing a nymph; Venus disarming Love; and Hercules strangling a lion. The Chapel Royal, though altered in the eighteenth century, still displays its original decoration with scenes from Francesco Colonna's *Hypnerotomachia Poliphili* (usually translated as 'The Strife of Love in a Dream'). Elsewhere a frieze in high-relief displays the fleur-de-lis and the collar of the Order of St Michael, surmounted by an imperial crown and the salamander. In its ruinous condition, the main elements of Villers-Cotterêts are somehow purified, giving an impression of such concentrated beauty that perhaps here, more than anywhere else, one is left astonished by the world Mary Stewart inhabited.

Life for the young couple continued merrily, though Mary more than once alarmed her family with fainting spells and vague illnesses. The court were quick to interpret anything from pallor to fainting as proof that Mary was carrying an heir to the French throne. Then September brought an untoward incident. The nine Scottish commissioners returning home were suddenly taken violently ill; four died, probably from food poisoning, and the Scots regarded the incident as an ill omen. It had been agreed during the marriage negotiations that Francis would have the crown matrimonial, that is, during the marriage he would rule jointly with Mary, and on official documents they were 'Francis and Mary, King and Queen of Scots'. Even from the first moment of her marriage, as soon as the benediction was pronounced, Mary called her husband King of Scotland. But when Henry II demanded that the Scottish crown be sent to France so that the Dauphin could be officially crowned King of Scots, there were endless delays and the crown remained in Scotland.

In 1557 Philip II of Spain, with the help of English forces, had invaded France from the north, taking Saint-Quentin where the army was under the command of Constable Montmorency. Montmorency was taken prisoner and it was feared that Philip would march on Paris. The Duke of Guise, who had been fighting unsuccessfully in Italy, was recalled to save his country. He reached Paris in October and was made Lieutenant General of the kingdom, with almost unlimited powers. He then made preparations for the siege of Calais where the hitherto impregnable fortress and town were taken, after six days of fighting, on 6 January 1558. Calais had been held by England for 220 years, the last English foothold in France. The Duke of Guise went on to capture Guînes, Thionville and Arlon, and Mary could once again take great pride in being a member of the Guise family.

In England, other momentous events were taking place. In November 1558 Queen Mary of England, wife of Philip II, died childless, and, following Henry VIII's will, her half-sister Elizabeth became Queen. Elizabeth was the daughter of Henry VIII and his second wife, Anne Boleyn. But in the eyes of the Catholic Church Henry's marriage to his first wife was still valid at the time of his second marriage; Elizabeth was, therefore, illegitimate, and her cousin Mary Stewart, being both a granddaughter of Henry VIII's sister, Margaret Tudor, and legitimate, had a stronger claim to the throne of England. For this reason Henry II of France, with strong support from the Guises, had Mary's cloth of estate, silver plate and other regalia emblazoned with the arms of England, quartered with those of Scotland and France. She assumed the style and titles of the ruler of England, even when she later became Queen of France, an intoxicating concept for a young person taught to believe that monarchs were divinely chosen and responsible only to God. A wedding hymn by René Guillon proclaimed that the union of the Dauphin and the Queen of Scots crossed the white lily of France with the white rose of Mary's Yorkist ancestors. Now, the wave of poetical propaganda supported not only Mary's claim to the English throne, but also the Dauphin's claims through marriage to the thrones of both Scotland and England.

The year 1559 began with celebrations for the wedding of Princess Claude, the Dauphin's sister, to the Duke of Lorraine, and Mary and Francis took part in all the festivities. In April, the treaty of Cateau-Cambrésis was signed between Spain, England, France and Savoy. The peace treaty provided that Italian territories taken by the French should be surrendered, and was sealed by two more royal weddings. Marguerite of Valois, the unmarried sister of Henry II, was to wed the Duke of Savoy following the wedding of Princess Elisabeth, Mary's childhood companion, to Philip II of Spain. The weddings entailed elaborate galas and pageantry including a series of jousts. The forty-year-old King practised every day 'at the tilt' for the coming tournament, as did the sickly Dauphin. On 30 June the King, clad in the black and white colours of Diane de Poitiers, entered the tiltyard to the cheers of the court and onlookers. He rode at the lists three times. During the last foray, his opponent, the Comte de Montgomerie, Captain of the Scottish Guard, thrust forward his lance which shattered on the King's breastplate, lodging splinters in his right temple and eye. The King reeled with pain, then became weak and had to be helped from his horse. He was then carried to his bedchamber in the Palace of the Tournelles. Henry's wounds were obviously grave. He lingered for ten days, attended by his family, including Mary, but died on 10 July 1559.

The Dauphin was now Francis II, King of France, and Mary was Queen of France. She ignored her own distress at losing someone she had grown to love, and consoled Catherine de' Medici and the rest of the family. When the Spanish Ambassador arrived to present Philip II's condolences, it was Mary who received

Below Drawing, *c.* 1559 of Mary's coat-of-arms, showing the arms of England quartered with those of Scotland and France.
Opposite background Tournament in June 1559 in which Henry II was fatally wounded.
Opposite Mary (in profile) with her husband Francis at the foot of King Henry II's deathbed, detail from a woodcut, 1559.

TOVRNELLES

Above and right On this coin, minted shortly after their marriage on 24 April 1558, Mary and Francis face each other. Above their heads is the new Scottish crown of the fleur-de-lis between crosses. On the reverse are the combined arms of Mary and Francis.

him on behalf of the family, making an appropriate reply to his speech. It was also Mary who ordered that an inventory be made of the late King's jewels so that they could be reclaimed from Diane de Poitiers, who had by now firmly aligned herself with the Guises' rival, Montmorency.

Henry II was buried at the cathedral of St-Denis, and in September Francis II was crowned at Reims. But the young King was more concerned with hunting than ruling, exasperating the Cardinal of Lorraine and the Duke of Guise in their attempts to explain matters of state. All the same, his lack of interest meant that the Guises could rule France with little hindrance. The English Ambassador reported: 'The House of Guise ruleth and doth all about the French King'; and it was not long before Charles Cardinal of Lorraine, was described as both Pope and King of France. The royal accounts for April to June 1560 are full of Guise expenditure.

During the spring of 1560, Mary and Francis with the court visited Blois and Amboise. Since the accession of Francis II, many, including the Calvinist and Huguenot nobles, had been unhappy about the now unrivalled power of the Guises. A conspiracy to overturn their government and remove the King from power was formed at Nantes. The Guises were warned of the plot (possibly by Catherine de' Medici who had, at one stage, been party to the rebel plans), and were ready when the château of Amboise was attacked on 19 March 1560. Several conspirators were killed outright and large numbers were taken prisoner. Guise vengeance was merciless. For a whole week there were tortures, quarterings and hangings of some 1,200 men, their bodies and remnants tossed into the Loire. Mary, who had an aversion to bloodshed, may or may not have witnessed the gruesome spectacle, but she would certainly have been aware of the proceedings. Not surprisingly, the events at Amboise became an embarrassment to France and inspired bitter hatred of the Guises.

It was a difficult time for the young Queen, who in June 1560 suffered the loss of her mother, Mary of Guise. The Venetian ambassador had earlier remarked that the Queen of Scots 'loved her mother incredibly, and much more than daughters usually love their mothers'. Overcome with sorrow, Mary spent the day passing 'from one agony to another'. It was Catherine de' Medici's turn to offer consolation; the two were – according to outward appearances – becoming close. They discussed Francis's health, went to chapel together and shared a dining chamber.

Right This engraving shows Catherine de' Medici with the Cardinal of Lorraine and Francis, Duke of Guise, either warning the brothers of the plot to attack the government at Amboise, or preparing countermeasures.

Below The brutal Guise revenge for the attack on Amboise on 19 March 1560, a contemporary woodcut.

As a demonstration of unity and joy that the young King was secure after the Amboise conspiracy, Catherine staged a grandiose celebration at Chenonceau in honour of her son and daughter-in-law. She had recently reappropriated the château from Diane de Poitiers and, on 31 March 1560, she welcomed Francis and Mary to her new estate with fireworks, a drum tattoo and waving banners. Along the avenue leading to Chenonceau were fanciful obelisks, columns, statues and fountains designed by Primaticcio; the path was strewn with violets and pinks. The couple passed through triumphal arches, then a young woman representing Fame stepped forward to congratulate the King, while an Athena – the protector of civilized life, the embodiment of wisdom, reason and purity – scattered bouquets of flowers to the wind; 900 servants looked on. In front of the château, statues of nymphs gushed with red wine, and the way to the forecourt was lit by a beacon in the form of a pillar, the symbol of imperial power. The young King and Queen were invited to wander in Diane's garden, passing on their way an altar decorated with branches of cypress, pine, pomegranate and boxwood (Pluto's sacred trees). On a column above the altar a golden Medusa's snaky head was reflected in Athena's shield – perhaps signifying hope. Yet, just over eight months later Mary would compare her life to 'darkest night'.

Left *The Bath of Diana*, School of Fontainebleau, attributed to François Clouet, thought to be a pastoral on the triumph of the Guises on Mary's marriage to the Dauphin in 1558. The Guises and Diane de Poitiers had, by that time, become enemies, and Mary is celebrated as the new Diana. She seems to appear twice in the painting – in the centre as the goddess Diana, attended by the wife of Duke Francis, and on the right as a nymph. Seated is a youthful-looking Catherine de' Medici. If this interpretation is correct, the horseman is the Dauphin and the two satyrs are Mary's uncles, Francis and Charles.

On 5 December 1560 Francis II died of an illness brought on by an ear infection. The English Ambassador, Sir Nicholas Throckmorton, wrote that the young King 'had departed to God, leaving as heavy and dolorous a wife as of good right she had reason to be, who, by long watching with him during his sickness [which lasted nineteen days], and by painful diligence about him, especially the issue thereof, is not in the best time of her body, but without danger.' Mary had grown to love her childhood companion, and would regard Francis as her true husband all her life. On his death, she wrote a lengthy 'sad, quiet song' which included the following lines:

Whether in wood or meadow,
Whether at dawn of day
My heart feels ceaselessly
Grief for his loss to me.

Below and opposite

Mary Queen of Scots in White Mourning, artist unknown. This painting on panel is based on the black-and-red chalk drawings by François Clouet, *c.* 1559–61, of Mary in '*deuil blanc*'. Within a period of eighteen months she suffered the deaths of her mother, Mary of Guise; her father-in-law, Henry II; and her husband, Francis II.

The traditional period of mourning for a Queen of France was forty days. Mary, three days before her eighteenth birthday, again put on white garments and shut herself in a darkened room; no light but torchlight was permitted to enter. There, after the initial convulsions of grief, she began to consider her future. In verse she wrote: 'He who was my dearest, already is my plight.' Her role in the Valois court, though honourable if she chose to remain in France, would certainly be less exalted, and Catherine de' Medici had waited only a day after her son's death to retrieve from Mary the crown jewels. Would it be better to become the consort of another powerful, continental monarch? After only two weeks of mourning, the Queen of Scots was beginning to consider a second marriage. Several candidates were considered – publicly by the court, privately by Mary and the Guises. Francis II's younger brother Charles, now King Charles IX, had become entranced by her and though only eleven years old, was a possible second husband. 'Happy brother!' he would exclaim whenever he gazed at Mary's portrait; 'though your life and reign were so short, you were to be envied…the possessor of that angel, and the object of her love.' Brantôme recorded that the King of Navarre wanted to abandon his wife in order to marry the widowed Queen of Scots, and a son of Constable Montmorency (also married) was thought to be in love with her. There were other candidates, among them the heir to the throne of Spain, sixteen-year-old Don Carlos. The Spanish prince was a superb political choice, but there his attractions ended. Physically, he was misshapen, undersized, had epilepsy and a speech impediment; he later developed tendencies towards homicidal mania. Mary nevertheless favoured the match, and the advantage to Spain, one of France's old adversaries, would be in gaining a potentially useful ally. But Catherine de' Medici

Opposite and above
Mary Queen of Scots, by
Ponce Jacqio, *c.* 1559/60.
This bronze bust shows
an idealized likeness of
Mary, then about 17 years
of age, when she was also
Queen of France. On her
head she wears the closed
imperial crown made of
linked fleurs-de-lis. The
bust is in the Mannerist
style of northern Italy
which was very popular
at the Valois court.

would not have it. With the death of Francis II, the Guises had lost much of their
power; Catherine, who now ruled as Regent on behalf of Charles, had no intention
of restoring their ascendancy with a Spanish marriage, nor did she wish to see her
daughter Elisabeth, wife of Philip II, one day overshadowed by Mary. Catherine
persuaded Elisabeth to convince the King of Spain that such an alliance would
be both dangerous and costly, and by June 1561 it was generally known that there
would be no marriage between Don Carlos and the Queen of Scots. Mary was
bitterly disappointed.

The situation in Scotland was hardly enticing, although, according to
Throckmorton, the Queen of Scots' difficulties were no greater than those faced
by other sovereigns: 'Madam, your realm is in no other case at this day than all the
other realms of Christendom are; the proof whereof you see verified in this realm
[France]'. The previous two years had been crucial in the history of Scotland. Mary
of Guise had been deposed as Regent by the Prostestant Lords of the Congregation
in October 1559, and her authority transferred to a Council of Regency led by the
Duke of Châtelherault (James Hamilton). With the help of French troops, Mary
of Guise struggled to regain the Regency and, she had some success. But, after
several months, both sides were lacking resources and the conflict came to a standstill.
The Protestant lords turned to England for help, signing the Treaty of Berwick in
February 1560, which provided the lords with money and troops. The English gains
were the promotion of Protestantism north of the Border, and, potentially, the
removal of the French who still maintained important strongholds in Scotland.
In June 1560, Mary of Guise died, and the hostilities ended. The Queen of Scots
had done nothing to check the ever-increasing power of the lords; by failing to act,
she effectively handed them control of the country. And it was the Protestant
lords, 'the Great Council of the Realm', who benefited most from the Treaty of
Edinburgh, signed in July 1560, between England, Scotland and France. By this treaty
both the English and the French were to leave Scotland; the position that France held
in Scotland since 1548 (the year the Queen of Scots was sent to France) was lost. Mary
refused to ratify the treaty which also required her to recognize Elizabeth as the
rightful Queen of England by giving up quartering the English arms with her own.

Then in August the Scottish parliament met to clarify the religious situation.
The Scottish lords authorized a new Protestant Confession of Faith, abolished
the power of the Pope in Scotland, and made both the saying and the hearing of
Mass unlawful; all acts previously protecting the old Church were invalidated. But
there were still large numbers of Catholics in Scotland whose hopes for reinstating
Catholicism as the official religion were dampened but not extinguished, and there

Right and opposite

Mary's Book of Hours, undoubtedly a gift from her husband Francis, Printed in Paris by Renauld and Claude Chaudière in 1549. The front displays an armillary sphere surrounded by the words *'unus non sufficit orbis'* ('one world is not enough'). The back displays the arms of the Dauphin of France and King of Scotland, crossed with those of Mary. In 1561, en route to Calais, and her departure for Scotland, Mary stayed overnight at the abbey of St-Pierre-les-Dames where she gave this book as a parting memento to her aunt Renée, the Abbess.

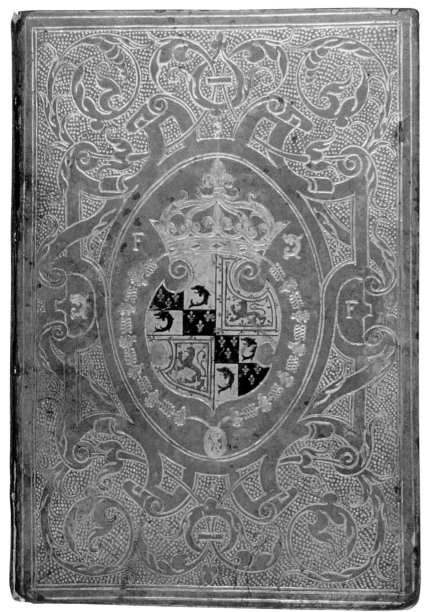

were perceptible disagreements between the Protestant lords. Representing Scottish Catholics, John Leslie, later Bishop of Ross, assured Mary that if she returned to her own country she would find a warm welcome there. He also suggested that, as a Catholic monarch, Mary should initiate a counter-Reformation in Scotland by entering the country not in Edinburgh, but in the north at Aberdeen. By so doing she would receive the support of the powerful earls there, particularly the Earl of Huntly, which would promise an army of 20,000 Catholics. Mary refused to entertain Leslie's suggestion. Throckmorton, who had many interviews with the young Queen observed: 'That she is both of great wisdom for her years, modesty and also of great judgment.'

James Stewart, Mary's illegitimate half-brother, then aged thirty, spent five days with her in April 1561. After her period of mourning Mary had travelled with the court and visited her Guise relations probably to canvass their views regarding her future. When James caught up with her, the two allegedly argued against each other's religion: Lord James asked Mary to renounce Catholicism and embrace the Protestant faith; she declined, suggesting in turn that if he became a Catholic she would see that he soon wore a cardinal's hat; he also refused. The obligatory rhetoric dealt with, they got down to business. Mary's political attitude towards religion was to show tolerance, heeding James's words: 'Abuiff all things, Madame, for the luif of God, presse na matters of religion, not for any mans advice on the earth.' However, regarding her own religious observances, she would only return to Scotland if she was allowed to hear Mass in her private chapel. On condition that she recognized the Protestant Church, James agreed. John Leslie claimed that in return for Mary granting James's request for the earldom of Moray, it is likely that he offered to support Mary's claim to the English throne. A few months later he wrote to Queen Elizabeth pointing out that, 'by the law of all nations', Mary was the next descendant 'of the right line of King Henry the Seventh'. On 10 June Lord James concluded matters by writing to Mary, extending a formal invitation from the Protestant lords for her return to Scotland. The hope of a continental marriage exhausted, Mary made up her mind to accept.

In preparation for her departure she sent a request to Queen Elizabeth for safe passage through English waters. But Mary had not ratified the Treaty of Edinburgh recognizing Elizabeth as Queen, and the pass was, therefore, denied. Mary was all the more eager to make the voyage, and told Throckmorton:

If my preparations were not so well advanced as they are, perhaps the Queen your mistress's unkindness might stop my voyage, but now I am determined to adventure the matter, whatsoever comes of it. I trust the wind will be so favourable as I shall not need to come to the coast of England, but if I do, then, Monsieur l'Ambassadeur, the Queen your mistress shall have me in her hands to do her will with me, and if she be so hard-hearted as to desire my end, she may then do her pleasure and make sacrifice of me.

Four days of farewell festivities were held in Mary's honour at Saint-Germain-en-Laye. Then, on 25 July, she made her farewells to Catherine de' Medici and Charles IX, and set out for the port of Calais via Reims, where she paid a final visit to her Guise aunt, Renée, Abbess of St-Pierre-les-Dames. On 14 August 1561, Mary, visibly unhappy, boarded the great white galley that would take her to Scotland. She was joined by three of her Guise uncles, leaving Francis Duke of Guise and Charles Cardinal of Lorraine to contend with the changing politics in France. A retinue of courtiers also accompanied her, including Brantôme and the four Maries – her playmates on the voyage made thirteen years earlier. As her ship pulled away from shore Mary wept uncontrollably. She kept to that part of the galley nearest to the French shore watching as the land so dear to her receded from view. Over and over, the eighteen-year-old Queen was reputedly heard to utter through her sobs, '*Adieu France!... Adieu, ma chère France!... C'en est fait!... je pense ne vous revoir jamais plus!*' ('Good bye, dear France.... It is done.... I think I will never ever see you again.')

One of Ronsard's finest poems, *Elégie à Marie Stuart*, laments the Queen's departure for Scotland. It recalls her portrait, 'a sacred image' in white mourning dress; the memory of Mary walking in the park at Fontainebleau her white veils 'billowing like sails from a mast'; then the scene changes as the galley takes her away from France.

ELEGIE SVR LE DES-
part de la Royne Marie retour-
nant à son Royaume
d'Escosse.

OMME vn beau pré
despouillé deses fleurs,
Comme vn tableau priué
de ses couleurs,
Comme le ciel s'il perdoit
ses estoilles,
La mer ses eaues:le nauire ses voiles,
Comme vn beau champ de son bled des-
couuert,
Et côme vn bois perdãt son mãteau verd,
Et vn anneau sa pierre precieuse,
Ainsi perdra la France soucieuse
Ses ornemens en perdant la beauté
Qui fut sa fleur,sa couleur & clarté.
Dure fortune indomptable & felonne
Tu es vrayement fille d'vne Lyonne,
Tu vas passant les Tygres en rigueur.

A 2

Left A poem written by Ronsard on Mary's departure from France in August 1561. He laments: 'Like a fine meadow stripped of its flowers,/Like a painting deprived of its colours,/Like the sky should it lose its stars,/The sea its waters, the ship its sails,/Like a beautiful field shorn of its wheat,/A wood losing its verdant mantle/And a ring its precious jewel,/So will grieving France lose all ornament in losing the loveliness/That once was her flower, her colour and her radiance.' The poet recalls Mary's portrait, a 'sacred image' in white mourning, and Mary walking in the park at Fontainebleau, her white veils 'billowing like sails from a mast', a harbinger of the ship that was to take her to Scotland. Ronsard had served in Scotland as a page of James V, 1537–39.

Her Majesty in Scotland

'Lady, whose sceptre (yours by long descent)
Gives Scotland now a happy government
By beauty, virtue, merit and sweet grace
Queen of your sex, star of our age, our race '

George Buchanan's dedication to Mary Queen of Scots (1562).

Left Falkland Palace
in Fife, showing the east
range overlooking the
pleasure gardens. Falkland
was the hunting palace
of the Stewart dynasty,
and a residence that the
Queen of Scots particularly
enjoyed visiting. Here, like
her father, she practised
archery and also the royal
game of tennis, and rode
out into the surrounding
hills and forest, hunting
stag and boar, and
hawking. It was recorded
that between 1561 and
1565 the Queen of Scots
played at being 'a country
girl in the park and woods'.

At about nine o'clock in the morning on 19 August 1561 two galleys – one white and one red, bearing aloft blue flags displaying the royal arms of France – sailed into Leith harbour, Edinburgh's port. The morning was dense with fog, a common occurrence along the North Sea coast, but one which the Scottish reformer John Knox twisted to his advantage when writing about the event: 'The dolorous face of the heavens [foretold the] sorrow, dolour, darkness and all [the] impiety' that Mary would bring to Scotland. Her initial reception was certainly disappointing. When the galleys fired a salute announcing the Queen's arrival, a ragtag of townspeople and dock workers squinted through the gloom in stunned silence; Mary had not been expected until the end of the month.

She was taken to the house of a local merchant to rest and take refreshment while Edinburgh was alerted to the Queen's arrival and the royal Palace of Holyrood made ready. That evening, 'sundry noble men and the town of Edinburgh', including the Duke of Châtelherault, his son James Hamilton, 3rd Earl of Arran, and Mary's half-brother Lord James, escorted the Queen and her resplendent entourage to Holyrood. There was, perhaps, not a glaring contrast between the finery of the French and the attire of those Scottish nobles who had visited the Valois court (though Brantôme thought the Scots drab). But when Mary saw the horses provided for her uncles

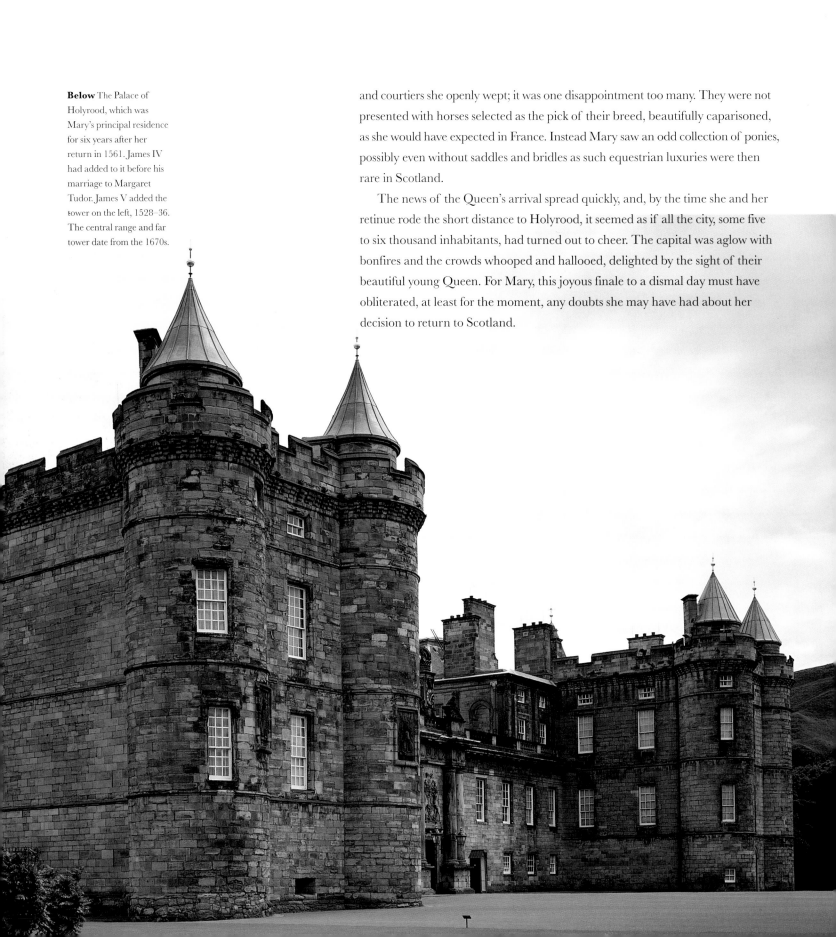

Below The Palace of Holyrood, which was Mary's principal residence for six years after her return in 1561. James IV had added to it before his marriage to Margaret Tudor. James V added the tower on the left, 1528–36. The central range and far tower date from the 1670s.

and courtiers she openly wept; it was one disappointment too many. They were not presented with horses selected as the pick of their breed, beautifully caparisoned, as she would have expected in France. Instead Mary saw an odd collection of ponies, possibly even without saddles and bridles as such equestrian luxuries were then rare in Scotland.

The news of the Queen's arrival spread quickly, and, by the time she and her retinue rode the short distance to Holyrood, it seemed as if all the city, some five to six thousand inhabitants, had turned out to cheer. The capital was aglow with bonfires and the crowds whooped and hallooed, delighted by the sight of their beautiful young Queen. For Mary, this joyous finale to a dismal day must have obliterated, at least for the moment, any doubts she may have had about her decision to return to Scotland.

Above Holyrood, the ruins of the Abbey Church are overshadowed by 'Arthuris Sete'. Founded as an Augustinian monastery in 1128, it became the quarters of succeeding Scottish kings as Edinburgh became recognized as Scotland's capital. Mary of Guise was crowned in the Abbey Church, and Scottish kings and members of the royal family were buried here.

By the time Mary's father, James V, had come to power, Edinburgh had long been established as the centre of government. Scotland was a poor country, but Edinburgh, with its busy port, was prosperous and cosmopolitan. The Royal Mile, the main street extending between Edinburgh Castle and Holyrood, was paved with dressed stone and bordered by tightly packed stone houses, with wooden galleries extending above the thoroughfare. Off the Royal Mile 'stretched an infinity of small streets, all adorned with tall houses in which dwelt the gentry…. There is nothing humble or rustic but all is magnificent.'

Mary had inherited five principal royal residences: the Palace of Linlithgow, Stirling Castle, Falkland Palace, Edinburgh Castle and the Palace of Holyrood. Holyrood, situated on the eastern side of the city, is surrounded by parkland

Left Mary's bedchamber at the Palace of Holyrood. Mary's apartments, on the upper floor of James V's tower, consisted of an outer chamber which led to her bedchamber and two smaller rooms. Important guests were received in the outer chamber, and in one of the smaller rooms. Mary entertained her more intimate friends with supper parties, poetry readings, board games and music.

Right Detail of an oak cupboard, 16th century, with 16 carved panels, which Mary probably inherited from her mother, Mary of Guise.

and overshadowed by a vast mound of rock, Arthur's Seat. Originally an Augustinian monastery founded in 1128, the Abbey of Holyrood took its name from its most precious relic, a fragment of the True Cross. As kings made increasingly comfortable lodgings in the abbey, preferring the cosiness of the park to the exposed position of Edinburgh Castle, palace buildings eventually eclipsed the abbey's. Despite a variety of architectural styles, the final composition nevertheless achieves a natural harmony. James V's first major building work was at Holyrood. In 1528 a massive tower was begun in the north end of the main façade, containing a comfortable apartment on each of the two upper floors. Later, another extension of apartments was added, with great expanses of windows and glazed oriels. Mary's apartments in the upper floor of the tower were agreeable enough; two or three years before her return a new ceiling was added, oak-panelled and painted with heraldic symbols. But the furnishings left behind by her mother were few and worn in comparison with the luxuriously appointed rooms Mary had grown accustomed to in France. Mary immediately set her tapestry-makers and embroiderers to work on repairs, and the production of new wall and bed hangings, linens, blankets, cloths of estate, cushion covers and chapel furnishings.

During the Queen's first night at Holyrood, she was treated to an impromptu entertainment, which Brantôme described as 'five or six hundred marauders' from the city, serenading her with 'evil' fiddles and rebecs, to which they sang 'psalms very badly'. Knox was more generous, reporting that 'a company of most honest men, with instruments of music, and with musicians gave their salutations at her chamber windows, and that the Queen said that the melody liked her well, and she wished the same to be continued some nights after.'

Mary had arrived on a Tuesday, and the celebrations went on until the following Sunday when she attended Mass in the palace's private Chapel Royal, accompanied by her uncles and her predominantly French household; the service was conducted by a French priest. It soon spread that the Queen was to hear Mass, and seemingly in an instant the effusive goodwill of the citizens of Edinburgh was transformed into outrage, and cries rang out for the lynching of the 'idolatrous priest'! A servant

Crucifix and rosary (now at Traquair House) said to have belonged to Mary.

Opposite Plan of the city of Edinburgh *c.* 1582. After the Scottish Reformation of 1560, Catholicism was illegal in Scotland, but Mary was assured that she would be allowed to practise her religion in private. Yet when she attended Mass in Holyrood's private Chapel Royal, the citizens of Edinburgh were outraged. Between 1561 and 1565, the Queen was tolerant towards the Protestants, but her increasingly pro-Catholic attitude in 1565 and 1566 led the most powerful Protestant nobles to insurrection and violent reprisals.

carrying the altar candles was shoved and jostled, his candles snatched by the crowd and other altar ornaments were trodden into the ground. Mary had been assured by her half-brother Lord James that she would be allowed to practise her religion in private, and he was as good as his word, standing at the threshold of the chapel to thwart the mob's entry. He was assisted by Mary's other half-brothers, Robert and John. But even with their protection, the Mass was conducted in an atmosphere of mortal terror, the priest with limbs so tremulous he could scarcely lift the chalice during Communion. The next day Mary issued a proclamation announcing that there would be no 'alteration or innovation of the state of religion which Her Majesty found public and universally standing at Her Majesty's arrival in this her realm.' She herewith acknowledged the ecclesiastical revolution and allowed the Scots to continue attending Protestant sermons. But she also maintained her right to participate in private Catholic services; no one was in any way to molest her servants. John Knox used the skirmish at Holyrood as the basis for a sermon condemning the Mass and the Queen's observance of it.

Mary made her grand entry into Edinburgh, the ritual of spectacle and theatre that takes place when a ruler takes formal possession of a city, on 2 September 1561. She dined at Edinburgh Castle, and afterwards made a stately procession down the Royal Mile to Holyrood. It was a far cry from the extravaganza staged for Henry II's entry into Rouen which she remembered from her childhood, but for Scotland it was elaborate. 'In farces, in maskings and in other prodigalities, fain would fools have counterfooted France,' was Knox's comment on such events. Mary proceeded to Holyrood on a litter beneath a canopy of purple velvet, fringed with gold and held aloft by twelve representatives of the magistrates. Before her walked fifty men disguised as Moors, wearing black masks, black caps, and yellow taffeta suits, bedecked with golden chains. Wine flowed from the fountain at the Market Cross, and there were maidens dressed as the Virtues while others re-enacted mythological and religious dramas. A dragon was slaughtered with great ceremony and figures from the Old Testament were seemingly burned to death. Cannons were fired from the castle, children sang with angelic voices and there were speeches of welcome. But among these cheerful tableaux were also presentations that caused the Queen to 'frown'. It was said that her subjects had intended to burn an effigy of a priest and had only been stopped at the last moment by the Catholic Earl of Huntly. More significantly, when Mary passed

EDENBVRG.

Castrum puellarum

EDENBVRGVM
SCOTIAE
METROPOLIS.

Below John Knox, the energetic Reformer and author of the *First Blast of the Trumpet against the Monstrous Regiment of Women*. He had five confrontations with Mary. At their first meeting he questioned her fitness as a monarch, and pointed out that subjects ruled by a Catholic had a duty to be disobedient. This portrait, from a woodcut, is believed to be the only authentic likeness of Knox.

through a richly decorated arch, a child dressed as a cherub descended from a painted cloud and presented her with the Bible, in English instead of Latin, and the Protestant service book, both clear symbols of the Reformed faith. Mary was perturbed, but showed gracious appreciation for the city's gift of a gilded cupboard. Then came another rebuff; a group of children admonished the Queen to renounce the Mass. She knew who to blame for these insults and summoned John Knox to Holyrood for an interview, the first of five dramatic confrontations.

After his release from France's galleys Knox had moved to England, but, with the accession of Catholic Mary Tudor, he fled to the Continent and on to Geneva, becoming an ardent follower of John Calvin. He returned to Scotland temporarily in 1555 and permanently in 1559, where his evangelism – so energetically delivered – made a powerful contribution to the Scottish Reformation. Mary was aware that Knox had tormented her mother, and his book of 1558, the *First Blast of the Trumpet Against the Monstrous Regiment of Women*, directed at Mary Tudor, did little to endear him to any other female regent or monarch:

To promote a woman to bear rule, superiority, dominion or empire above any realm, nation or city is repugnant to nature, contumely to God, a thing most contrarious to his revealed will and approved ordinance, and, finally, it is the subversion of good order, of all equity and justice.

Mary regarded Knox as the source of 'subversion of good order', and she intended to mitigate his influence.

At their first meeting only Lord James, who kept in the background, and two of the Queen's ladies were present. The eighteen-year-old Queen confronted Knox, at forty-seven well over twice her age. She began by accusing him of civil disturbances and inciting her subjects to rebel against their rightful monarch. Her experiences in France had taught her that Protestants fell into two categories: agitators who stirred up the populace to rebel against their sovereign, and honest subjects deluded and led astray by ill-intentioned men. It was a sovereign's duty to keep them on the right pathway. They must obey their ruler, as must he. She went on in this vein for some time while Knox remained silent. Then, when she paused, he interjected his favourite topic: did Mary, as a woman, have any right to sovereignty? He conceded that he would not 'farther disallow than within my own breast' that of which the people approved. But subjects should not give their allegiance to a monarch who was ungodly; those who were ruled by a Catholic had a duty to be disobedient. Mary was shocked. Having never encountered such plain speaking she became too vexed to respond. She 'stood as if amazed, more than a quarter of an hour' said Knox. Lord

Above James Stewart, Earl of Moray; portrait by H. Munro, 1925, after an unknown artist. Mary's half-brother, a Protestant, was her principal adviser during the first four years of her reign. He later became her enemy. Adam Blackwood, Mary's zealous supporter, called Moray 'The foxe…in natour so ambitious that he would hawe no pacience till he had killed her Maiestie, either with poyson, sworde or by some other indirect, oblique and sinister meanes.'

James came closer and asked what had offended her. 'Well,' she said to the preacher when she had regained some composure, 'then, I perceive that my subjects shall obey you and not me; and shall do what they wish and not what I command. And so must I be subject to them and not they to me!' They then debated their own religious views to a stalemate; there could never be any understanding between them. After their meeting, Knox levelled his opinion of the Queen: 'If there be not in her a proud mind, a crafty wit and an indurate heart against God and his truth, my judgment faileth me.' Some weeks later he added, 'In communication with her I espied such craft as I have not found in such age.'

The English ambassador Sir Thomas Randolph reported that John Knox 'knocked so hastily upon [Mary's] heart that he made her weep'. But Knox's views were not representative of all Scots, and, although Mary's return to Scotland presented something of a threat to what Protestants had achieved, Mary's willingness to be accommodating in allowing Scotland to keep the Reformed faith was winning her support. To her Privy Council she appointed leading nobles, nearly all Protestants, and her executive and judicial officers continued in roles they had held during the previous administration. The Queen frequently attended meetings of her Council, sitting in the background, sometimes working a piece of embroidery, and now and then offering an opinion. Her principal advisers were her half-brother Lord James Stewart and William Maitland of Lethington. Lord James Stewart was a formidable politician, having been a leader of the revolution of 1559–60, and later in negotiating Mary's return to Scotland. Since early childhood, he may have played the role of domineering older brother, for he was described as dealing with her 'rudely, homely and bluntly'. The day before his wedding to Lady Agnes Keith in 1562 – celebrated with elaborate splendour – he was created Earl of Mar.

Maitland – Mitchell Wylie (Machiavelli) as he was known to the Scots – had been Secretary of State to Mary of Guise, deserting to the Lords of the Congregation in October 1559; three days later Mary of Guise was removed from the Regency. A brilliant intellect, he had been instrumental in the success of the Lords of the Congregation; had engineered the Treaty of Berwick; and had persuaded the Scots to accept the terms of the Treaty of Edinburgh. Maitland's grand design was permanent Anglo-Scottish harmony. In September, just after her arrival in Scotland, Mary dispatched Maitland to London to reaffirm her wish for improved relations between the two kingdoms. Maitland hoped that Elizabeth would now recognize Mary as her heir and that the Treaty of Edinburgh could then be ratified. Elizabeth insisted on ratification first. Maitland dealt with Mary 'delicately and finely', while Mary was 'patient to hear and beareth much'. Although Mary refused to ratify

Above and opposite
George, 5th Lord Seton, holding a staff with the royal monogram 'MR', indicating his office as Master of the Queen's Household (he was appointed in 1563). The splendid garments he wears were undoubtedly made in France. He was a resolute Catholic, and Mary's loyal supporter and friend. His half-sister was one of the Queen's 'four Maries'. He had been in France for the Queen's marriage to the young Dauphin Francis in 1558.

the parliamentary legislation making the Mass illegal, her administration was conducted in a manner that seemingly agreed to the acts of 1560.

Once again being conciliatory towards the Protestants, in 1562 she agreed to a plan wherein one-third of the revenues of most benefices were collected by crown officers and used to pay stipends to the clergy of the Reformed church. The money was also used, in part, to increase Mary's own revenues – royal poverty would be a perpetual aggravation – but the Protestants also benefited and Mary was gaining their approval. Knox began to speak of his dwindling followers, which he blamed on Mary's charm; the Queen's warm personality was a useful asset, but it was her policies during the early years of her reign that were creating a favourable opinion of her. With regard to her own faith, she would continue to hear Mass, but, as the years passed, Mary was not uncomfortable attending a Protestant baptism or marriage. She would sometimes listen to a sermon of the Reformed faith – as long as it was not delivered by Knox – and would even go so far as to express favourable views of the Church of England. However, it must be said that Mary's desire for the throne of England was an abiding obsession, and no doubt reflected her attitude towards that country's religion. Even her beloved uncle, Charles, Cardinal of Lorraine, urged her to 'embrace the religion of England'. Charles was at this time a member of the Gallican party at the French court, which represented the middle ground between the heretics and recognition and acceptance of the Calvinists. When a papal envoy arrived in Scotland in 1562 Mary was unable to encourage him with her plans to lead Scotland back to the 'true faith'. Nor did she arrange for Scottish representation at the final session of the Council of Trent, from which the Counter-Reformation was organized, particularly against England. Continental Catholics expected more from Mary in the cause of their faith, and even Scottish Catholics expressed some disappointment. But John Leslie, the Catholic Bishop of Ross, was content with the Queen's reign; in his estimate, she 'tendered her subjects so lovingly, as that she would use herself toward them as a natural mother toward her children'.

The Queen's 250-strong household was predominantly French and paid for from her revenues as Queen Dowager of France. There were also a few Italians: the Queen's French secretary was replaced by the Italian David Riccio, and Timothy Cagneoli was treasurer. Her furrier was French, as were her apothecary, her *parfumier* and her master cook who prepared meals for Mary and her immediate circle. Frenchmen were appointed to military posts, and when the Queen's bodyguard of archers was organized in 1562 it included several French names.

In 1563 when her heroic uncle, *le balafré*, was assassinated, shot by a Protestant, Mary's tears flowed like rain. She later confided to the English Ambassador – to

whom she spoke 'much of France' – that she felt almost bereft of friends. Certainly she had more family in France, and they had surrounded her with love and affection. Her half-brother, Lord James Stewart, was probably too austere for her taste but she still addressed him as '*mon frère*'. Her half-brother Robert, Commendator of Holyrood, who, like James and John, had been in France with the Queen, she called '*mon frère de Ste Croix*'. But of the three half-brothers (the illegitimate sons of James V), Mary was probably closest to the lively John, Commendator of Coldingham, who shared Mary's sense of humour. She was present at his wedding at Crichton Castle in January 1562, when he married Jean Hepburn, sister of the Earl of Bothwell. With Jean he had a son, Francis, probably named after Mary's first husband, and Mary was the child's godmother. Lord John died within a year of his marriage, causing Mary considerable distress – 'God always took from her those persons in whom she had the greatest pleasure.' Mary had formed a close attachment to her half-sister Jean, the playmate of her earliest childhood. Jean, married to the Earl of Argyll, preferred court life to her husband's estates, causing something of a scandal. Mary acknowledged that her half-sister was 'not so circumspect in all things as that she wished her to be'.

Closest of all to Mary were the *demoiselles* of honour, her four Maries, the childhood companions who, except for a brief period, had always been a part of the Queen's household in France as well as in Scotland. They thoroughly enjoyed the dancing and festivities of court life, adding their extra sparkle to the fun, and many observers commented on the pleasing picture they made riding in procession behind their mistress. Within a period of eighteen months during the years 1556–67, three of the four Maries were married. Mary Fleming, described by Leslie as 'the flower of the flock', became the bride of William Maitland; Mary Livingston, nicknamed 'the Lustie' wed John Sempill (John Knox claimed that she was pregnant at the time of her marriage); and dark-eyed Mary Beaton, the eldest of the four Maries and known by them as 'the Duenna' wed Sir Alexander Ogilvie of the Boyne. Only the pious Mary Seton remained single; she remained in the Queen's service until 1583. Mary Seton's brother, George, 5th Lord Seton, had been in France in 1558 for the wedding of the Queen to the Dauphin Francis, and Mary appointed him master of her household in 1563.

Though the Queen of Scots had been socially at ease with the royalty of France and the princes of Lorraine, she appears to have been less comfortable in the company of the earls of Scotland. With those not seeking political favours she was able to relax. Among servants Mary maintained a gracious familiarity; again and again in the records of Mary's life there is mention of her generosity. Her kindliness put her in good standing with her subjects, as did language – while Mary preferred to speak French, she would when necessary, speak most agreeably in Scots, although she did not speak Gaelic, the language of the Highlands. In short, the Queen of Scots was in her policies of the first four years of her reign, in her engaging personality and physical beauty, considered 'very lovesome'.

John Knox, ever brisk with criticism, attacked the pastimes of the Queen and her courtiers. Mary explained that she had been brought up in 'joyousity' in France, and so naturally wanted to extend the same ambience to her court in Scotland; in this she succeeded. Sir Thomas Randolph describing the amusements of the Queen's court, reported that 'devilish devises are imagined upon' and entertainments 'continued with joy and mirth, marvellous sights and shows, singular devices: nothing left undone either to fill our bellies, feed our eyes or content our minds'. What Knox found particularly heinous was dancing, which Mary could not do without. He claimed that in December 1562 she danced 'beyond midnight' out of sheer joy at the news that persecution of the Huguenots had resumed in France. If Mary was carefree in her dancing, always ready to take to the floor with her ladies, her movements were never less than graceful and becoming.

Some evenings, members of the Queen's court dressed up in imaginative costumes and danced by torchlight in masques. On one occasion the Queen and her ladies dressed up as burgesses' wives and travelled the streets begging money for banquets. Randolph said they later enjoyed a banquet where he himself was lodging. The other guests and townsfolk taking in the scene were transfixed with amazement. At Castle Campbell in midwinter 1563 there were gentlemen disguised as shepherds clad in white damask while others played 'sweetly' upon lutes. In May, these frolics took place around a little lake in the park at Holyrood. Mary's well developed sense of fun led her to dress herself and her four Maries as men for a banquet given for the French Ambassador one Easter Monday at Stirling. The Treasury records of 1561–62 show payment of nearly £21 for 38 yards of red and white taffeta delivered to the Queen's French tailor 'to be maskin claithis'. Her masquing costumes also included armour – twelve breastplates, twelve backplates, helmets, shields – and there were three Egyptian hats of red and yellow taffeta.

Mary would often disguise herself as a man to wander incognito in the streets, mixing with her subjects, and perhaps partaking in their amusement – just as her father had done. These adventures no doubt provided welcome relief from the limelight, but in so doing Mary could also learn of her subjects' concerns, so there was probably an intelligence element as well. Brantôme believed that only ladies of flawless face and form could carry off male disguise so that no one could discern

'to which sex she really belonged, whether she was a handsome boy or the beautiful woman she was in reality'. One might wonder at Mary's penchant for male clothing, which was more than likely just the high spirits of youth. The Valois had, perhaps, a more defined taste for novelty; Mary's brother-in-law, the future Henry III, was keen on wearing bodices. For playing tennis – there were royal tennis courts at Stirling, Holyrood and Falkland Palace – Mary reputedly donned doublet and hose. Indoors the Queen's diversions included card and dice games which usually involved a wager – a crystal jewel, a ring, a brooch. She played backgammon and chess, and it seems the Queen enjoyed billiards and was also fond of puppet shows, a new craze from Italy. The Twelfth Night pastimes – or *la fête des Rois* – included choosing kings and queens. The choice was made by a bean hidden in a cake. In 1563 Mary Fleming enjoyed 'the great solemnity and royall estate of Queen of the Beene'. English envoy Thomas Randolph reported: 'That day yt was to be seen, by her princely pomp, how fite a match she wold be…to contend with Venus in beauty, Minerva in witt, or Juno in worldly wealth…. The Queen of the Beene was in a gowne of cloth of silver, her head, her neck, her shoulders, the rest of her whole body, so beset with stones, that more in our whole jewell house wer not to be found.'

While living in France Mary had reserved two hours a day for reading and improving her mind. In Scotland she read Livy every day under the guidance of the humanist and Latin scholar, George Buchanan, who wrote verse honouring Mary. The Queen's library, brought with her from France, was housed at Holyrood in a room carpeted with green cloth. Her books – 240 of them – were catalogued under Greek, Latin or modern languages, the greatest number of which were in French including two volumes of *Lancelot du Lac*, works by Pierre de Ronsard, Joachim du Bellay, Clément Marot, Rabelais, along with the *The Cardinall of Loyranis Oratioun at the Assembly of Poesy* and *One Oratioun to the King of Franche of the Quenis awin hand write*. The Greek authors included Euripides, Herodotus, Homer, Plato and Sophocles. Among the French translations of the classics were Plutarch, Ovid and Cicero. There were also books in English, such as *The Institutions of Astronomie*, and in Scots, Spanish and Italian. Among the Italian volumes were the *Decameron*, Ariosto's *Orlando Furioso* and a translation of Marcus Aurelius. In her will the Queen left her Greek and Latin books to the University of St Andrews, and her French and English books to Mary Beaton. 'Thre buikis of Musik' were listed in Mary's library, and music was never absent from her court. Italian minstrels were again employed, as were five viola players and three lute players. Some of the Queen's valets of the bedchamber had musical talent, soothing her evening hours with melody and song, and her valet – later her secretary – David Riccio had musical ability that may, in part, have influenced the Queen to

Left *Mary Queen of Scots*, copied from a miniature painted in France, *c.* 1565. It appears that the Queen of Scots never sat for her portrait during the years she ruled Scotland. The Queen's wardrobe included hats of black velvet, grey felt and embroidered taffetas, and here her bonnet is adorned with a feather and pearls – pearls are also strung around her collar, added to a net for her hair, sewn into her gown and sleeves, and hang from her ears.
Opposite The attire of a Scotswoman from *Recueil de la Diversité des Habits*, 1562. Cold weather in Scotland is not confined to winter. To keep warm Mary would wear long, woollen 'hieland mantills' – one blue, one white and one black.

choose him. Mary herself liked to sing, as she had done in France, accompanying her voice – admired by all – on the lute and virginals. In 1562, Randolph reported that Mary was desolate over the lack of music at her Mass on Christmas Day, but by 1565 for Easter High Mass 'she wanted…neither trumpets, drum nor fife, bagpipe or tabor'. Also included in the Queen's library at Holyrood were *The Buik of Hunting* and *A Little Buik of the Chas*. For one memorable hunt 'two thousand red deer, besides roes and fallow deer' had been gathered together for the Queen's sport. But when Mary let her dog loose on a wolf, the leading stag took fright and mayhem ensued. In the stampede two men were killed and several others injured. Besides hunting, Mary had a passion for hawking, golf, tennis, archery, croquet and, as a spectator, a few months after her arrival in Scotland, she had watched a Guise uncle and her half-brothers John and Robert taking part in the gentlemen's feat of 'running at the ring'. In this instance, there were two teams of six equestrians and, for added fun, one team was dressed as women, the other as 'strangers' decked out in an assortment of costumes.

Alexander Scott's poem 'Ane New Yeir Gift' presented 'to the Quene Mary when sche come first, Hame' at the beginning of 1562, contained the lines:

**Let all thy realm be now in readiness
With costly clothing to decoir thy court.**

Courtiers, for their costly attire, were to be the target of much extreme Reformist criticism. It was recorded that at least one of the Maries, Mary Beaton, wore gowns of 'ormosing taffties' (taffeta from the Isle of Ormuz in the Persian Gulf). An inventory of the Queen's wardrobe in 1562 lists 131 items, including 60 gowns of silk, satin, velvet, cloth of gold and cloth of silver; 14 cloaks are included, some described as being of the Spanish fashion, and 2 royal mantles – one of purple velvet, the other trimmed in ermine. With these she would wear long woollen 'hieland mantills' – one blue, one white and one black, to keep out the cold. There are 16 fronts or stomachers, the list also includes robes for mourning and her costumes for masques and other fancy-dress capers. Beneath her dresses Mary wore silk doublets and *brassières* made of both black and white silk, and farthingales (petticoats of cloth and colourful embroidered satins stretched over birdcage-like hoops). Her 'woven hose' were made of silk, often entwined with gold and silver thread. Her hats or caps were of embroidered taffetas, black velvet and grey felt, and some sported feathers; the Queen's luminous veils were all in white.

Mary, for the most part, wore black mourning in Scotland until her second marriage in 1565, but there are a considerable number of white garments in the list. Perhaps influenced by Diane de Poitiers or Henry II, the Queen combined the two colours, dressing herself and all her attendants in black and white for a Shrovetide banquet in 1564, served by a boy with bandaged eyes dressed as Cupid, while servants sang an Italian sonnet. In addition to a preponderance of white and black, the inventories of the Queen's wardrobe include crimson velvet, green velvet, orange damask embroidered with silver, yellow satin trimmed with fur and silver braiding, and blue and purple satin. To preserve her complexion against the sun, Mary walked beneath a kind of parasol, 'a little canopy of gold and cramoisie satin furnished with fringes and tassels, and many painted buttons all serving to make a shadow before the Queen'. The Queen's pet dogs had their share of the regalia too, appearing elegant in blue velvet collars.

As dress added distinction to a monarch, so too did glitter, and many monarchs appeared to measure their esteem in jewels. The Queen of Scots' jewels were internationally famous. When she returned to Scotland Mary possessed 159 pieces, 43 of which were kept in her own private cabinet under the care of Mary Seton. The Queen had returned the royal jewels of France to Catherine de' Medici after the death of Francis, retaining only items belonging to the Scottish Crown and those that were by right her property as Queen Dowager. Among these was the Great Harry diamond, the prize of her collection. An enormous stone set with a large cabochon ruby in an 'H', it had been a gift from Henry II on the Queen of Scots' marriage to Dauphin Francis. After returning to Scotland Mary had the diamond mounted in the crown of Scotland. When the Queen later fled the country leaving most of her jewels behind, the Great Harry had to be retrieved from the clutches of Lord James's wife Agnes. Mary's son, who eventually became King of England, mounted the stone in a royal jewel called the Mirror of Britain. But, under the Commonwealth, Mary's precious diamond vanished without trace. Mary's uncle Charles, the Cardinal of Lorraine, may have had the stone in mind when, at the Queen's departure from France, he had urged his niece to leave the bulk of her jewels in his safe keeping, rather than risk them at sea. The Queen retorted that if she herself were safe in undertaking the voyage to Scotland, then so were her jewels.

By 1562 Mary had increased her collection with the acquisition of some twenty additional pieces. She had redeemed, for a sum of £1,000, a gold cross set with diamonds and rubies that had once belonged to her mother, and she

Above, centre and above right The Penicuik Jewels: necklace, earring, pendant and locket, said to have been owned by Mary.
Below Pearl necklace, reputedly once belonging to the Queen of Scots. She acquired ropes of Scottish pearls, thought to be the finest in Europe.
Opposite top Pendant jewel, *c.* 1565, bearing a French cameo of Mary on a locket of enamelled gold set with rubies and diamonds. It may have been a gift from the Queen to one of her supporters.
Opposite centre Two views of a gold enamelled pendant of French workmanship, set with crystal showing the Queen of Scots' arms.
Opposite bottom Gold pomander believed to have been Mary's. The compartments were filled with aromatic herbs, and it was worn from a chain encircling the waist.

had also acquired ropes of Scottish pearls, thought to be the best in Europe; their pale iridescence made them symbols of purity, virginity, and were thus coveted by Queen Elizabeth who would later order the purchase of some of Mary's pearls. There were also rubies with pearls and rubies with diamonds – for which Mary's crimson velvet gowns were the perfect foil. Sapphires and other gemstones were represented in the Queen's jewelry collection, including belts, pomanders and brooches – which, like pendants, could be pinned to Mary's velvet caps. She soon acquired twelve neck furs of ermine and sable which were listed among her jewels due to their valuable gold bejewelled heads and feet. Other trinkets would seem to fit the category of *objets d'art:* four small gold fruit baskets; a crystal vase enriched with gold, turquoise and rubies; a small gold cage with a parrot; a gold pigeon with black and white enamel; a little gold dog, also enamelled black and white; a small ship enamelled white – perhaps a reminder of the galley that brought the Queen back to Scotland; a small gold apple containing a miniature of James V; a jewelled torch with jewelled flames; and the somewhat startling entry of 'two serpents' tongues'!

The Queen was eager to see and be seen by her subjects; she remembered little of the country of her birth. A royal progress would allow Mary to see the extent of her kingdom while providing publicity for her monarchy along the way. But there were other reasons for the royal progresses. It was necessary to vacate a palace at regular intervals on sanitary grounds, given Mary's extensive household and the primitive conditions of the period. Food was also a consideration, preferably consumed where it was produced, and there were building repairs that were best carried out when the court was absent. During these years Mary spent the spring in Fife. In the summers of 1562 and 1564, she went north to Aberdeen and Inverness. She was in the west in Argyll and Ayrshire in the summer of 1563, and in the autumn in both 1565 and 1566 the Queen made her progress in the south-west and south. While travel was never easy during the sixteenth century, the appalling state of the roads – if those 'foul ways' can be so distinguished – meant that carriages, and for the most part litters, were out of the question; Mary would ride. Happily, for one to whom the outdoors and a saddle were second nature, travelling on horseback posed little discomfort; indeed, the Queen had expressed a yearning for the easy unfettered life of a man – able to rough it in an open field beneath the stars, spending his days going about the town wearing a helmet and sword.

Opposite Falkland Palace,
the twin-turreted tower of
the gatehouse, the final part
of the extensions and
improvements that James V
made to the palace. The
gatehouse is linked to the
south range where the
Chapel Royal is located
on the first floor. Passing
through the gatehouse is
to emerge from a medieval
castle into the courtyard
of a Renaissance palace.
It was at Falkland that
James V died in 1542,
making the infant Mary
Stewart Queen of Scots.

Between August 1562 and September 1563, Mary covered a distance of
1,200 miles, and 460 miles between July and September 1564, across a landscape
practically denuded of trees, a scarcity that forced parliament to make the unlawful
felling of trees a criminal offence. For the Queen the countryside must have appeared
bleak in contrast to the lushness of the Loire Valley. There were, however, forests to
be found near the city of Aberdeen and in the vicinity of royal palaces, and the rivers
were so thick with salmon that nobility shunned the delicacy as being too common.
Yet, instead of discovering abundance, sixteenth-century visitors from Europe found
Scotland a barren scene, perceptibly uninhabited. The population of France during
the mid-1500s was around fourteen million, whereas in Scotland, during Mary's
reign, there were only 700,000 inhabitants. The people were poor, most of them
living in makeshift hovels with turf roofs which they shared with their cattle as a
means of adding warmth and of securing the animals from thieving raids, which
were the scourge of lowland Border districts.

Lawlessness was not however unique to southern Scotland. The overlords of
the Highlands, such as the Earl of Huntly in the north and the Earl of Argyll in the
west, had been delegated by the Crown powers of life and death, thus maintaining
a semblance of order, while saving the sovereign a good deal of travelling and risky
campaigning in harsh conditions. In so doing it was necessary for the great overlords
to raise armies from their own clan followers, which could sometimes outnumber
the sovereign's forces. The problem with the clans was the complete loyalty the
Highlanders gave to their chiefs; the system often led to bloody feuds carried on
from generation to generation. Clan chiefs ostensibly owed their allegiance to the
sovereign, but the reality was quite different. When feuds became intense to the point
of anarchy, the sovereign would then intervene, having raised troops by proclamation.
Mary had no standing army at her command. When the raising of troops took place
in Edinburgh, all men between sixteen and sixty, providing their own 'victuals', had
to serve the Queen as required. To do otherwise risked forfeiture of life, lands and
goods. Sir Nicholas Throckmorton had told Mary that the difficulties of her kingdom
were really no greater than those faced by other monarchs, which may have been
true in the matter of religion. But while the monarchs of Europe were increasing
their power and curtailing that of the nobles, as Henry VII had done in England,
the clan networks had actually increased their power over two centuries. Added to
this was the greed of lords both north and south for the lure of English money;
bribery was a useful tool in Queen Elizabeth's Scottish policy, just as it had been
during her father's reign. The misfortune of Scotland was its nobles – 'so divided
and disturbed' – as Marco Grimani had written describing the political state of

the country around the time of the infant Queen's
coronation in 1543; money and family ambition
had rendered many nobles incapable of taking
a more altruistic view – striving for nationhood.
Eighteen years later, this situation was unchanged.
Having been raised in France in the belief that
a sovereign's command was supreme, ruling a lawless
land where royal claims over her nobles, had at
times little validity, must have felt, at the very least,
daunting. That the Queen's choice of worship ran
contrary to the country's official religion
compounded the difficulty.

During Mary's first royal progress, her priests
celebrated High Mass in her presence in the Royal
Chapel at Stirling. This led to another angry scuffle;
the Queen's clergy emerged with 'broken heads and
bloody ears' and Mary's half-brother James, even had
a share in dealing the blows. Along the route north
the Queen visited Perth where she happily received
the city's offering of a gold box in the shape of a heart
filled with gold coins. But later Mary swooned after
observing some pageants staged for her welcome,
some of which were hostile to the Catholic Church.
The Queen had to be carried from her horse to
nearby lodgings, assailed with the vague illness
that she was 'often troubled with, after any great
unkindness or grief of mind'. The following day
Mary travelled on to Dundee, and from there
to St Andrews, where a priest had allegedly been
murdered the previous Sunday. In or near St Andrews
an unpleasant quarrel ensued between the Catholic
Earl of Huntly and Lord James. Huntly claimed that,
at the Queen's command, he would have the Mass heard in three counties, but Mary
would have had more sense than to make such an order.

On her travels north, the Queen stayed at Falkland Palace in Fife; nestled at the
foot of the Lomond hills, Falkland was to become Mary's favourite country retreat.
James V, employing Scottish and continental masons, had carried out extensive

Palace of FALKLAND

alterations to the palace, which, by 1541, had become the most architecturally advanced building in the whole of Britain. The external façade has a fortified appearance, relieved by finely carved statues, now gone, but which had probably been Biblical in nature, set in five niches above consoles carved with images of Christ's Passion. Passing through the gatehouse to the courtyard, one changes cultures, for here the building is all Renaissance elegance and balanced proportions. The courtyard façades were, and to a considerable extent still are, articulated with pilaster buttresses fronted by columns, explicitly classical details. Above the columns were carved stone figures and statues, now demolished or worn away. Still visible are some of the portrait medallions grouped in pairs between upper-storey windows. A few of the portrait figures seem to lean out of their portholes to scrutinize passers-by; the game is to guess who they represent – kings, queens, deities, friends of the

Background The
courtyard of Falkland,
1530s, from *Theatrum
Scotiae* (1693). The façades
were decorated with
classical details – pedestals,
columns and sculpted
medallions – the work
of French masons.
Right Detail, with a
pilaster buttress fronted
by a column, and portrait
medallions, perhaps of
kings, queens, deities or
friends of the Stewarts.

Stewarts, or some mischief-maker of the court? For relaxation there was Falkland's chief attraction – hunting. Surrounding the Palace was a great forest into which boar, stags, roebucks and hares were released for the chase, but not killed, so they could provide future sport. The deer were actually transported along with the endless stream of provisions and furnishings that moved with the Queen from one royal residence to the next.

The Queen's furniture, bedding and tapestries were generally reinstalled only at her principal residences. Several items remained *in situ*, but there was nevertheless a staggering number of goods to be transported, and each undertaking required detailed advanced planning. An inventory of the Queen's possessions made at Holyrood in 1561 listed 186 items, including 45 beds, 23 sets of tapestry, 36 Turkey carpets, 81 cushions, 10 cloths of estate, 4 table covers and 2 folding stools. Also included in the inventory are 10 paintings, one of the Muses, another of 'Grotesques or Conceits' and 8 entitled the *New Doctors*. There are, in addition, maps and globes, gold and silver clocks that chimed the hours, lamps of silver and chess-tables of ebony inlaid with mother-of-pearl. Only one table, painted and gilded, is entered, and one chair of estate covered in velvet and cloth of gold. Among the 45 beds is the Bed of Amitie hung with cloth of gold and silver and swags of violet and grey silk embroidered with cyphers and garlands of leaves; the canopy of the bed was edged with a gold and silver fringe. Another listing – canvas – is 'for a bed to a female Fool'. Nichola, or *la jardinière*, the Queen's Fool, had travelled with Mary from France. Treasury records show payments to fools of both sexes.

In addition to the principal palaces and a palatial guest house at Dunfermline, the Crown possessed castles throughout the kingdom, including Blackness on the

Right Falkland Palace, stained-glass window, 1890s, bearing the Queen of Scots' coat-of-arms.

Opposite The oak entrance screen, dating from James V's reign, that leads into the Chapel Royal at Falkland Palace. Much of the painted decoration, including the ceiling, was executed for the visit of Charles I of England in 1633. The tapestries within are 17th century, and tell the Biblical story of Joseph and Benjamin. It is the only existing Catholic Chapel Royal in Britain and is still used for worship.

MARY QVEEN OF SCOTS.

Forth; Doune, north of Stirling; Inverlochy; Lochmaben near Dumfries; and
Rothesay on the Firth of the Clyde. The most obvious feature of Scottish buildings
of any pretension compared to those of England during the mid- to late sixteenth
century was that in Scotland, with its feuding nobles and renegades, defence was still
very much a part of domestic architecture; the wealthy necessarily lived in fortresses.

Within only a few days of Mary's first visit to Falkland she had to return to
Edinburgh. There the Town Council had issued a proclamation ordering 'monks,
friars, priests, nuns, adulterers and fornicators and all such filthy persons' to leave
the city – a clear challenge to her authority. Mary waited a few days before
responding, then issued a counter-proclamation declaring that all her law-abiding
subjects were at liberty to move about the towns as they wished; the city's provost
and bailies (magistrates) were replaced.

Background and opposite The red sandstone ruins of Edzell Castle, built in the early 16th century. During her three-month northern progress of 1562, Mary spent two nights here. On the 25 August – the day of her departure to Aberdeen and Inverness – a meeting of the Privy Council was held here. The primary aim of the 1562 progress was to curb the power of the Earl of Huntly who controlled the north-east of Scotland. Today, the parterre garden is laid with triangular beds of box, with designs based on the Scottish thistle, the English rose, the Irish shamrock and the French fleur-de-lis.

Mary's progress of 1562 ultimately took her to the Highlands where the Crown was brought into armed conflict with George Gordon, 4th Earl of Huntly, a Catholic, and one of the most powerful men in the kingdom. Huntly was irked, partly over the Queen's decision to confer upon her half-brother, Lord James, the earldoms of Mar and Moray – properties within Huntly's vast holdings. When Mary reached Inverness, Huntly's son, Alexander Gordon, the captain of the town and castle, refused the Queen entry – a treasonable act. The townspeople and others from the surrounding countryside came to Mary's aid, and Alexander Gordon was rapidly seized and hanged from the castle ramparts. Mary proceeded to Aberdeen having first taken the precaution of augmenting her forces with horsemen and retainers on foot. Huntly and his third son, Sir John Gordon, did likewise, intending to block the Queen's progress to Aberdeen. Her entourage was harassed by Sir John Gordon's cavalry, but Mary arrived in Aberdeen unscathed. Huntly was summoned before the council to explain his actions, but failed to appear, and was declared an outlaw. Sir John, who had been accused of previous crimes, was already a fugitive from justice. Huntly and his Gordon army marched on Aberdeen to face Mary's forces (whose numbers had again been increased) led by Lord James, Earl of Moray, and Maitland of Lethington. Mary offered to put on armour and lead her troops from the front, which was naturally rejected. Battle ensued at Corrichie near Aberdeen on 28 October 1562. The Gordon forces were completely routed, some 200 men were slain and 120 taken prisoner, including the Earl of Huntly himself – the man who had offered, the previous year, to put so many Catholic troops at Mary's disposal to help her return the country to Catholicism. After his capture the Earl suffered a massive stroke and fell down dead. Sir John Gordon and his brother Adam, a boy of seventeen, were taken prisoner. Huntly's mansion stronghold Strathbogie was sacked, and Mary confiscated enough loot to entirely fill the ship that later transported the items to Edinburgh: valuable pieces of tapestry, embroidered sets of hangings and furniture, including fifty items of chapel furnishings – later altered for the Queen's domestic use. Huntly's corpse was embalmed and preserved until parliament met the following year, when the act of forfeiture and attainder was formally passed upon it, and Huntly's place as Chancellor was given to James Douglas, Earl of Morton. Sir John Gordon confessed under torture to his part in the rebellion, and was executed in the Queen's presence on 2 November. Mary had a deep aversion to witnessing human suffering and fainted during the hideous ordeal, but it had been necessary for her to attend the execution in order to silence the general talk which blamed Lord James for launching the campaign against the Gordons without her approval. The youth, Adam Gordon, was pardoned. The eldest of Huntly's sons, Lord George Gordon, who had no real part in the conflict, was later captured, tried for treason and sentenced to be hanged, drawn and quartered – a sentence that was commuted to a term of imprisonment. He was set free in 1565, and, like his brother Adam, became one of Mary's supporters.

For Mary the affair was not over when the battle was won; she was at pains to explain her actions to Catholics in Scotland and abroad. The Cardinal of Lorraine, having received a lengthy letter from Mary, pointed out her position to the Emperor: the Queen of Scots had not failed Catholicism, she had merely dealt with a rebellious subject, and was now at liberty to be more completely dedicated to the Catholic cause.

Sir John Gordon, who had been a handsome young man, had once been in love with Mary, or perhaps with her power, formulating schemes to persuade the Queen to marry him. The Venetian ambassador wrote that the Queen of Scots was a princess who was 'personally the most beautiful in Europe', and Knox claimed that she had magical powers of enchantment 'whereby men are bewitched'. The so-called bewitched included not only Sir John Gordon, but also James Hamilton, 3rd Earl of Arran, the eldest son of the Duke of Châtelherault, and a Protestant. He had been rejected as a suitor for the young Queen of Scots, suggested for the daughter of Diane de Poitiers, and unsuccessfully proposed marriage to Queen Elizabeth.

Before Mary left France, Arran sought her hand once more, a proposal that had Knox's blessing as an opportunity to bind the Queen to the Protestants, but the Earl was promptly turned down. In Scotland, it seems he had openly threatened to kidnap Mary from Holyrood, presumably in the hope that she would, under duress, agree to be his wife. Having heard of the scheme, one of Mary's Guise uncles, René, Marquis of Elboeuf, her half-brother Lord John Stewart and James Hepburn, Earl of Bothwell, retaliated by attempting to pursue Arran's mistress, Alison Craik. This in turn led to skirmishes and reprisals, but at length Arran met with Mary, and made an emotional plea for reconciliation; all was forgiven. Unfortunately, it soon became evident that the Earl was mentally unbalanced: 'so drowned in dreams and so feedeth himself with fantasies, that either men fear that he will fall into some dangerous and incurable sickness, or play one day, some mad part what will bring him to mischief'. He later became completely insane, and was confined for the rest of his life.

Another of the love-crazed was one of her aristocratic French courtiers, poet Pierre de Boscotel de Châtelard. He had travelled with the Queen's court to Scotland in 1561, returned briefly to France, then again made his way to Scotland. En route he passed through London where he had confided to a friend that he was on his way to see his lady love. When he arrived in Scotland Mary greeted the young man with her customary warmth, and lent him a sorrel gelding and perhaps money. It was observed that the Queen delighted in Châtelard's company, and was, some thought, too familiar with 'so unworthy a creature and abject a varlet', and 'too much to have been used to his master himself by any Princess alive'. But Mary was fond of poetry, and of poets who were indulged to a considerable degree in the Valois court. Young Châtelard, besotted with the Queen, and probably reading too much into her friendliness, was emboldened to enter her apartments at Holyrood and hide under the bed. He was soon discovered during a routine search and dragged away. Mary did not learn of the incident until the following morning, when she had the unhappy young man banished from the court. Foolishly, Châtelard then followed Mary on her journey towards St Andrews. At Rossend Castle near Burntisland he suddenly burst into the room where she was about to disrobe and go to bed. Mary was only accompanied by two of her gentlewomen, and her startled reaction was to scream which brought Lord James rushing to her aid, dagger drawn. The Queen probably forestalled the young man's summary execution, and had him put under arrest. Knox, of course, put the worst possible interpretation on the incident. The poet was taken in chains to St Andrews, where he was tried, convicted and hanged in the market place. From the scaffold he recited Ronsard's hymn to death:

Je te salue, heureuse et profitable mort …
… puisqu'il faut mourir
Donne-moi que soudain je te puisse encourir
Ou pour l'honneur de Dieu, ou pour servir mon Prince….

I salute you, happy and profitable Death …
… since I must die
Grant that I may suddenly encounter you
Either for the honour of God, or in the service of my Prince….

And with his final breath he cried out, 'Adieu the most beautiful and cruel princess in the world!' Under interrogation the poet had confessed to being a Huguenot, sent back to Scotland for the purpose of compromising Mary; subsequent investigations appear to bear out his admission. And yet, a poem written by Châtelard to the Queen of Scots, would seem to confirm that the young man's passion for Mary was genuine. The work was preserved among the memoirs of French courtier Mauvissière de Castelnau, who had travelled with the Queen on her return to Scotland; Castelnau's *Memoirs*, including Châtelard's poem, were published in London in 1725 in Samuel Jebb's *De Vita & Rebus Gestis*. Written in French, in the Renaissance style of Ronsard, with allusions and transformations to the elements – air, water – the poem consists of nine stanzas, in which the following verses are included:

I wish to sing of the great sorrow that
makes me grieve…. But who can
hear my sigh, or understand
my languishing pain? Will it be this grass,
or the running water, beside the bank, flowing
with the tears streaming from my eyes?
…or these deserted retreats…
lonely places and secret hills
that are the only confidants of my piteous regrets?

Alas, no! for the wound vainly seeks a healing,
and for relief keeps struggling without change.
My lament had rather tell of its bitter sting
to you, the one who has filled my soul
with such torment.

After the incident, the Queen, as a safety precaution, began sleeping with Mary Fleming.

The matter of the Queen's marriage was continually discussed during the early years of her reign: as John Knox put it, 'the marriage of our Queen was in all men's mouths'. It was a monarch's duty to marry and produce a lawful heir, and Mary herself was eager to make a suitable match. For a female sovereign, choosing a partner was complicated by the fact that by marrying she not only took a husband but also a King for her people. George Buchanan wrote: 'Many were of the opinion that it was more equitable that the people should choose a husband for a girl, than that a girl should choose a King for a whole people'. Mary's first choice and that of the Guises was still the son of Philip II, Don Carlos. In spite of Catherine de' Medici's earlier meddling, Philip once more entertained the idea, promising that, if Mary became his daughter-in-law, he would support a Catholic insurrection in England to depose Elizabeth and put Mary on the throne. While the Queen of Scots found this suggestion interesting, her more immediate aim was to obtain Don Carlos's assistance

In France, the widowed Queen of Scots had sought a marriage with Don Carlos, Philip's son, but this was opposed by Catherine de' Medici, whose daughter, Elisabeth, had become Philip's third wife. In Scotland, Mary revived this marriage plan, with the approval, remarkably, of many of her Protestant lords. Philip secretly promised that once Mary was his daughter-in-law, he would back a Catholic insurrection to put her on the English throne. But discussions came to an end in 1564. Don Carlos's madness was making him dangerous.

in ruling her kingdom until he inherited the throne of Spain and diverted his attention there. Remarkably, many of the Queen's Protestant lords favoured the marriage, and she continued the negotiations with determination. John Knox, of course, harangued her over the match, and Elizabeth would not countenance it under any circumstances. The Spanish negotiations dragged on for nearly eighteen months, while at the same time other candidates were being considered, such as Archduke Charles of Austria, brother of the Emperor; and again Charles IX of France, now twelve. But the Queen of England, fearful of a powerful European alliance north of the border, preferred that the Queen of Scots marry an English subject, if, indeed, she wanted her to wed at all. Elizabeth, in the spring of 1564, put forward Lord Robert Dudley – a suggestion that was more of a snub than a plausible choice. Dudley's father had been executed for treason, and his own reputation was besmirched with the accusation (not the conviction) of the murder of his first wife, Amy Robsart. Moreover, the Queen of England's name had long been romantically linked with Dudley which made her 'dear Robin' seem something of a cast-off. Elizabeth, then, seemingly to improve his desirability, enhanced Dudley's social standing by conferring upon him the title Earl of Leicester. She also dangled the hope that if Mary wed 'to her satisfaction she would not fail to be a good friend and sister to her and make her heir' – Mary's cherished ambition. Soon after her return to Scotland, Mary had sent Maitland to England to assure Elizabeth of her friendship and to persuade the Queen of England to recognize Mary as her successor to the English throne; Maitland would return to England, on the same mission, several times. Mary followed up these entreaties with flattering letters and costly gifts. In 1561 she presented her picture to Elizabeth and two years later they exchanged portraits. One of her letters included a heart-shaped diamond ring accompanied by a poem which she had composed (originally in French) – 'The Diamond Speaks':

And thus from Queen to equal Queen I'll pass at length
O would I could join them with an iron band alone, and unite their hearts as one.

Nevertheless, Elizabeth insisted she ratify the Treaty of Edinburgh before the subject of the English succession could be broached. But from Mary's point of view signing the treaty was to disclaim her rights as a granddaughter of Henry VII. She suggested that an entirely new treaty might be written, and most of all Mary hoped for a meeting – Queen to Queen – so that Elizabeth would 'mair clearly perceive the sincerity of her good meaning'. A year after Mary sent her heart-shaped ring to Elizabeth, she, in turn, received a ring from the Queen of England. The ring was delivered by Randolph, which he reported the Queen of Scots 'marvellously esteemed, oftentimes looked upon, and many times kissed'. At length, Elizabeth

agreed to meet Mary and preparations were laid for a meeting of the two monarchs in 1562 at York, between 20 August and 20 September, at a cost of £40,000, which would have made it one of the most extravagant entertainments ever authorized by Elizabeth. For this epic event the English planned to stage an allegorical tableau dramatizing the imprisonment of figures representing False Rumour and Discord at the request of Prudence and Temperance. During the entertainment Peace was to enter in a chariot pulled by an elephant, bringing everlasting harmony to the world. But this was to be tested by the appearance of Evil Inclination astride an enormous serpent and Disdain who would ride upon a wild boar. Happily, Valiant Courage was to defeat them. Elizabeth's formidable Secretary of State, William Cecil, personally sifted through the script for hidden meanings or language that might be misinterpreted by the Scots. As the climax to the entertainment the two Queens were to put down their 'Evil Inclinations', which, presumably intended for Mary, would imply that she was to renounce her claims to the English throne, and ultimately, Catholicism.

While plans were under way for Mary's safe conduct to York, civil war broke out in France with the Huguenots once more fighting against the Catholic Guises, and with the prospect of Spain and other powers entering the fray. Elizabeth cancelled the York meeting and went on to name the Guises as the perpetrators of the conflict in France. When Mary learned from Maitland that her long hoped-for meeting with the Queen of England was not to take place, she reputedly collapsed, needing several days' confinement in her room. When Mary emerged, Elizabeth's envoy, Sir Henry Sidney, confirmed what she had already been told, but she had evidently been unable to come to terms with the disappointment, for the Queen of Scots responded to Sidney's news not only in words 'but in countenance and watery eyes'. Sir Henry did explain that the event was not in fact cancelled, but merely delayed due to the trouble in France, and that Elizabeth hoped to reschedule the event for the following summer. But then, as it happened, within a few months the Queen of England was contemplating war against Mary's beloved Guise relatives. In March, the Duke of Guise had ordered an attack upon a Protestant prayer-meeting in Vassy, precipitating war between French Catholics and Huguenots. There followed an interlude of peace before hostilities were resumed on 12 July 1562. It was thought that Spain would enter the war on the side of the Catholics, at which point England was prepared to join the Huguenots. The seriousness of the situation made it impossible for Elizabeth to venture north, and the meeting with Mary had to be cancelled. The two monarchs were destined never to come face to face.

On top of this frustration, on 6 August 1564 Philip II announced that the Spanish marriage could not take place. There were political reasons, and perhaps it was also

Above and opposite
Henry Stewart, Lord
Darnley, *c.* 1566. A quasi-
Catholic, and Mary's
cousin, Darnley had a claim
to the English throne. Like
Mary, he was tall (between
6 ft 1 in. and 6 ft 3 in.),
and he was handsome,
if somewhat effeminate.
He soon won Mary's heart,
and she married him on 29
July 1565 – he was 19 and
she was 22. Politically, he
was a reasonable choice,
even though Elizabeth I
was decidedly against
the marriage as were some
of Mary's Protestant
nobles. But his behaviour
made him unsuitable as
co-ruler and as husband.

becoming increasingly apparent that his son's insanity was making the young man dangerous. Randolph reported to London that 'some think the Queen's sickness is caused by her utterly despairing of the marriage of any of those she looked for'.

There was, however, another young man in the background, Henry Lord Darnley, an English subject whom Mary may have been considering as early as November 1561, three months after her arrival in Scotland. He was the eldest son of Matthew Stewart (changed to Stuart), 4th Earl of Lennox – the man who had participated in nine-month-old Mary's coronation at Stirling, then defected to England, and who himself had once been suggested as a bridegroom for the young Queen. Mary had distant blood ties with the Earl of Lennox, and Darnley's mother, the Countess of Lennox, Margaret Douglas, was her aunt. Margaret Douglas was a daughter of Margaret Tudor (Mary's grandmother) and her second husband, the 6th Earl of Angus. Thus the Queen of Scots and Darnley were cousins. More important was the fact that Margaret Douglas and Lord Darnley stood next to Mary in line to the English throne, and some thought Darnley's claim was the stronger as he was, in effect, an Englishman. The marriage would therefore greatly strengthen Mary's claim as Elizabeth's heir. Mary gave the Earl of Lennox permission to return to Scotland in September 1564 and restored his estates in the west of Scotland. The following February Darnley crossed the border from England – with Queen Elizabeth's permission.

The court was in Fife when he and Mary met each other for what was the third time. Darnley at the age of thirteen had gone to France for the coronation of Francis II in 1559, returning again, when the young King died in December 1561, to offer Mary his family's condolences. Margaret Douglas had had her son well educated, envisaging his future role as King of England, then later, when Mary's husband died, as King of Scotland – sharing the throne with the young widow. He was very tall, fair-haired, a somewhat beautiful nineteen-year-old, accomplished in all the courtly graces, and a good sportsman. What is more he could express himself in verse. He wrote to Mary in the summer of 1565:

If langour makes men light
I am for evermore
In joy, both even and morrow....

The turtle-dove for her mate
More dolour may not endure
Than I do for her sake....

When Mary saw her cousin on Saturday 17 February 1565 in Fife she 'took well with him, and said that he was the lustiest and best-proportioned long man that she had seen, for he was of high stature [he was taller than Mary]…and small [slender], even and erect, from his youth well instructed in all honest and comely exercises'; though lacking in an overt manliness for it was said 'no woman of spirit would make choice of such a man that was more like a woman than a man…beardless and lady-faced'. Darnley was soon going everywhere with the court. For Mary it was initially more of a warm friendship than love. But the young man became ill with measles, suffering episodes of dangerous fevers. Mary nursed him through his sickness, making bedside vigils until midnight, and by April the Queen of Scots had lost her heart. Mary's love for Darnley marks a turning-point in her reign, and the beginning of her downfall. He was spoilt and arrogant, easily influenced, and his assumed importance made him many enemies. Mary became defiant towards those who attempted to point out Darnley's obvious shortcomings, and all the more determined to make him her husband. On 22 July the banns for the marriage were read and Mary made her fiancé Duke of Albany. When she then made it clear before their wedding that Darnley would be styled the King of Scots – a status that was not in her legal power to grant since it rested with a decision of parliament – the lords were alarmed by her wilfulness. Furthermore, the matter of religion again raised general concern. Darnley's mother was well known to be a devout Catholic, and the young man's faith – Protestant or Catholic – was flexible. At this time he professed to be a Protestant; still, it was necessary for Mary to issue a proclamation maintaining the religious status quo. But her hopes of an understanding with Elizabeth disintegrated. While the Queen of England had seemingly urged Darnley towards Mary, her manoeuvring had been a diversion to play for time while avoiding a Scottish-European alliance. When the marriage became likely, Elizabeth was vociferous in her objections. In the view of Mary's friends – and her enemies – the Queen of Scots' behaviour was becoming reckless, no less so when disguised as a man she sauntered about the streets of Edinburgh with her fiancé, and before their marriage spent two nights with Darnley at the home of Lord Seton: 'This manner of passing to and fro gave again occasion to many men to muse what might be her meaning.'

Ignoring all pleas to reconsider her plans, the Queen of Scots and Darnley were married on 29 July 1565. The bridegroom placed three rings on the Queen's finger, the centre ring set with an enormous diamond. They knelt side by side while Mary's Catholic priest said prayers for their union, then Darnley, whose Protestant principles would not allow him to remain, kissed his bride and left the private chapel at Holyrood as the Queen heard Mass. Mary had worn black mourning during

the ceremony, representing the widow's life she was leaving behind. Afterwards her ladies helped her out of her black garments, making a playful show of it as each pin – each link with the past – was removed. Etiquette demanded that the Queen feign reluctance before cheerfully accepting brightly coloured, jewel-encrusted attire. Compared to her first wedding in Paris, the Queen of Scots' second marriage was decidedly low-key. A trumpet fanfare resounded through the corridors of Holyrood as the newlyweds walked in procession to the Great Hall where they dined upon a magnificent feast. Outside, crowds cheered and leapt at gold coins scattered 'in great abundance' – a gesture signifying good fortune. When the wedding party had eaten and drunk their fill and had been entertained with a masque on the powers of love and marriage, they danced. The Queen and King with their stately height, dazzling clothes and youthful beauty were charming to watch as they moved across the floor of the torchlit chamber, stepping and twirling to the music with practised elegance. They took more refreshment, and more dancing, 'and so they go to bed'. The festivities continued throughout the next two days.

The wedding was the cause of fierce resentment amongst Mary's Protestant nobles. Her half-brother Lord James, the Duke of Châtelherault, the Earl of Glencairn, the Earl of Morton and Lord Ruthven – all had signed a bond agreeing to join together to prevent the marriage. These lords had not been pleased to see a Lennox, the family who also had claims to the throne of Scotland, back in the country, and Darnley's increasingly irresponsible and profligate behaviour made his unsuitability as co-ruler all too evident. A particular antagonism had existed between Lord James and the Queen's husband almost from the moment Darnley had first set foot in Mary's Scottish court. By the time of the marriage there were rumours circulating that Darnley was plotting to murder Lord James, and James was said to be intent upon kidnapping the Lennoxes – father and son – and forcing them back to England. When Mary could stand their seething no longer she tenaciously took her husband's side and on 6 August denounced Lord James as

Above Double portrait
of Mary Queen of Scots
and her second husband,
Henry Stewart, Lord
Darnley, late 16th century.
With an army, Mary and
her new husband chased
the Queen's rebellious
nobles, including her
half-brother Lord James,
around the kingdom
(the Chaseabout Raid).
Mary wore a pistol tucked
in her belt, and Darnley
was resplendent in gilded
armour.

an outlaw. Brother and sister had nearly three years earlier taken to the field against the rebellious Huntly. Now the Queen's action meant that James and Mary would have to fight against each other. But the Queen of Scots, with all the bravado of one confident in the belief that she, and not an illegitimate Stewart, had been chosen by God to rule, declared that she would rather lose her crown than fail to be revenged upon Lord James for his disloyalty.

The Queen raised an army and on 26 August rode out of Edinburgh wearing a pistol tucked into her belt. She chased her half-brother and his army of two thousand men around the kingdom – the aptly named 'Chaseabout Raid'. Mary's courage was dauntless, even John Knox registered some admiration, noting that although 'the most part waxed weary, the Queen's courage increased, man-like, so much that she was ever with the foremost'. Lord James and his supporters eventually slipped across the border into England, beyond the Queen's reach. Throughout, Darnley had ridden at Mary's side, resplendent in gilded armour. At Dumfries another man joined the campaign – James Hepburn, Earl of Bothwell – Mary made him her Lieutenant General.

Mary had responded quickly to the crisis, and demonstrated an ability to take command. Though the nobles had objected to her marriage, the Queen of Scots still enjoyed popular support from the rest of her subjects. As if to create a second line of defence from more immediate supporters, she had before her wedding made another half-brother, Lord Robert Stewart, Earl of Orkney and Shetland, and Lord Erskine was raised to the earldom of Mar. After the rebellion she ordered the Edinburgh town council to depose its Protestant provost whom she replaced with a friend, Sir Simon Preston of Craigmillar; he was also admitted to her council. As Mary became distanced from most of the great nobles, she put her trust in lesser men; peers of the realm from whom the Queen of Scots now had support were her father-in-law the Earl of Lennox, the Earl of Atholl and the Earl of Bothwell. Meanwhile, Mary's policies drifted more openly towards Catholicism – the rebellion of Lord James and other powerful Protestant nobles had caused the Queen to seek support from Philip II and from Rome.

Darnley had been furious with the Queen for making Bothwell Lieutenant General instead of his own father. Mary considered Bothwell, a Protestant, the better political choice. It was one of several disagreements that led to heated arguments between the couple. And, far from being a helpmate, the young man was uninterested in affairs of state, preferring hunting excursions or the low-life and brothels of the city. He was so often absent from court that a stamp had to be made of his signature – official royal documents required the signatures of both the Queen and the King.

Sensibly, Mary had not granted her husband the crown matrimonial, which Francis II had enjoyed. This would have ensured that, should the Queen predecease him, he would continue as King of Scots, and if he then remarried, any children of this union would be in line for the throne. This omission, too, inflamed his anger. 'The Lord Darnley followeth his pastimes more than the Queen is content withall.' On one occasion his fondness for drink and resulting boorish behaviour caused him to overstep the bounds by reducing the Queen to tears in public; her love for her husband began to turn bitter. When a new silver coin was issued commemorating their marriage, it displayed the profiles of Mary and Darnley and the words, '*Henricus & Maria, Rex & Regina Scotorum.*' A *faux pas* may have been committed in putting Darnley first, though it appeared thus on many official documents. A new coin was swiftly minted showing Mary's name first, and displaying the emblem of a crowned palm with a tortoise crawling up the trunk; the crowned palm was meant to represent the Queen, and the tortoise Darnley. Moreover, Mary was becoming insensitive to her husband's claims, then demands, for power. He grew tiresome, spouting grievances of neglect by the Queen, and sulking for sympathy. Mary's enemies listened to Darnley's woes, then, taking advantage of his vain, suspicious nature, planted a more serious wedge between husband and wife: how was it that the Queen – a mere woman after all – had the audacity to exclude him from the government…to exclude him from her company? The Queen was playing him for a dupe – she was unfaithful. Darnley, easily pliable, believed their lies.

Mary's alleged lover was David Riccio, a Catholic. Of ancient aristocratic lineage, the Riccios had come down in the world. David was the son of a musician from Pancalieri near Turin and had come to Scotland in 1561 in the company of the ambassador to the Duke of Savoy. He was an accomplished musician, but it was his pleasing singing voice that first attracted the Queen's notice: he became the bass needed to complete a quartet of singers engaged to perform in her private chapel or in the royal apartments during informal supper parties and the leisure pastimes enjoyed by the Queen and her companions. Riccio was probably about thirty in 1565. He is said to have been deformed in some way and ugly, which was offset by his charm, at least in the Queen's company. From his role as singer-musician and valet of the chamber he advanced to be secretary of Mary's French correspondence. After Lord James's revolt, Mary no longer trusted her other principal adviser, William Maitland, and she began to take Riccio increasingly into her confidence. Proximity to the sovereign tended to be associated with political power, which brought rich benefits to David Riccio – and danger. It became necessary to obtain this 'base-born' adviser's permission for admittance to the Queen's presence. Nobles to whom the

Opposite A silver ryal of Mary and Henry minted in 1566, after their marriage. The crowned palm represents the Queen, and the tortoise crawling up the palm symbolizes King Henry (Darnley). The reverse bears the royal coat-of-arms. This coin replaced an earlier version on which Darnley's name appeared before Mary's, and which was speedily withdrawn. By now Darnley's insufferable behaviour was ruining the affection that Mary had genuinely felt for her husband.

Queen's door was firmly shut hated him. Riccio also invited hostility by assuming a manner and style exceeding his station; his costly apparel and jewels were said to be finer than the King's. The rumour that he received bribes was later confirmed by the discovery of money in his possession far exceeding the amount Riccio would have earned for dealing with correspondence. Another rumour that, as a Catholic, Riccio may have been in the employ of Philip II of Spain to persuade the Queen to start a Catholic revolt, was making the man's life precarious. Sensing ill-will, Mary urged courtiers to be kind to her secretary; she said he was 'hated without cause', but her entreaties could not subdue the hostility. The Protestant lords involved in the Chaseabout Raid were eager to return to Scotland, and plotted with others to destroy Riccio; Darnley, ripe for revenge, and his father were drawn into the scheme. Parliament was scheduled to meet in March 1566; during the assembly Lord James and his confederates were to be charged with treason, their land and titles forfeited. The Queen's friends realized that such a measure would hasten a potentially violent reprisal, and urged Mary to pardon the lords; she would not. But after receiving messages from Elizabeth on behalf of Lord James, and after further pleas from her supporters, Mary relented to a degree – the meeting of parliament would be postponed.

Then the scenario took another turn, influenced, perhaps, by Mary's uncle, the Cardinal of Lorraine. At the 1562–63 meeting of the Council of Trent, the Catholic Princes had established firm Catholic doctrines to aid their crusade against Protestantism; these were enacted in 1564. The Cardinal had written to his niece urging her to join them. Mary had not sent a representative to Trent, but the previous January she had written to Pope Pius V explaining that, when the time was right, she would restore Catholicism to Scotland; the Queen even went so far as to suggest the possibility of its extension into England. After receiving the Cardinal of Lorraine's letter, Mary became more determined in pursuing Catholic policies. She now ordered the meeting of parliament to go ahead as planned, at which the Queen requested legislation be enacted permitting Catholics throughout Scotland to worship freely. Lord James and the rest of the exiled rebels were summoned to appear before parliament on 12 March; their plans could no longer be delayed. The rebels drew up a bond agreeing that by some means an unspecified person was 'to be tane away'. The exiled lords – Argyll, Glencairn, Rothes, Boyd and Ochiltree – put their names to the bond along with Darnley. Lord James's signature was not there though he was undoubtedly involved. The rebels planned to secure the crown matrimonial for Darnley, who, in return, was to assure that parliament would not proceed against them, and to support the lords in promoting the Reformed religion.

On 9 March 1566, two days before the rebels were scheduled to appear before parliament, David Riccio was savagely murdered in front of the Queen. She had been enjoying supper at Holyrood in a small room or cabinet off her bedchamber, accompanied by her half-sister Jean, Countess of Argyll, her half-brother Lord Robert Stewart and others. The master of her household was also in attendance, as were the Captain of the Guard, her apothecary, a few domestic servants and David Riccio himself. Soon after they had begun eating, the party was disturbed by a sound from the narrow stairway connecting the room with Darnley's apartments – situated directly below the Queen's. A tapestry concealing a door to the stairway was suddenly flung aside and Mary's husband appeared. Everyone was astonished, as the strain

between King and Queen was such that Darnley was unwelcome at these gatherings. But Darnley would have his revenge. Lord Ruthven later claimed that, although the signatories to the bond planned to murder Riccio, the assassination was to take place in the secretary's own chamber; it was all Darnley's insistence that Riccio be 'taken at supper-time, sitting with her Majesty at the table, that she might be taunted in his presence, because she had not treated her husband according to her accustomed manner as she ought of duty'. The King's behaviour with the Queen and her friends was flippant, his nerves having been fortified with drink. He made some light small-talk, then playfully sat down beside the Queen, putting an arm around her waist. They were then startled by the entrance of Lord Ruthven in full armour, his face ghastly white. 'May it please Your Majesty to let younder man Davie come forth of your presence,' Ruthven ordered, 'for he has been overlong here!' 'What offence hath he made?' cried Mary. 'Great offence!'

Mary now understood what was about to happen, and angrily turned to her husband demanding what he knew of the 'enterprise'. Darnley replied that he knew nothing. She then commanded Ruthven to leave at once, or be charged with treason. If Riccio had been guilty of any crime, she herself would see that he was punished according to the law. Ruthven then looked at Darnley, 'Sir, take the Queen your wife and sovereign to you,' he ordered. Mary got to her feet, and heroically stood in front of Riccio, while Darnley, instead of seizing his wife, began to protest his innocence. The secretary then drew his dagger and leapt to the embrasure of a window behind Mary, clinging to the folds of the Queen's gown. 'Justice! Justice! Save me, Madam! Save me!' The Queen's attendants responded by lunging towards Ruthven who drew his own weapon shouting, 'Lay no hand on me for I will not be handled!' Then, as if his words had been a signal, the room filled with armed men. Lord Ruthven grabbed hold of Riccio, and George Douglas, Darnley's uncle, snatched his nephew's dagger from his belt and stabbed the secretary. The first thrust, according to Mary, was over her shoulder, and so close to her neck that she could feel the coldness of the steel, while a loaded pistol was pressed to her stomach. The frenzy increased, they 'dragged David with great cruelty forth from our cabinet', Mary later recalled, 'and at the entrance of our chamber dealt him fifty-six dagger wounds'. The mutilated body was thrown down the stairs and hauled to the porter's lodge where it was slung across a coffer; the porter's servant then stripped Riccio of his rich clothes. The same night, a Dominican friar attached to the Queen's household was also murdered.

When Mary had recovered some scrap of composure she accosted Darnley: 'What offence have I made you, that ye should have done me such shame?' 'Ye regarded me not, neither treated me nor entertained me after your wonted

Opposite The Queen's bedchamber at Holyrood, a 19th-century drawing. During the 18th century, visitors to Holyrood began to focus on Mary's apartments, 'perhaps the most interesting suite of rooms in Europe', soon embellished and shown for a fee. An early 19th-century guidebook reads: 'Strangers visiting the palace are usually led to Queen Mary's apartments…[where] her bed still remains…a piece of wainscot…hangs upon hinges, and opens a passage to a trap-stair…. Through this passage Darnley and his accomplices rushed in to murder the unhappy Rizzio [the old spelling of Riccio].'

Overleaf *The Murder of Rizzio*, by Sir William Allan, 1833. The violence of Riccio's assassination in Mary's presence convinced her that her own life and that of her unborn child had also been endangered. The murder had been provoked by Mary's pro-Catholic policies, and by her reliance on foreigners 'of base degree'. John Black, a Dominican friar in the Queen's household, was also murdered that night.

fashion,' he retorted. Mary soon stifled her husband's reproaches with a declaration: 'My Lord, all the offense that is done me, you have the wite [knowledge] thereof, for the which I will be your wife no longer, nor lie with you any more, and shall never like well till I cause you have as sorrowful a heart as I have at this present.' The Queen of Scots was at this time six months pregnant with Darnley's child.

Riccio's assassination precipitated Mary's fears for her own life, and that of her unborn child; Darnley too became frightened. The morning after the murder he was full of contrition, weeping forth a confession to the conspirators' plans, and showed the Queen a copy of the bond that he had signed. She learned that they intended to take her to Stirling Castle, keeping her prisoner until the heir to the throne was born. King Henry (Darnley) would rule with the firm guidance of the lords, and Mary would remain their captive until she died. There was no other recourse; Mary could only avoid the treacheries by planning an escape, although in the advanced stages of pregnancy. And what is more, she would have to take Darnley with her – for all his gross defects, he was still father to the heir of Scotland's throne. Playing for time, Mary pretended to be in premature labour. So convincing was the Queen's performance that Ruthven and the others sent for a woman to attend her. Mary also managed to get a message to Lords Bothwell and Huntly, who had escaped earlier through back windows of the palace, to wait for her at the home of Lord Seton.

Meanwhile, the conspirators issued a proclamation in Darnley's name, cancelling the forthcoming parliament, making it safe for them to return to Edinburgh. Shortly after his arrival in the city, Lord James was summoned to the Queen's presence. When he arrived at Holyrood, Mary embraced her half-brother, and was all affection. She may have been motivated to separate him from the other lords, but her tenderness was possibly genuine, remembering the past when they had been on closer terms. Mary exclaimed that if he had been at court 'they would not have seen her so uncourteously handled'. For his part, Lord James was 'so moved that the tears fell from his eyes'. Mary put the blame on Darnley for the exile of the Protestant lords, and her half-brother then claimed that, until he reached Edinburgh, he had known nothing of Riccio's murder. Their meeting ended, but Lord James, with his co-conspirators, later returned for a formal discussion with the Queen. On bended knee, except for Lord James, the conspirators through their spokesman, the red-bearded Earl of Morton, asked pardon for the murder of Riccio. Darnley had earlier expressed to Mary his view that granting the conspirators a pardon was the only means of getting them both out of danger. She was wary of such an easy solution, and sought to play for time. The conspirators could not immediately be granted what they asked, but, if by their future honourable behaviour they tried

to efface the past, then, 'I give you my word that on my part I will endeavour to forget what you have done.' Lord James then gave a passionate lecture on the virtues of clemency. Mary was incautiously sarcastic with her response, and, before their exchange became volatile, she resorted to theatrics – again pretending to be stricken with excruciating pain, she called out for her midwife to help her to her bedchamber. The lords, bewildered, withdrew to formulate a set of articles for their security which they later handed to Darnley on the promise that he would give the document to the Queen. Darnley then went off, seemingly with this intention, but had to return to the lords full of apologies. The Queen was too ill to read or sign anything, but would do so in the morning. With that they entrusted Darnley to guard the Queen – the conspirators had no intention of allowing her to go free – and they retired for the night.

During the early hours of the morning, Mary and her husband slipped through Darnley's chamber, through the quarters of her French servants, and with their help made their way through a side-door to the palace cemetery, and from thence to a gate where Lord Erskine and a group of Mary's friends were waiting with horses. They mounted and rode off. At Seton Palace more of the Queen's supporters were waiting, but, sighting them in the distance, the easily frightened Darnley mistook them for the enemy. 'Come on! Come on!' he shouted. 'By God's blood, they will murder both you and me if they catch us,' and he thrashed his horse and hers. Mary was exhausted and pleaded with Darnley to slow his gallop out of concern for her condition. He pointed out bluntly, that if she lost the child she was carrying, they would get others. Mary, near collapse, told her husband to ride ahead, and within a moment he had vanished. Five hours after her escape from Holyrood the Queen, weary, but alive, arrived with her companions at the safe fortress of Dunbar Castle where Bothwell awaited them.

More supporters soon rallied to Mary's aid, and she wrote letters to Queen Elizabeth and to her friends on the continent, with all the details of Riccio's murder and asked for their help. Mary offered to pardon the rebels involved in the Chaseabout Raid, but separated them from the conspirators to Riccio's murder who would not be pardoned. When the assassins and others connected with the plot realized that Darnley had deserted them and was apparently reconciled with the Queen, they fled the capital. Morton, Ruthven and another conspirator, Lord Lindsay, went to England; Maitland, whose involvement was suspected but not proven, went north to the Highlands, and John Knox, who had also been a supporter of the plot, retreated to the west of Scotland. With her enemies scattered, Mary returned like a conquering heroine to Edinburgh, where she lodged with Lord

Herries in the centre of the city. She would not, just then, go back to Holyrood, with its images of horror and entrapment still vivid. But Mary still feared that the lords would yet attempt to seize her child as soon as it was born, and she left Lord Herries's hospitality for the greater safety of her fortress on the rock, Edinburgh Castle.

She accepted Lord James back into her council along with Glencairn and Argyll, and Maitland, too, was soon welcomed back into the inner circle of the Queen's advisers. After all the upheaval, Mary was trying to get her government under

Opposite Edinburgh
Castle, towering over
the city from a cliff of
basalt rock – an extinct
volcano. This castle was
the strongroom of the
kingdom, the crown jewels
were usually kept here as
well as the national records.
The rectangular Great
Hall, lit by large windows
(seen here centre top) was
added on the orders of
James IV. The royal
apartments were located
in the upper south-east
corner (upper left), and
were remodelled for the
Queen of Scots and King
Henry (Darnley). A sign
at Edinburgh Castle
commemorates Mary
of Guise's death here on
11 June 1560: 'A lady of
singular judgment, full of
humanity, a great lover of
justice, helpful to the poor'.

control, trying to create some balance by separating her recalcitrant nobles – better
to have the most powerful among them within view – and she did much to reconcile
friends and enemies. Darnley joined his wife in Edinburgh, but the couple's recent
peril had failed to make any impact on his wretched behaviour. Lord James called
him 'a young fool and proud tyrant'. The young man seemed incapable of winning
approval, or unwilling to try. Sir James Melville acknowledged that he 'past up and
down on his own and few durst bear his company'. There were soon rumours that
the Queen would divorce her husband; an English visitor observing the couple
declared that Mary's hatred for Darnley was such that the King could not safely
remain in Scotland. But by June 1566 all the Queen's attention was focused upon
the birth of their child.

On 3 June Mary began her ceremonious confinement at Edinburgh Castle in
a great bed hung with blue taffeta and blue velvet. Ten lengths of Holland cloth were
used to cover the baby's cradle. She took the precaution of sending to Dunfermline
for the relics of St Margaret, believing these would protect her during the birth,
and the further precaution of drawing up a will. If Mary died, survived by her child,
everything was to go to the child. If they both died, her jewelry and other valuables,
253 articles, were to be distributed according to her wishes, with the most impressive
or costly jewels going to the Scottish crown in memory, she said, of the allegiance
between Scotland and the house of Guise-Lorraine. Thereafter the beneficiaries
were: fourteen of her Guise relations; the four Maries and their families; her
illegitimate Scottish relations; various Scottish and French nobles; servants; and Lord
Darnley who was to receive, among other items, Mary's diamond wedding ring – 'It
was with this that I was married,' she wrote, 'I leave it to the King, who gave it to me.'
Another ring was left to Riccio's brother, Joseph, who was to deliver it to one whose
name the Queen had secretly imparted to him.

On 18 June Mary went into a difficult labour in a small room – easier to keep
warm – off her larger chamber. During her agony the Queen called out that she
wished she had never been married, and as the pains became yet more intense she
prayed aloud for God to spare her child rather than herself. The Countess of Atholl
summoned the black arts, attempting to cast the Queen's suffering upon Lady Reres,
who responded by lying in bed seeming to writhe with her mistress's pangs.
Witchcraft had long played a part in Scottish society; in this instance the Countess
of Atholl's attempts were unsuccessful.

At last, between ten and eleven in the morning on 19 June 1566, Mary gave
birth to a healthy son. The baby was said to have been born with the 'lucky caul' –
a fragment of amniotic sac – over his head, which according to folklore guaranteed

that he would not die by drowning. Weakened though she was, it was crucial for the Queen to protect the heir to the throne from the slur of illegitimacy. She summoned Darnley to her chamber, and in the presence of her assembled household she unwrapped the newborn, displaying him to all, particularly to his father, who had, with the child's birth, moved farther down in the succession. 'My Lord', she said, 'God has given you and me a son, begotten by none but you.' Drawing a cover from the baby's face, she continued: 'Here I protest to God, as I shall answer to him at the great day of Judgment, that this is your son and no other man's son. I am desirous that all here, with ladies and others bear witness.' Then she added, unable even at

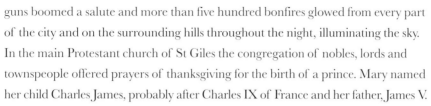

Opposite and below
After the birth of their son, in 1566, Mary and Darnley, with their son Charles James, visited Traquair House in Peeblesshire. Mary slept in this room and her child slept in the cradle at the foot of the bed. The four-poster bed, used by the Queen of Scots, was brought to Traquair in 1890 from Terregles Castle where, in 1568, she had been a guest of Sir John Maxwell, 4th Lord Herries.

that moment to conceal her contempt for Darnley: 'For he is so much your own son that I fear it will be the worse for him hereafter.'

Outside the castle, all Edinburgh was rejoicing. It had been almost thirty years since a male heir had been born to Scotland's throne (the young sons of James IV and Mary of Guise had died before Mary Stewart was born). The castle guns boomed a salute and more than five hundred bonfires glowed from every part of the city and on the surrounding hills throughout the night, illuminating the sky. In the main Protestant church of St Giles the congregation of nobles, lords and townspeople offered prayers of thanksgiving for the birth of a prince. Mary named her child Charles James, probably after Charles IX of France and her father, James V.

Now that the baby was born, anxiety for her own and the infant's safety increased. She was well aware that Scottish nobles had a predilection for obtaining possession of the royal heir, and ruling during the child's minority. Hence, Mary paid little regard to the custom of immediately placing royal infants in their own household nearby, but kept her son's cradle in her own chamber. Mary was a good mother, attentive to her baby. She had an intuitive ability with children and enjoyed their company. Darnley, however, still 'vagabondized every night', and his movements meant that the castle gates had to be continually opened at irregular hours, putting them all at risk. The stress for Mary was becoming unbearable, and, two

months after Charles James's birth, she decided to move her son to the safer stronghold of Stirling Castle, just as she herself had been moved there so many years before. The baby was placed under the protection of John Erskine, who had been made Earl of Mar in 1565 when Lord James had forfeited the title by his rebellion. For her child's nursery Mary commanded that every detail was to be 'the finest that can be gottin', including blue plaid to adorn his cradle, fustian for his mattress and feathers for his pillow. She also had copes and other vestments of

Above Ceiling of the small room in Edinburgh Castle where Mary gave birth to her only child, Prince Charles James. During her son's coronation ceremony on 29 July 1567, the name 'Charles' was dropped and the baby became James VI of Scotland, and in 1603 James I of England. The painted decoration of the ceiling was added in preparation for the 'homecoming' of James VI and I in 1617. Beneath the royal arms of Scotland is a doggerel verse in Old Scots: 'Lord Jesu Chryst that Crounit was with Thornse/ Preserve the Birth quhais Badgie heir is borne/ And send Hir Sonee Successione to Reigne still/ Lang in this Realme, if that it be Thy Will/ Als grant O Lord quhat ever of Hir proceed/ Be to The Glorie Honer and Prais sobied.'

Background Hermitage
Castle in Liddesdale.
In October 1566 Mary
rode twenty-five miles
across the wild countryside
of the Borders to visit her
lieutenant, Bothwell, who
was lying wounded in this
remote fortress. Mary's visit
to his bedside was later
used to slander her.

Opposite James
Hepburn, 4th Earl of
Bothwell, and his first
wife, Jean Gordon, whom
he married in 1566. This
double miniature by an
unknown artist is thought
to be the only existing
likeness of Bothwell. In
1567 Jean divorced her
husband, and their
marriage was also annulled
on the grounds of the Earl's
adultery with his wife's
serving maid.

cloth of gold cut up to make bed hangings for the cradle, and the walls were hung all round with tapestries. Lady Reres, who had already proved to have a sympathetic nature, was appointed as wetnurse for the baby. The honour came with its own accoutrements, plaid for the cover and canopy of her bed.

For the sake of her child and the kingdom Mary made some effort, according to her own account, to patch up her marriage by spending more time with Darnley and sharing his bed. During that August of 1566, either before or after their child's removal to Stirling, Mary and Darnley were together for a hunting excursion at Traquair House near Peebles. The couple's host, Sir John Stewart, Captain of the Queen's Bodyguard, was forced to rebuke Darnley when Mary excused herself from the chase because she thought she was pregnant. 'What!' Darnley exclaimed, 'ought we not to work a mare when she is in foal!' King or no King, Sir John could not ignore the young man's insolence, and told Darnley, in no uncertain terms, to treat his wife with more respect.

The Queen of Scots who had hoped for a husband who would be her companion, her adviser and helpmate in governing Scotland, had clearly not found the man to share her burden, but had, instead, added to it. She now turned to someone else to fill that role – thirty-year-old James Hepburn, Earl of Bothwell. She increasingly sought his counsel. Whereas Darnley was foppish, the swarthy Bothwell was tough and masculine. He was six inches shorter than Mary, and not generally considered handsome. The genteel George Buchanan found his appearance disgusting, 'Like an ape in purple.' Yet the Earl of Bothwell had a sexual magnetism that had attracted a string of mistresses, and a wife. He had been well educated, was well travelled, had spent time at the court of France and was fluent in French. By nature Bothwell was impulsive, a swashbuckling adventurer, but also turbulent and given to fits of anger. Like most nobles he was acutely ambitious for his family. The Hepburn dominions spread across south-east Scotland, and the family also possessed the wardships of royal castles, including Dunbar to which the Queen had ultimately fled from Holyrood. When poverty threatened Bothwell's position, he married Jean Gordon, of the wealthy Huntly family; the settlement in their wedding contract was in this instance the obligation of the bride. Lord Herries described him as a man 'high in his own conceit, proud, vicious and vainglorious above measure, one who would attempt anything out of ambition'. No one trusted him, except the Queen.

Darnley let it be known that as a result of his wife's treatment of him he was considering leaving the country. Such public effrontery towards the Queen would not do. The Privy Council made an occasion of pointing out the King's great good fortune in having a wife of such esteem, imbued with wisdom and virtue. In front of everyone present, Mary took her husband's hand and pleaded with him to state clearly any reason she may have given him for wishing to leave. His answer was equivocal. In October the Queen left Edinburgh on a progress through the Borders, holding justice ayres (royal judicial courts). She had expected Darnley to accompany her, but he refused, preferring to stay in the capital where he might find an audience for his laments, and he continued to let it be known that the Queen was causing him to seek solace abroad. To the Kings of France and Spain, the Cardinal of Lorraine and the Pope he wrote letters complaining that Mary was no longer a good Catholic; this from a man who had on occasion insisted that he was a devout Protestant.

When she reached the Border town of Jedburgh in her progress, Mary learned that Bothwell had been seriously injured in a skirmish with 'Wee' Jock Elliot, one of a gang of reivers (Border outlaws) and was lying at the point of death in Hermitage Castle. The Queen was distressed that her loyal supporter was in danger, but took no action until five days later, on hearing that Bothwell was recovering, she went to see him. Together with Lord James and several courtiers she rode twenty-five miles across wild, uneven countryside to the complete solitude of the Hermitage. The brooding fortress looms like a giant against the stark landscape – since the thirteenth century the castle had served as the 'guardhouse of the bloodiest valley in Britain'. Remarkably, it took its name, indirectly, from an Irish hermit who had travelled to the desolate valley spreading religion. A tributary of the Liddel Water, called Hermitage Water, was named after the hermit, and the castle came to be named from its proximity to the river. An ever present wind blows across the hills and rushes through the valley, making a whirling sound punctuated by water tumbling over rocks in the riverbed, and there is the cry of birds, forlorn rather than pleasing, but hypnotic; at Hermitage Castle it is difficult to judge whether to pitch one's conversation at the level of a shout or a whisper. The atmosphere exudes intrigue, and George Buchanan, whose verse had so often praised Mary's virtue, later, at a critical moment, used Mary's visit to Bothwell's bedside at Hermitage to assault her reputation. The castle was not equipped for offering hospitality to exalted guests, so Mary and her party had to ride back to Jedburgh that same evening, covering fifty miles over all. She had been feeling unwell before the Borders progress, and after the trip to Hermitage Castle her illness became alarming. She began to have convulsions, and, fearing that she would die, sent for her nobles to give them her final wishes. Darnley was not to have the crown, the infant Prince would be the next King and he was to be brought up by good example, schooled in honourable principles, and kept away from unsavoury company. To her half-brother, Lord James she pointed out that she had never persecuted Protestants, and bade him be equally tolerant towards Catholics after

her death. On 25 October Mary became unconscious, her body rigid and cold. Her French physician struggled to revive the Queen by bandaging her big toes, her legs and her arms. He then forced wine down her throat and gave her an enema. She began to stir and was able to swallow a tincture, after which she vomited blood. Mary's recovery took a long time, but when she had a little strength, Lord Bothwell called upon her. Darnley didn't visit his wife until a week later.

Mary blamed the constant stress of her relationship with her husband for her illness. Maitland went further, telling the Scottish ambassador in France that Darnley 'has recompensed her with such ingratitude, and misuses himself so far towards her, that it is a heartbreak to her to think that he should be her husband, and how to be free of him she sees no way out'. In November she was still far from well and together with her general weakness began to suffer bouts of depression. To Lord James and Maitland she confessed that 'unless she was free of him in some way she had no pleasure to live, and if she could find no other remedy, she would slay herself'. From Jedburgh with a train of 'a thousand horse' she was carried on a litter through the Borders making various scheduled stopovers before returning to Edinburgh. Just south of the capital, at the residence of Lord Preston, Craigmillar Castle, Mary and her advisers, including Bothwell, spent long hours in discussion over the problem of Darnley. Annulment was not possible, for the Queen had obtained a dispensation from the Pope which had sanctioned her marriage to her cousin. Furthermore, if her marriage was made invalid, their child would be declared illegitimate. Nor was divorce a desirable solution; apart from the stigma inherent in this arrangement (regardless of regal precedence such as Henry VIII and a few Continental monarchs), for Mary's Catholic principles meant that she would merely live apart from her husband, and in the eyes of God she would still be Darnley's wife. A third alternative was that Lord Darnley be removed by other means without disadvantage to her son. Maitland told Mary that Lord James would be willing to 'look through his fingers thereto, and will behold our doings saying nothing to the same'. Mary may not have realized during these discussions at Craigmillar, that the course of action being decided upon by her advisers was specifically murder. There had been talk of charging Darnley with high treason on the basis of his complicity in the conspiracy to seize the Queen at the time of Riccio's assassination, a solution that had the comfort of providing a legal means to his death. In any event, their plan could not be carried out until after the baptism of Prince Charles James.

The royal baptism was to be the most spectacular occasion of Mary's personal reign. It was modelled, in part, on the elaborate fête staged at Bayonne in 1565, marking the meeting between Charles IX and representatives of the court of Spain.

Opposite Craigmillar Castle, three miles south-east of the centre of Edinburgh. The construction of the castle was begun in the 15th century by the Catholic Preston family, lairds of Craigmillar. Sir Simon Preston became Edinburgh's provost, at Mary's insistence, in 1565, and served as one of her privy councillors from 1565 to 1567. Mary stayed at Craigmillar in 1563 and again in November 1566 when she arrived from Jedburgh to convalesce. Before she left on 7 December, Mary and her advisers, including Bothwell, spent long hours discussing the problem of Darnley.

Opposite At Stirling Castle, a gilded stone lion, part of a 1990s restoration of the Great Hall, completed by James IV in 1503, when four heraldic beasts – two lions and two unicorns – were placed along the roof's skyline. The exterior walls were coloured with an ochre lime-wash and glistened with twenty-six principal windows set with stained-glass roundels. Inside, the magnificent hammerbeam roof stretched across the 138 x 47 ft rectangular space. There was an oak screen and a gallery carved with floral motifs; there were five fireplaces and four spiral staircases. On 17 December 1566 Mary's son was baptized in a Catholic ceremony at Stirling. The guests adjourned for dinner in the Great Hall where Protestants and Catholics served each other in an atmosphere of reconciliation. On the third day of the festivities, celebrating the power of the Stewart monarchy, the guests were seated at a round table, emphasizing Scotland's links with King Arthur. For Mary, the 1566 baptism and celebrations at Stirling were probably the high point of her reign.

In the style of a Renaissance triumph, the festivities presented Mary as a hero and reconciler and would show England, as well as all of Europe, that the Queen of Scots knew how to put on a display glorious enough for the Valois court. But to do so she had to borrow £12,000 from the merchants of Edinburgh. Her valet Bastien Pagéz stage-managed the sequence of theatrical tableaux, masques, banquets and other entertainments after Mary had first studied every detail of his plans. The baptism took place on 17 December 1566 with full Catholic ritual. The Comte de Brienne, representing Charles IX of France, the baby's godfather, carried the Prince to the chapel where they were met by John Hamilton (the illegitimate brother of the Duke of Châtelherault), Archbishop of St Andrews, who led the procession of Catholic prelates all splendidly arrayed in ornate vestments. One part of the traditional ceremony had been prohibited by the Queen, the spitting into the infant's mouth by the officiating priest – Mary may have heard that the Archbishop was syphilitic.

Queen Elizabeth was represented by the Protestant Earl of Bedford, who stood outside the chapel during the Catholic ceremony. The Earl had a second mission in coming to the baptism, namely to lodge England's protest against the Scottish poet Patrick Adamson's *Genethliacum…Iacobi VI*, a Latin poem of thanksgiving for the child's birth, published in Paris. Adamson, a strong supporter of the Queen and the Stewart dynasty, referred to James as '*Serenissimus princeps*' of Scotland, England, France and Ireland; rightful heir to the English throne in place of its illegitimate possessor, Elizabeth. The Queen of England and the House of Commons were outraged. The King of France, responding to the furore, had the poem suppressed, and was ultimately obliged to have Adamson imprisoned for six months. Mary herself could not help but rejoice, albeit with considerably more restraint, for the birth of a healthy son could only serve to strengthen her and her son's position in the English succession.

Elizabeth had also sent the showpiece of the service, a magnificent font made of gold and set with precious jewels – it weighed 28 pounds. The Countess of Argyll held the child on the Queen of England's behalf, and the Duke of Savoy, another godparent, was represented by Philibert du Croc. Most of the Scottish Protestant nobles also remained outside the chapel, refusing to take part in the Catholic ritual, though they had been happy with the luxurious garments provided for them at the Queen's expense, and finer than many of them had ever worn before. Lord James was dressed in green, Argyll in red and Bothwell in blue; other lords wore cloth of silver and cloth of gold. After the solemnities, there was a banquet in the Great Hall accompanied by music, followed by two hours of dancing and revelry. On the third day of celebrations, there was a dinner at which the focal point – reminiscent of

Stirling's legendary past – was Arthur's Round Table. The food was served from a moving stage pulled by satyrs, while musicians dressed as maidens accompanied the feast with music and song. There was a moment of unpleasantness when the Satyrs began wagging their long tails in the direction of the English guests who interpreted their nonsense as an insult. Happily, all was well for the presentation of an allegorical siege by Moors, Highlanders, Centaurs, Lanzknechts and Fiends upon an enchanted, pasteboard fortress, constructed in front of the castle. A lavishly decorated gallery had been made for the Queen and her company – the ambassadors of France, England and Savoy – to watch the event. At nightfall came the climax of the celebrations – a pageant of fireworks, exploding streaks and curlicues of luminous red and yellow into the freezing darkness, then hissing with spent combustion – again, again, again; it had taken forty days to assemble the firework exhibition.

The Prince's father Darnley had, throughout, kept to his apartments. A few days later he abruptly left Stirling for the Lennox family estates near Glasgow, and Mary departed for Drummond Castle near Crieff. Among the courtiers who accompanied the Queen was Bothwell. Mary was becoming increasingly dependent upon the Earl; they were together so often that malicious rumours speculating on the exact nature of their relationship began to spread.

Shortly after Charles James's baptism, the Queen granted the Protestant church more benefices and a gift of £10,000, perhaps a tactic for girding support, for a few days later Mary restored to Archbishop Hamilton full powers to hold courts, under canon law; in so doing she risked a Protestant uprising. Mary's reason for such a rash action seems to have been her conviction that, after all, the only realistic means of being released from her marriage was to divorce. The Hamiltons were life-long foes of the Lennoxes, and the Archbishop would oblige the Queen, whereas the Pope might not. But in a couple of weeks Mary again changed her mind and revoked her commission to the Archbishop, Lord James impressing upon her the potential danger, and she had also received messages from Europe stressing that she must not divorce her husband. To do so was to lose the support of Catholics in England, and Darnley would become the spearhead of all those who wished to plot against her. Another important decision made by the Queen at this time was to allow the conspirators in Riccio's murder to return. They had remained abroad for two years, presumably on good behaviour. Mary now wanted them back. Only two of them were still excluded for expressly threatening the Queen's life.

Before the end of December 1566 Darnley was reported to have been stricken with 'a great fever of the pox'; he was probably in the secondary stages of syphilis. It would have been years before he actually died of the disease. When Mary learned that her husband was really very ill, she sent her physician to see him and visited Darnley herself on 22 January 1567. He was a pathetic sight – too weak to move from his bed, emaciated, his face covered with a taffeta mask concealing the eruptions that now ravaged his features. His condition appeared to rekindle the Queen's sympathy, and her protective nature came to the fore. She spoke with tenderness to her husband saying that she was willing to take him back to Edinburgh, and that when he had recovered, they would be a couple again. Her feelings for Darnley in his helpless condition may have been genuine, and were quite in character. But, apart from an emotional response to suffering, there were practical reasons for a reconciliation. Divorce was out, so why not make the best of a difficult situation? It was also rumoured that Mary was pregnant, but not by Darnley, in which case the need to resume her relationship would have been essential in order to establish the legitimacy of the child. There was also a third reason, she had heard from London that Darnley was definitely plotting against her. If true, Mary would have to charm him away from schemes that were a danger to her and the kingdom. By the end of January Darnley was being carried on a litter to Edinburgh. Mary could not receive him at Holyrood for she had recently moved her son there from Stirling, and, not knowing the nature of her husband's disease, she was anxious to avoid the possibility of infecting their baby, so she made arrangements for Darnley to be taken to Craigmillar. Her husband, however, vehemently protested that he would not go there. Perhaps he had learned of the discussions of his demise that had taken place at Craigmillar or perhaps the somewhat isolated location of the castle made him uneasy for his safety. No, he would go to Holyrood and only Holyrood. With soothing words Mary managed to bring him around to a compromise. Darnley would instead have his convalescence at a house at Kirk o' Field, just inside the town walls, and much nearer to Holyrood than Craigmillar. Kirk o' Field was situated in a quadrangle formed by gabled houses on three sides of the square and a large house on the fourth. The quadrangle had been attached to the collegiate church of St Mary-in-the-Field, which over the years had come to be called Kirk o' Field.

The house that Darnley was to occupy was the Old Provost's Lodging, consisting of two bedrooms, one above the other; a room to be used as Darnley's presence chamber; two *garderobes*; and a kitchen with vaulted cellars below. It had its own garden, and there were pleasant walks and an orchard close to the house where he could take exercise when he was stronger. So that the King's lodgings would be comfortable, furnishings were sent down from the palace: several sets of tapestries, a Turkish carpet, cushions of red velvet, a table covered with green velvet, a chair of estate covered in purple velvet, and a bed that had belonged to Mary of Guise, given to Darnley by the Queen the previous summer, draped with violet-brown velvet, embroidered with flowers and ciphers of gold and silver – this bed replaced a black bed which was, according to Darnley's taste, too paltry. A bath was also sent over from the palace and placed beside the King's bed, bathing being part of the treatment for Darnley's condition. The chamber beneath the King's was furnished for Mary with a bed hung with green and yellow damask silk, and later a fur coverlet. Darnley was installed at Kirk o' Field on Saturday 1 February, attended by his valet and two other servants who lodged with him. Within days he was regaining health, all due to 'my love the Queen', he wrote to his father. Mary appeared to be making every effort to be kind to him. He still feared treachery from the nobles, and when he became quite overcome with anxiety, Mary agreed to spend the Wednesday night and then Friday night in the room below his. During the day Darnley was entertained by a stream of courtiers who had come to pay their respects to the patient, to converse, play cards and listen to music. Amid all this pleasantry, Lord Robert Stewart, the Queen's half-brother, well aware of the taut animosity surrounding the King, warned Darnley that if he did not flee the city at once, it would cost him his life. Darnley immediately confronted Mary, who with apparent distress questioned Lord Robert. Her half-brother, no doubt afraid himself of revenge, denied disclosing anything to the King. Anyway, Darnley was so much recovered that he planned to move into Holyrood the following Monday, where he would feel safer.

Sunday 9 February, the last Sunday before Lent, was a busy day in Mary's social calendar. The morning began with the wedding of her favourite valet, Bastien Pagéz to Christian Hogg, and the Queen was present at their wedding breakfast held at noon in Holyrood. At four o'clock she attended a farewell dinner given by the Bishop of the Isles at his house in the Canongate for the ambassador from Savoy. Bothwell, Huntly, Argyll and others accompanied Mary, but not Lord James who had left Edinburgh earlier in the day upon receiving news that his wife had miscarried. After the Bishop's dinner Mary and her companions rode to Kirk o' Field to amuse Darnley with all the day's happenings. There were table games and music, laughter and casual chatter. Mary had planned to stay the night with her husband but at around ten or eleven o'clock a courtier reminded the Queen that it was time for Bastien's wedding masque, which she had promised her valet she would attend. So the group made their good-byes to Darnley and set off back to the palace. The King protested at being so hastily deserted, and, before she left, Mary gave her husband a ring as a token of her rekindled affection, then went downstairs and out into the courtyard. When the Queen was about to mount her horse she was startled to see Paris, formerly a servant of Bothwell. 'Jesu, Paris,' she exclaimed, 'How begrimed you are!' His face was apparently smeared with soot. Paris said nothing, but looked guilty. Mary hesitated, studying the man, then mounted her horse and rode off with her courtiers to the palace. When Mary got back to Holyrood the festivities were almost over, but they were in time for the ceremonial high-jinks of bedding the bride and groom. Sometime after midnight Mary retired, and had been deeply asleep, it was said, when at about two in the morning she suddenly jerked awake at the sound of a massive explosion that shook the city. Mary cried out for assistance, thinking that what she heard was gunfire. Bothwell, in his capacity as Sheriff of Edinburgh, sent messengers to learn what had caused the blast. Inside the city wall townspeople were crowding around Kirk o' Field where the Old Provost's Lodging had been; there was now nothing but rubble. A moaning sound was heard, and there on the parapet of the city wall was the blackened but very much alive figure of Nelson, Darnley's manservant, who had been thrown clear in the explosion. The crowds then began to dig in the rubble and discovered the corpses of two more servants, but not the King. Perhaps an hour later Darnley's body was discovered in the orchard, and a few feet away was the corpse of his valet Taylor. Near their unmarked bodies was a chair, and on the ground near it were a dagger, coat and cloak. Like the bodies, the articles were unmarked by the explosion. Doctors who later examined the two corpses came to the conclusion that the Queen's husband and his valet had been strangled. Darnley was only twenty years old. Once more, Mary was faced with a crisis. It is possible that Mary had no knowledge of the plot to murder her husband. Yet, she would be suspected of having been involved. With the death of Darnley, Mary's life entered a series of crises from which she could not recover. Her judgment failed, and for the most part she ceased to be an effective ruler.

Mary had never entirely recovered from her illness at Jedburgh which left her dispirited, and given to prolonged periods of melancholy. A week after Darnley's death, her nerves near breaking-point, she left the claustrophobic atmosphere of mourning – the forty days that propriety required – for the 'wholesome air' of Lord Seton's residence; a change of environment that had been suggested by the Queen's physicians. Upon leaving Holyrood she left her son in the care of Bothwell and his brother-in-law, the Earl of Huntly. Her choice of guardians had been ill-judged, and the day after the Queen left the capital, a placard appeared charging Bothwell with the murder of Mary's husband, and implicating the Queen, implying that she had acted under the spell of witchcraft. More hostile was the placard that appeared on 1 March showing a hare – the animal on Bothwell's family crest – and a mermaid – the sixteenth-century symbol commonly used to represent a prostitute. So that the meaning of the placard would be unmistakable, the hare was surrounded by a circle

of swords, and the mermaid wore a crown. Thereafter, the rumours that the Queen's lover Bothwell had murdered the King could not be stopped. For Mary's part, she did little to assuage the tongue-wagging. She continually appeared with Lord Bothwell in public, and rewarded her steadfast supporter with costly jewels and furs.

Though it was clearly in the Queen's interest to prosecute her husband's murderers, it was left to Lord Lennox, Darnley's father, to accuse the perpetrators; he immediately named Bothwell. A trial before parliament was fixed for 12 April; the Earl of Bothwell, as a member of the Privy Council, helped to make the arrangements. Darnley's father, with an army of three thousand men, marched from western Scotland towards the capital. But at Linlithgow he was told that he could only enter Edinburgh with six supporters. Bothwell, had taken the precaution of filling the city with his own men, and Lennox had no choice but to go back home. On the morning of the trial, the Earl of Bothwell mounted his horse in the forecourt of Holyrood, then glancing up at Mary's window he waved his hand; the Queen acknowledged his gesture with a friendly nod. The court proceedings dragged on for over eight hours, but, in the absence of Lennox or the Queen, there was no one to accuse the defendant – at least no one brave enough to come forward – and Bothwell was acquitted. Four days later, when the Queen made her ceremonial opening of parliament, he was prominent in the procession, carrying the royal sceptre.

That spring, Bothwell on several occasions asked the Queen to marry him. Though he already had a wife, his ambition to be King seemed to override that technicality, and indeed Lady Jean appeared willing to release him. Mary rejected his proposals; she later said that her regard for Bothwell was as 'a man of resolution, well adapted to rule'. Her refusals of his offers of marriage suggest that – at least initially – she did not want him to be her consort, and her friends (those who truly had the Queen's interest at heart) strongly advised against it. Bothwell, however, would not be discouraged. He organized support from some of the most powerful figures in the country, including Maitland, Morton, Argyll and Huntly, twenty-nine signatories in all who put their names to the so-called Ainslie Tavern Bond, agreeing to support his claim to marry the Queen, and if force was necessary, so be it.

Mary attended parliament on 19 April and formally took the Reformed Church under her protection. She also ratified gifts to her leading nobles, who apart from Bothwell, were Lord James, Lord Robert, Maitland, Morton and Huntly; actions interpreted as an attempt to gain the support of these influential men. Prince Charles James, now ten months old, had been moved back to Stirling Castle, and on 20 April Mary went to visit him there. She spent two days enjoying her baby before the return journey to Edinburgh, unaware that she would never see her child again. The Queen and her retinue of some thirty courtiers, including Maitland, Huntly and Sir James Melville, returned to the capital via Linlithgow where they spent the night. The next day they proceeded to Edinburgh. About six miles from the city they were intercepted by a small army with Bothwell at the lead. The Earl seized the bridle of Mary's horse saying that there was danger in the capital, and that for safety's sake the Queen must accompany him to Dunbar. Mary may have gone along with Bothwell by choice, or she may have been unwilling. When members of the royal party objected to her being taken away, Mary silenced their protests saying that she would have no more bloodshed. Huntly, Maitland and Sir James went with the Queen to Dunbar where Sir James later claimed that Bothwell 'ravished her and lain with her against her will', and that as a result 'the Queen could not but marry him'. Of Bothwell, Protestant poet John Sempill wrote:

Such beastly buggery Sodom has not seen,
As ruled in him who ruled Realm and Queen.

Two weeks later Mary wrote to the Bishop of Dunblane about the incident saying that: 'Albeit we found his doings rude, yet were his words and answers gentle.' Two days after Mary was taken to Dunbar, Lady Bothwell, accusing her husband of adultery, began proceedings for a Protestant divorce. The next day, Bothwell applied for an annulment to the marriage. By 3 May 1567 Lady Bothwell was divorced and on 8 May the marriage was also annulled. Neither the Protestant Church nor the Catholic Church could now object to the marriage between the Earl of Bothwell and the Queen of Scots. On 6 May, when the minister of the parish church of Edinburgh was commanded to announce the banns for a Protestant marriage between the couple, he would not do so, believing Mary had been coerced into the match against her will. The following day the minister was given a document from the Queen saying that she had been neither held captive nor raped. The announcement was duly made, but the minister would not withhold his views of Bothwell, articulating the common opinion: 'I laid to his charge, the law of adultery, the ordinance of the Kirk, the law of ravishing, the suspicion of collusion between him and his wife, the sudden divorcement, and proclaiming within the space of four days, and last the suspicion of the King's death which her marriage would confirm.' Three days before her third marriage the Queen made Bothwell Duke of Orkney and Lord of Shetland. With her own hands Mary placed the ducal coronet upon his head.

At ten o'clock in the morning on 15 May 1567 the Queen of Scots and the Earl of Bothwell were married by Protestant rite in the Great Hall at Holyrood. The wedding day was without the usual joyous celebrations and pageantry. The Queen

Preceding pages
A contemporary sketch of the scene after the murder of Darnley at Kirk o' Field in February 1567. At the top on the right are the corpses of Darnley and his servant in the gardens, with a chair, a cloak and a dagger beside them. Centre left are the houses attached to St Mary Kirk o' Field, and, in front of the town hall, the house where Darnley had stayed – a heap of rubble after the explosion. Below left, Darnley's body is carried away as a crowd looks on. Prince Charles James is in his cradle, top left, with the words: 'Judge and Avenge my cause, O Lord.'
Opposite On 1 March 1567, a placard appeared in the capital with a mermaid (the symbol for a prostitute) with a crown and flanked by Mary's initials. Below it was a hare – from Bothwell's family crest – encircled with swords.

wore a black gown decorated with gold braid, and later a yellow gown refurbished with white taffeta. The wedding breakfast was a solemn affair, with little or no conversation. Outside the palace, a placard was erected bearing a Latin quotation that translates: 'Wantons marry in the month of May'. It was generally held that Mary had been deeply in love with her seducer and welcomed his sexual advances. In Protestant literature she was regularly addressed as Clytemnestra, Delilah, Jezebel, and 'her lecherous life' was condemned. To her credit, the Queen's confessor, Mameret, later declared to the Spanish Ambassador in London that until her marriage to Bothwell, he had never met a woman of greater virtue, courage and uprightness.

On 17 June 1567, Bothwell's servant was allegedly seized by the Queen's enemies, and under threat of torture produced a silver casket containing Bothwell's personal papers, which were soon destroyed. It was later claimed that the casket contained letters (known historically as the Casket Letters), incriminating Mary in Darnley's murder, and sonnets written by the Queen to Bothwell. Most historians agree that the incriminating letters were faked by Mary's enemies. Similarly, the validity of the sonnets remains a matter of debate. With regard to the sonnets, Robin Bell, editor and translator of *Bittersweet Within My Heart* (now sadly out of print), the collected poems of Mary Queen of Scots, argues that: 'The Bothwell sonnets, are consistent with Mary's characteristic, slightly unorthodox syntax and her wordgames, puns, sideways leaps in thought and conventional piety mixed with deep emotions. They have the same themes of duty, devotion, honour, constancy and suffering that recur in her later writing.' The Bothwell poems probably represent Mary's first attempt at the sonnet form. 'Enemies faking poems', continues Bell, 'would have been far more likely to copy her earlier ode or rhyming couplets, rather than guess the form she would adopt later in her career!' But then, he goes on to suggest that 'the sonnets may have been tampered with and their order shuffled'. George Buchanan, previously her tutor, and the author of many court entertainments, became one of Mary's most outspoken enemies, later insisting that the sonnets were written before Darnley's murder.

There are twelve sonnets to Lord Bothwell. In the first, Mary (or whoever wrote them) acknowledges that in her commitment to Bothwell she has alienated family and friends, and sacrificed her reputation:

For him, my conscience and good name to chance I've cast:
I would renounce the world, were it his whim:
I'd gladly die if it should profit him.
What more is there to prove my love steadfast?

In the second sonnet, Mary writes of her jealousy of Lady Jean, Bothwell's first wife:

She made your acquaintance through her family;
I bring you love and thus defy my kin.
But nonetheless you doubt if I be true
And place your trust in her loyalty to you.

Her jealousy continues in the third sonnet, and in the fourth she faces her feelings:

My love for him is growing and shall grow
Throughout my life as long as there's a part
Where it can grow to greatness in that heart.

In the fifth sonnet, Mary talks about Bothwell's raping her at Dunbar:

And I have shed for him so many a tear.
First when he took my body and made it his own
Although my heart was not yet won....

For him, I've gambled conscience, rank and right
For him, all friends and family I've fled,
And all respectability I've shed:
In short, with you alone will I unite.

The sixth sonnet conveys desperation:

I call you my sole sustenance of life
Only because I seek to make it true;
Thus I dare force myself in all I do
In order to win you despite all the strife.

In the seventh sonnet, she submits to the marriage:

Into his hands and wholly in his power
I place my son, my honour and my all,
My country, my subjects, my surrendered soul....

After his marriage to Mary, Bothwell continued to see Lady Jean. In this eighth sonnet Mary's jealousy becomes cattish:

In her dress, she showed without a doubt,
She never feared bad taste might blot her out.

In sonnet nine there is more fun: Mary discovers letters to Bothwell from Lady Jean, and believing the woman incapable of 'a learned tone' suggests that Jean had borrowed words from another author:

And she would fain deceive my friend
With writings tricked out in a learned tone
That could not be the product of her brain
But borrowed from the works of some great man....

The jealousy continues in sonnet ten, but also indignation at being considered fickle:

You trust in her; alas I see too well you do!
And you cast doubt upon my constancy,
(You, who are the only joy and hope for me.)
And I cannot persuade you I am true.
You think I'm fickle, it's plain to see,
And thus you will not grant your confidence.

Bothwell had to be absent from the Queen in order to rally support for their cause. In the eleventh sonnet Mary fears that her husband may not truly understand the sincerity and depth of her feelings for him. She also comes to understand that they will not be allowed to have a normal life together. Thereafter she is consumed with fear for Bothwell's safety:

And sometimes I fear a mishap on the way
Has turned my lover from his true intent
By some adversity or accident.
May God turn all such evil signs away!

Mary did not finish her twelfth sonnet to Bothwell:

I do not know what your judgment may be,
But I know well which one of us loves best.
You'll clearly tell which one shall gain the most.

Immediately after her marriage to Lord Bothwell, the Queen became morose. She had no faith in the Protestant ceremony by which she had sacrificed her principles and her honour. Two days after the wedding Mary asked for a knife to kill herself, and when her equerry Arthur Erskine made every attempt to soothe her, Mary said that she would commit suicide by drowning instead. She was indeed jealous of Lady Jean, the cause of many arguments between the Queen and Bothwell. Bothwell, too, would become enraged with jealousy over her behaviour, which he considered fickle and overly flirtatious. To appease him Mary gave up all her particular pleasures – music, card games, hunting, hawking, golf, and so on. In public Bothwell sometimes treated the Queen with exaggerated cordiality, going bareheaded in her presence when he alone among all the courtiers had the right – and so he was expected – to keep his head covered. Mary oftentimes grabbed hold of Bothwell's bonnet and plumped it squarely on his head. In the relative privacy of their apartments Bothwell was often indifferent towards his new wife, and used extremely coarse language.

The Queen's advisers were still less pleased with the arrogant Earl whose marriage gave him superior standing. As public and private opinion increasingly turned against Bothwell, the nobles now pledged to free Mary from his grasp. On learning that a number of lords were mustering forces to march on Edinburgh, the couple went on 6 June 1567 to Borthwick Castle, a massive fifteenth-century tower situated about twelve miles south of Edinburgh. For their comfort, the Queen's chamberlain sent a silver basin and ewer, when what was really needed was adequate arms and military support. They soon resorted to planning an escape. As a diversion Mary spoke to the lords, refusing their invitation to escort her back to Edinburgh, while Bothwell slipped away unnoticed. The next morning, Mary, dressed as a man, managed to sneak through the castle gates and rode off to join her husband at a prearranged rendezvous, possibly Hailes Castle. From there they rode to Dunbar Castle. For the next few days they were busy raising their own army, mostly from the Borders. Foreseeing that her marriage to Bothwell would signal a revolt, Mary had already ordered that the gold font used for the Prince's baptism be melted down to pay for the hire of mercenaries. Whether the order was carried out is uncertain.

On 15 June the two forces, almost equal in number, met at Carberry Hill near Musselburgh. The insurgents held aloft a banner painted with the corpse of Darnley below a tree and in front of the body his son, kneeling, with the caption: 'Judge and Avenge my cause, O Lord.' The day was hot, and the two armies stood facing each other, sweltering beneath the sun, for some hours. Eventually, a single horseman advanced towards the Queen's camp, Philibert du Croc, the French Ambassador, acting as the nobles' intermediary. The Ambassador informed Mary that if she would abandon Lord Bothwell the lords would restore her to her rightful position. Mary firmly rejected their offer. After all, were these men who now stood opposite not the very nobles who had in the Ainslie Tavern Bond urged her marriage to Bothwell in the first place? Their change of mind was certainly no reason for her to do likewise. Du Croc returned to the rebel lines with the Queen's response. Bothwell then favoured settling the conflict by single combat – himself against whomever

Opposite Hailes Castle on the Tyne, twenty-two miles east of Edinburgh. One of the oldest stone castles surviving in Scotland, it was probably built shortly before 1300, and in the 14th century came into the hands of the Hepburns, who eventually refortified the castle, creating 'a house of verie good strength'. To this tranquil setting, Bothwell may have first brought Mary after 'seizing' her near Edinburgh in April 1567. And it was probably at Hailes Castle that Mary joined Bothwell after she had slipped away from Borthwick, making her way along the river. From here they went to Dunbar Castle and on to Carberry Hill.

IHS

Judge and avenge my caus o lord

HER MAJESTY'S STATE PAPER OFFICE

Above A contemporary drawing of the banner carried by the army of Mary's insurgent nobles on 15 June 1567 at Carberry Hill. Prince Charles James kneels besides his father's body, with the words: 'Judge and Avenge my cause, O Lord.'
Opposite Contemporary drawing of Carberry Hill. Bothwell is by the cannons, Mary is on horseback being led to the rebel lords by Kirkcaldy of Grange.

would take him on. Mary would not have it. As the day wore on, many of the Queen's supporters became discouraged and began to wander off. Seeing her army was dwindling, Mary realized that her situation was hopeless. She relented and agreed to the rebels' proposition. If they were true to their word and restored her to her proper place, then she would send her husband away, and go with them. Bothwell protested, but Mary persuaded him that it was the only way they could save themselves. He must stay away until parliament had a chance to meet and investigate Darnley's murder. If he were proved innocent, then 'nothing would prevent her from rendering to him all that a true and lawful wife ought to do', but should he be found guilty, 'it would be to her an endless source of regret that, by their marriage, she had ruined her good reputation, and from this she would endeavour to free herself by every possible means'. Bothwell finally agreed. Before

he left, he handed Mary a bond signed by Morton, Maitland and others agreeing
to murder Darnley. Swearing that he had only done so on their advice – these lords
who now opposed him – he cautioned Mary to keep the document safe, then rode
off. Kirkcaldy of Grange then approached the Queen, and she said to him: 'Laird
of Grange, I render myself unto you, upon the conditions you rehearsed unto me,
in the name of the Lords.' She gave him her hand to kiss, then he seized her horse's
bridle and led the Queen to the rebel camp. Hot and dishevelled though she was,
Mary sat regally in her saddle as she advanced towards the lords, her servants
trailing behind, anticipating an honourable reception. What she received, however,
was hatred. 'Burn the whore! Burn the murderess of her husband!' rang the insults
hurled in her direction. Mary in turn threatened to hang the lot of them for their
impudence. Eventually, Kirkcaldy and others drew swords on the rabble, whose
taunts then became silent, but the atmosphere remained tense. Mary was put under
the guard of two particularly churlish men who held high the insulting banner

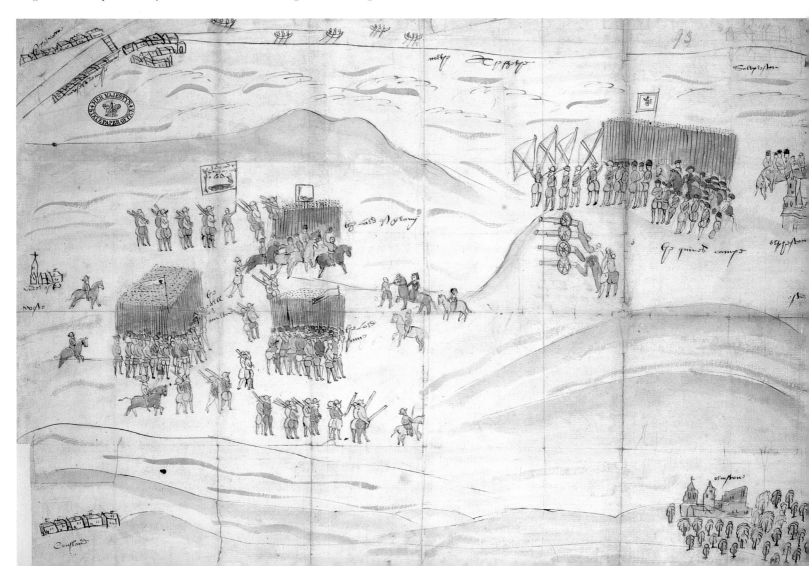

displaying the murdered Darnley. On the return to Edinburgh, fatigue and distress began to affect the Queen, who struggled to remain upright in her saddle – she was two months pregnant at the time. About ten o'clock at night the rebel lords with their captive re-entered the city. Crowds of men, women and children gathered around the pathetic figure, exhausted, her hair tumbling down, her garments torn; they shouted every sort of crude insult and there were cries of 'Kill her! Drown her!'

Instead of the Palace of Holyrood, the Queen was taken to the Lord Provost's house and kept under guard in a small, sparsely furnished room. Looking from the window of this chamber Mary could see the rebels' insulting banner. After a night and a day of further dejection and humiliation, the Queen was taken under cover of darkness to Lochleven Castle, an island stronghold owned by Sir William Douglas, half-brother to Lord James, Earl of Moray; Lady Margaret Douglas, James's mother, acted as chatelaine. Mary would not denounce Bothwell as Darnley's murderer, nor would she disavow her marriage. If the Queen were to be put on trial there was the risk that she would produce incriminating evidence of the nobles' own complicity in the murder of Darnley, therefore she had to be removed to some isolated place. Kirkcaldy of Grange was uneasy, having promised Mary that she would be restored to the throne. The Earl of Morton then produced a love letter purportedly written by the Queen to Bothwell the previous night in her prison chamber at the Lord Provost's house. In the letter – now believed to be a forgery – Mary called her husband 'dear heart' and pledged to stand by him. Kirkcaldy was persuaded to forego his promise.

In 1561 Mary had first visited Lochleven Castle as a guest, and she had returned again on at least one other occasion; now she was prisoner there. Her secretary in later years described the Queen's first weeks of imprisonment:

At the edge of the lake she was met by the Laird and his brothers, who conducted her into a room on the ground floor, furnished only with the Laird's furniture. The Queen's bed was not there, nor was there any article proper for one of her rank. In this prison, and in the midst of such desolation, Her Majesty remained for fifteen days and more without eating or drinking or conversing with the inmates of the house, so that many thought she would have died.

Queen Elizabeth on the other hand received reports from the lords that implied Mary was beginning to adjust to her situation, taking 'both rest and meat', indeed, she danced and played cards, and 'she is become fat'. But then, Elizabeth had been most upset that a lawful monarch should be so ill-treated. She sent Sir Nicholas Throckmorton to Scotland to see if he could intervene. Throckmorton could only manage to smuggle messages to Mary, warning her of conditions outside her prison

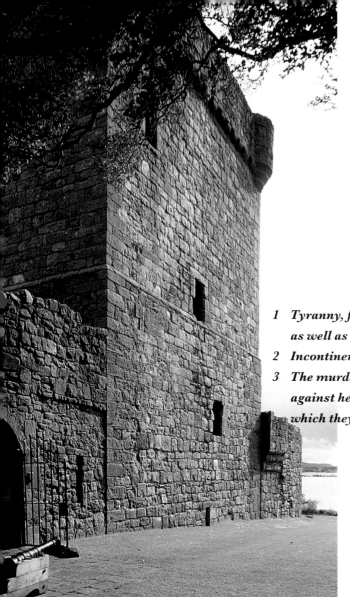

walls, of 'the great rage and fury of the people against her', that she must save herself by immediately divorcing Bothwell. But she would rather die than cast off her husband for 'taking herself to be seven weeks gone with child, she should acknowledge herself to be with child of a bastard and to have forfeited her honour'. Throckmorton then began to fear the lords would kill the Queen. Soon after, he learned that they were demanding her abdication, but Mary steadfastly refused. Throckmorton now pleaded with her to agree to their demand in order to save her life, for an abdication obtained by force was not legal, and could be rightly disclaimed when Mary was free. Even then she refused. Maitland told Throckmorton that if Mary refused to sign the abdication documents they would bring her to trial on three charges:

1 *Tyranny, for breach and violation of their laws and decrees of the Realm, as well as that which they call Common Laws as their Statute Laws.*
2 *Incontinency as well with the Earl of Bothwell as with others.*
3 *The murder of her husband, whereof (they say) they have as apparent proof against her as may be, as well by the testimony of her own handwriting which they have recovered [the Casket Letters], as also by sufficient witnesses.*

It was not until the Queen suffered the miscarriage of twins and massive haemorrhaging that her captors, taking advantage of Mary's distraught and weakened condition, bullied her into signing, on 24 July, the Deeds of Abdication of the Scottish throne by which she resigned her crown to her son, naming the Earl of Moray as Regent. Lord James was abroad at the time of Mary's abdication, and she further agreed that Lord Morton and others would rule until her half-brother returned. As Mary put her name to these papers, she repeated over and over again that she would not be bound by their contents. Five days after Mary's abdication, thirteen-month-old Prince Charles James was crowned at Stirling; for only the second time in Scottish history, the ceremony involved changing the name of the monarch. John Knox preached the sermon and Morton took the oath on the child's behalf.

The Earl of Bothwell, meanwhile, fled north to the isles of Orkney and Shetland where he gathered together a few supporters and vessels and began attacking shipping. His pirate fleet was eventually broken up, and Bothwell narrowly escaped to Norway where he was ultimately imprisoned. In 1578 he died insane, probably due to the harsh conditions in which he had been confined.

After her abdication Mary was moved to the main tower of the castle complex, where she had greater comfort but also close surveillance – Lady Margaret Douglas's granddaughters shared the room in which the Queen slept. Mary, it seems had only been allowed to take a limited number of possessions and clothing to Lochleven. By September, some of her ladies, including Mary Seton, were permitted to join her, and the previous months she had been sent parcels of clothing and other provisions. Soon after arriving on the island, Mary's private property in Edinburgh had been plundered. The furnishings of her private chapel were ransacked as were her clothes, jewelry, gold and silver plate; twenty-seven of the larger pieces of silver plate were sent to the Edinburgh Mint to be converted into coinage. Lord James then had the pick of her jewels, and sold others. A letter written by Mary from Lochleven on 3 September requesting provisions suggests that she and her maidens continued to lack many items necessary to their comfort. She requested:

One doublet and skirt of white satin, ane aither...incarnet and blak and the skirts with thame...togither with the cameraige [cambric] and lynyn claith whereof I gave you a memorial, and if the schone [shoes] be not reddy made...send thame with some other eftir. Cause Servais [Servais de Condé, her chamberlain, responsible for furnishings and certain needlework materials] to send two pair sheets...all the dry damas plums [plum preserves] that he has, togither with the pens [pins] he has...ye shall cause make one dozen rasene nedillis [netting needles] and mowlis [gauges]; and speir at Servais if he has only aither covering of beddis to me nor [except] green and send me to put under the tother covering.

Servais records that between June 1567 and April 1568 he sent a red satin skirt with white stripes, trimmed with fur; six bodices, including one of crimson satin; two bodice fronts; a chemise; a holland cloak; black silk hose; white serge hose – possibly breeches – and a pair of hose or breeches in red woollen cloth, along with linen for making underclothes; handkerchiefs; ruffs; pairs of sleeves; black boots and five pairs of shoes; and perukes or hairpieces. For the Queen's needlework he sent the needles and sewing gauges as requested, several skeins of silk thread in various colours as well as thread of silver and gold, and a canvas painted with flowers outlined in black. The plum preserves were recorded as being sent, also pins, soap, boxes of scented powder, a small casket covered with crimson, decorated with a silver 'F', representing Francis II, and an alarm clock.

Lord James had gone to the continent shortly after Darnley's murder. If Mary had entertained the hope that upon his return to Scotland he would come to her aid, she was soon to be disillusioned. He visited the Queen in August 1567, and in the evening strolled with Mary in the castle gardens, and thereafter they engaged in a lengthy discussion: 'Sometimes the Queen wept bitterly, sometimes she acknowledged her unadvisedness and misgovernment, some things she did confess plainly, some things she did excuse, some things she did extenuate.' Furthermore Mary was shocked to find Lord James being addressed as 'Your Grace'. Her attitude only made him disagreeable,

Preceding double page The island stronghold of Lochleven Castle, Mary's prison for nearly a year. Mary's jailer, Sir William Douglas, was half-brother to Lord James, Earl of Moray, and cousin to the Earl of Morton – another rebel. It was here that Mary was forced to abdicate in favour of her infant son. The Venetian Ambassador to France reported in 1568: 'Guard was continually kept at the castle day and night, except during supper, at which time the gate was locked with a key.'

Opposite The tower house of Lochleven Castle built in the 14th century as the main lodging; the arched doorway leads to the inner courtyard. On previous visits to Lochleven, Mary had gone hawking, had debated with John Knox and had dined with Darnley. On the night of 2 May 1568, she disguised herself in shabby clothes and, assisted by two confederates, escaped from the island.

and he lectured her sternly. She was opposed to his accepting the Regency (which he had already accepted); her attitude made him hostile, he pointed out that the Queen's position was such that she should be 'in hope of nothing but God's mercy'. The next day the mood was friendlier between them, but then Mary shot back, telling her half-brother that if the lords would not obey their born Queen and rightful sovereign, how could he possibly expect them to give their allegiance to a King's bastard! 'He who does not keep the faith where it is due will hardly keep it where it is not due.'

On 8 December 1567, Mary celebrated her twenty-fifth birthday, the time when sovereigns traditionally took back grants of land made during their minority. For Mary to do so would have meant that the Earl of Morton and others would have lost valuable holdings. To prevent Mary from enacting what was deemed as her right, a parliament was quickly convened. Mary soon learned that parliament had been summoned and wrote to Lord James pleading for permission to appear before the assembled lords to clear herself of all the charges against her. Her half-brother, far from being her saviour, pushed through an Act of Parliament on 15 December declaring that 'inasmuch as it was clearly evident both by her letters, and by her marriage to Bothwell, that she was privy, act and part, of the actual device and deed' in Darnley's murder, thus, the conduct of the Queen's nobles had clearly been justified.

Mary smuggled out letters to Catherine de' Medici and to Elizabeth of England asking for support, while making more immediate plans for escape. It was clear that her rescuer would not be Lord James, so she showered her charm upon 'pretty Geordie', Sir William Douglas's brother, George, who had fallen hopelessly in love with her. With the assistance of his cousin, the equally besotted sixteen-year-old Willie Douglas, they planned Mary's escape. Willie procured the keys to the castle, and late on 2 May 1568, with Mary disguised in shabby clothes, he stole a boat and they made their way to the opposite shore, where George Douglas and a friend were waiting with horses. They quickly galloped away to meet Lord Seton who escorted them to his castle of Niddry, near Winchburgh. George Douglas was to serve Mary for many years, and Willie remained in the Queen's service until he died. As they rode to Niddry, rumours of Mary's escape had somehow spread, and people came out of their houses to cheer as she rode past. From Niddry she rode west to Cadzow Castle, home of the Hamiltons, where nine earls, nine bishops, eighteen lords and many others signed a document pledging their loyalty and aid to the Queen's cause. The religious acts of 1560 had finally been ratified, but there were many who were dissatisfied with the new government; thus Protestants and Catholics together, some

six thousand men, gathered in support of the Queen of Scots. Mary was exhilarated. Having consulted her advisers, the Queen was told, according to one account that there were two options; she could regain her throne either with support of parliament or by battle. 'By battle let us try it!' she shouted. She did eventually offer to negotiate a settlement with Lord James and the others, but was refused.

On 13 May the two armies came together at the village of Langside near Glasgow. Mary watched the battle from a nearby hill, and, when she saw that her forces were failing, she rode down to rally her soldiers and urge them on. It was later reported that Mary would have led her men in a renewed charge had she not been disillusioned by their quarrelling and exchanging blows among themselves. When defeat became inevitable, Mary fled the field. She was accompanied by a group of men, including Lord Herries who suggested that she seek sanctuary in his own lands in Dumfriesshire. They rode on through the night, and the next two nights stayed at Terregles Castle, where she wrote to her uncle the Cardinal of Lorraine:

I have endured injuries, calumnies, imprisonment, famine, cold, heat, flight, not knowing whither, ninety-two miles across the country without stopping or alighting, and then I have had to sleep upon the ground and drink sour milk and eat oatmeal without bread and have been three nights like owls....

Mary called a meeting of her band of supporters, and, after reviewing the situation, came to a decision – she would put her trust in Elizabeth and go to England. After all the English Queen had made some effort on Mary's behalf during the long months at Lochleven. 'Next to God,' she wrote to Elizabeth, 'I trust in you.'

The Queen could not be dissuaded from her decision to go to England, and a message was sent to Sir Richard Lowther, deputy-governor of Carlisle, requesting safe passage for Mary and her party. To disguise herself, the Queen 'caused her head to be shaved', and then she travelled on from Terregles to Dundrennan Abbey where she was to spend her last night on Scottish soil. On Sunday 16 May 1568, again without waiting for confirmation of safe passage, Mary and her loyal friends went down to the beach of the Solway Firth and boarded a small boat that carried them to England. The elegant young lady of the French court, now with her hair shorn, and wearing a jumble of borrowed clothes, boarded a humble fishing boat instead of a royal galley. According to tradition, during the four-hour voyage the Queen's supporters continued to urge her to sail for France, and at the last moment Mary was persuaded. But it was too late, the winds and currents had made their course unalterable – there was no other choice but to make shore on the Cumbrian coast of England.

Opposite Detail of a statue of an unknown abbot of Dundrennan Abbey. The figure bears evidence of murder and intrigue, for the abbot has a dagger plunged into his heart, and at his feet (not shown) is the disembowelled body of his assassin. The Cistercian Abbey of Dundrennan, near the Solway Firth on Scotland's south-west coast, was constructed in the second half of the 12th century. Mary may have seen the statue when she stayed at the abbey on 15 May 1568, her last night on Scottish soil. By then, the religious life of the abbey was over, ended by the Reformation of 1560.

Right *Elizabeth I* (detail), by or after George Gower, 1588.
Background The portcullis at the main entrance to Carlisle Castle in north-west England where Mary was first incarcerated. She was Elizabeth's prisoner in England for almost nineteen years until her execution in 1587. This portrait of Elizabeth I, painted the year after Mary's execution, acknowledges Elizabeth's greatness as the ruler of England, and hints at her power over other domains.

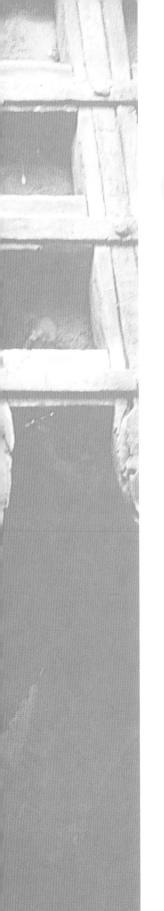

Prisoner of the English Queen

The daughter of debate
That eke discord doth sow
Shall reape no gain when former rule
Hath taught stil peace to growe.

From Queen Elizabeth's poem about the Queen of Scots, published in George Puttenham's
Arte of English Poesie, 1589.

The fishing boat carrying the Queen of Scots and her companions landed about
seven o'clock in the evening of 16 May 1568 at the port of Workington on the
Cumbrian coast of north-west England. When Mary stepped ashore she tripped
and fell, but, in high spirits and high hopes, the company interpreted the tumble as a
good omen – a sign that the Queen of Scots had come to take possession of England.

Mary's first refuge on English soil was the medieval fortress of Workington Hall,
owned by Sir Henry Curwen, a friend of Mary's supporter Lord Herries. From a
room in the north wing she wrote to Elizabeth:

**I entreat you to send for me as soon as possible, for I am in a pitiable condition, not only for a
Queen but for a gentlewoman, having nothing in the world but the clothes in which I escaped,
riding sixty miles in the first day, and not daring to travel afterwards except by night.**

She signed her letter, 'Your faithful and affectionate good sister and cousin and
escaped prisoner – Marie R'. Mary did not comprehend the predicament in which
she had placed Elizabeth by entering the country uninvited. The Queen of England
still struggled to cast off the yoke of illegitimacy – both the Pope and her own father,
Henry VIII, had declared her a bastard, the daughter of a strumpet, Anne Boleyn,
beheaded for treason. Now here in her kingdom was the very person who Catholics

Above When the Queen of Scots threw herself on the mercy of her cousin Elizabeth I in May 1568, she was first kept secure at Carlisle Castle in the north of England. The Captain's Tower (12th century) led to the inner baily and to Mary's quarters. The half-moon battery was built in 1541, during the reign of Henry VIII.

Opposite Carlisle Castle showing the entrance bridge (originally a wooden drawbridge), the outer gatehouse, and the massive bulk of the keep on the right, begun in the 12th century with a third floor added during the 16th century. Mary's quarters, demolished in 1834, were far right, beyond the keep.

believed was rightfully entitled to the throne of England. Nor had Elizabeth forgiven the Queen of Scots for having quartered the English arms with her own. Furthermore, after the Catholic rule of Mary Tudor, Elizabeth was still struggling to fully reinstate Protestantism. With the Queen of Scots in England, every Catholic rebel in the land would come to her aid, and, with support from Catholic Europe, Elizabeth's hold on the throne would be even more tenuous. If Elizabeth helped Mary regain the Scottish throne, she would infuriate important Protestants north of the border. The Queen of Scots' presence in England was clearly dangerous for Elizabeth and the security of the country; an extra anxiety was Mary's beauty and charm. An Englishman, Nicholas White who was to visit the Queen a few months later, reported that Mary had an 'alluring grace', and a 'searching wit, clouded with mildness', which might easily 'move some to deliver her' from captivity, and 'glory joined to gain might stir others to adventure much for her sake'. How then, was Mary to be received in England: as a prisoner, or as a royal guest? This was the question that no doubt troubled Richard Lowther, Deputy Governor of Carlisle Castle, who arrived at Workington Hall with four hundred horsemen to conduct the Queen and her small entourage to Carlisle. The next night they lodged at Cockermouth Hall, arriving at Carlisle Castle on 18 May. The Joan of Arc guise of the brave twenty-five-year-old Queen, with her French manner, shorn head and humble clothing, struck a note of sympathy in the Deputy Governor, who gave Mary a length of velvet for her wardrobe, and had a black dress made for her on credit. Lady Curwen, Mistress of Workington Hall also gave Mary some clothes. Mary had little money, and couldn't afford to pay her, but showed her gratitude with the gift of an agate wine cup. Lowther had ordered Mary's expenses at Cockermouth to be defrayed, and had provided geldings for the Queen and her company to ride to Carlisle Castle. On 20 May Mary wrote to one of her supporters in Scotland, the Earl of Cassillis, reporting that in England she had thus far been 'right well received and honourably accommodated and treated', and she was still confident of returning to Scotland at the head of an army of French, if not English, soldiers 'about the fifteenth day of August', as previously promised.

Carlisle was a frontier town on the border with Scotland. Called 'the key to England', it was enclosed within walls during the twelfth century and further fortified with a castle. The plan of the castle was Norman, with a strong tower, or keep, built upon a mound, surrounded by a defensive wall and water-filled moats. Over the centuries the castle continued to be refortified, and the town itself was so often under attack that every house and even some churches were built to withstand a siege. Following the Dissolution of the Monasteries in 1536, Henry VIII, fearing

an attack from Europe through Scotland, further improved the defences at Carlisle. Mary was lodged in a tower in the oldest part of the castle, her windows barred with iron gratings, and armed soldiers guarded the antechamber to her quarters. But she was allowed a certain amount of freedom. The Queen could leave the castle to attend church services in the town, and twice she watched football matches between her French servants and Scottish attendants, though wherever she went Mary was followed by a large company of English soldiers.

Yesterday hyr grace went owte at a posterne to walk on a playing greene toward Scotland, and we with 24 halberders of mast^r Reads band wth diverse gentlemen and other servants wayted uppon hyr. Where abowte 20 of hyr retinue played at footeballe before hyr the space of two hours very stronglye, nymbyllye, and skilfullye, without any fowle playe offered.

And once she rode out hunting the hare, but the Queen 'galopying so faste uppon everie occasion', it was decided that no more 'scotche Rydyng pastymes' would be ventured. Among Mary's retinue were ladies attendant upon her person, though they were acknowledged to be 'not of the finest sort'. Eventually, however, Mary Seton arrived, and set about dressing the Queen's cropped hair by skilfully manipulating wigs and hairpieces, creating attractive coiffures. Queen Elizabeth's loyal adviser, Sir Francis Knollys, who had been sent to Carlisle, noted with approval:

Among other pretty devices, yesterday and today she did set such a curled head upon the Queen that it was like to be a periwig that showed very delicately; and every other day she hath a new device of head dressing, without any cost, and yet setteth forth a woman gaily well.

Lack of regal attire continued to be a problem. Elizabeth sent her cousin a few, slightly threadbare garments, but Knollys, too embarrassed to admit that the gowns and pieces of black velvet had been intended for the Queen of Scots, passed off these trifles as hand-me-downs meant for her ladies. The Regent of Scotland, Lord James, was scarcely more compliant. To Mary's request that some of her fine gowns and other articles be sent to England, he only managed to send his half-sister one taffeta dress, a few cloaks and 'coverage for saddles'. Finally, in July, Servais de Condé was permitted to send more gowns and pairs of sleeves, including one pair embroidered with silver wire twisted into coils, and another pair made of silver net trimmed with black bows. He also sent handkerchiefs, chemises decorated with black embroidery, fifteen pairs of hose in various colours with six pairs of silk garters to hold them up. There were seven pairs of linen sheets and such little treasures as eighty pearl buttons, twelve pairs of ear-rings, a net coif made with gold thread to adorn the Queen's hair, and a parcel of silk cord to make a second coif along with eight parcels of ribbons and gold thread. Five months later the chamberlain despatched perfumed gloves, a gold pendant enamelled with black and white, and a small striking clock kept in a silver network bag.

It was important to Mary to maintain a sense of monarchy. Almost from the moment of her arrival in England she had been visited by nobles from all over the country, important Catholics amongst them, sympathetic to her plight; regal attire was necessary to her standing, and in a sense her politics. Mary also had to look her radiant best for her appearance at Queen Elizabeth's court. But while suspicion of complicity in Darnley's murder hung over the Queen of Scots, it was not possible for Elizabeth to receive her cousin. This was England's position conveyed with gentle diplomacy to Mary by Sir Francis Knollys. It had been a delicate business to persuade the Queen of Scots – who was not a prisoner, but certainly not at liberty, that she must clear her name before Elizabeth could come to her assistance. Sir Francis, a Puritan, accompanied by Lord Scrope, arrived in Carlisle and met Mary on 28 May, but instead of the brazen Catholic harlot described by John Knox and other Protestants, he found a 'notable woman' who had 'an eloquent tongue and discreet head'.

She seemeth to regard no ceremonious honour beside the acknowledging of her estate regal. She showeth a disposition to speak much, to be bold, to be pleasant and to be very familiar. She showeth a great desire to be avenged on her enemies. She showeth a readiness to expose herself to all perils in hope of victory. She delighteth much to hear of hardiness and valiancy, commending by name all approved hardy men of her country, although they be her enemies, and she commendeth no cowardness even in her friends.

He later added: 'the thing that most she thirsteth after is victory'. She therefore found her confinement increasingly frustrating, 'I am little else than a prisoner', she wrote to her uncle, the Cardinal of Lorraine. She then went on to lament the troubles of her faithful followers at the hands of Lord James and others who

demolish all the houses of my servants, and I cannot aid them; and hang their owners and I cannot compensate them, and yet they all remain faithful to me, abominating these cruel traitors. When I parted from my people in Scotland I promised to send them assistance at the end of August. For God's sake let them not be denied and deceived.... It is all one for myself, but let not my subjects be deceived and ruined, for I have a son, whom it would be a pity to leave in the hands of these traitors....

Mary ordered Lord Fleming to London to obtain Elizabeth's aid, but if that was not forthcoming he was to apply to France. She also sent Lord Herries to negotiate on her behalf, until Mary herself could personally solicit Elizabeth's help. Apart from the Cardinal of Lorraine, Mary also wrote to Catherine de' Medici, King Charles IX and the Duke of Anjou. In her letters she decried her circumstances, and her suffering as a devout adherent of Catholicism, making frequent mention of her need for money – there was revenue owing from her French estates. To Elizabeth she wrote more than twenty letters; she also wrote for her cousin a sonnet (originally in both Italian and French):

A longing haunts my spirit day and night
Bitter and sweet, torments my aching heart
Between doubt and fear, it holds its wayward part,
And while it lingers, rest and peace take flight.
Dear Sister, if these lines too boldly speak
Of my fond wish to see you, 'tis for this –
That I repine and sink in bitterness,
If still denied the favour that I seek.
I have seen a ship freed from control
On the high seas, outside a friendly port,
And what was peaceful change to woe and pain;
Even so am I, a lonely, trembling soul,
Fearing – not you, but to be made the sport
Of Fate, that bursts the closest, strongest chain.

While Francis Knollys dithered, confounded by Mary's charm – 'Nowe what is to be done with such a lady and princess, or whether such a princess and lady be to be nourished in one's bosom? or whether it be good to halt and dissemble with such a ladie' – Elizabeth decided to dissemble. On 8 June she wrote to Mary that it would be one of 'her highest worldly pleasures' to welcome the Queen of Scots into her presence once Mary had been acquitted of the crime that loomed over her. On the same day Elizabeth wrote to Lord James, Earl of Moray, accusing him of 'very strange' behaviour towards a sovereign prince who was now asking for her help and 'is content to commit the ordering of her cause to us'. Elizabeth was nevertheless willing to hear Moray's version of the business, as long as he ceased tormenting the Queen of Scots' supporters. Lord James knew that if Mary were to be found innocent of involvement in Darnley's murder, and returned to Scotland with Elizabeth's support, his position would become untenable. He therefore had to make the Queen of Scots' guilt a certainty, preferably without a trial, and in his response to Elizabeth he suggested that when the judges were appointed to try Mary, they should first read copies of incriminating letters (the 'Casket Letters') which would prove his half-sister's guilt in the matter. To further his case, he had already sent his secretary, John Wood, to London, to 'resolve Elizabeth's mind'. Wood was ordered to convince the English Queen of any aspect of the problem she might 'stand doubtful to'. Then, to make his task even more conclusive, Wood was provided with copies of the Casket Letters to show to Elizabeth. Establishing Mary's guilt would not only preserve Lord James, but would also give Elizabeth a means of escaping from a complex dilemma.

Below Silver-gilt casket, French, 15th or early 16th century, said to have contained incriminating letters from the Queen. The original Casket Letters vanished in the 1580s; the surviving copies are contradictory. It is generally accepted that the letters were false or at least tampered with.

Privately, Elizabeth's principal adviser, William Cecil, gave verbal assurances to John Wood that if the Queen of Scots were found guilty she would not be returned to Scotland.

By the end of June, the Earl of Moray was feeling secure and now favoured an English trial. Mary responded to Elizabeth's requirement for an enquiry with tears followed by outrage: 'She had no other judge than God...none could take upon them to judge her: she knew her estate well enough.' But in Scotland, George Buchanan, the scholar who had known Mary in France where he had celebrated her marriage to the Dauphin with warm phrases, and who had later in Scotland spent many an evening hour reading with the Queen of Scots, now became her traducer. The rebel lords, particularly Lord James, needed a guarantee of the Queen of Scots' moral decay and guilt, and the English needed to discredit her without weakening Elizabeth's stance of benevolent neutrality towards her reluctant royal guest. Buchanan, eagerly grasping the political opportunity, was commissioned to write his *Book of Articles* (originally in Latin, and later spiked with more venom for the publication of an English version) permanently to stain Mary's character, and in this he succeeded. Buchanan's diatribe stressed that the Queen of Scots' nature was of a type possessing 'vehement affection...they love with excess, and hate without measure; and to what side soever they bend, they are not govern'd by advis'd reason, but carried by violent motion'.

Meanwhile, it was decided that Mary should be moved further into England, to remote Bolton Castle in Yorkshire, forty miles from York and fifty miles from Carlisle. Mary was initially distressed by the removal, which increased the distance from her Scottish supporters, but soon came to adopt an attitude of placid resignation; her fate was in Elizabeth's hands. After six weeks in Carlisle the royal entourage, accompanied by an army of soldiers to guard them, travelled to Wharton, then on to Lowther Castle, arriving at Bolton Castle on 15 July. The fourteenth-century fortress, the property of Lord Scrope, overlooked the valley of Wensleydale, in a corner of the North Riding of Yorkshire. Mary's accommodation in the castle was piecemeal, with furnishings hastily borrowed from the house of Sir George Bowes, located some distance away from Bolton. But the absence of brightly hung, cushioned apartments was of little importance; the significant change in the life of Mary Queen of Scots was that she was now totally excluded from the political world. At the end of July, Lord Herries arrived at Bolton to put three proposals before the Queen. If Mary would agree to an enquiry (the word 'trial' was not actually used), then no matter the outcome Elizabeth would restore her to her former position in Scotland if Mary would:

1   Renounce her title to the English throne during Elizabeth's lifetime and ratify the Treaty of Edinburgh.
2   Abandon the alliance with France and enter into a league with England.
3   Give up the Mass in Scotland, 'receiving the common prayer after the manner of England'.

Mary agreed to all Elizabeth's demands, and even listened 'with attentive and contented ears' to the sermon of an Anglican chaplain. As a final stipulation, Elizabeth maintained that whatever the outcome of the quasi-judicial proceedings, the rebel lords could not be punished for their actions. Full of false hope, Mary's mood became confident, even cheerful, until she learned that she would not be permitted to appear at the enquiry in person, and that Lord James, Earl of Moray, was to produce irrefutable evidence of the Queen's guilt – letters found in a silver casket that demonstrated that Mary had been in love with Lord Bothwell while Darnley was still alive, and had lured her ailing husband from Glasgow to his death in Edinburgh. Mary was never allowed to see the letters. On 20 September Elizabeth wrote to Moray putting in writing what William Cecil had already confided to John Wood, that, regardless of her words to Mary, if the Queen of Scots were found guilty, she would not be allowed to return to Scotland.

Buchanan's English translation was prepared and widely circulated, and with all the political chess pieces in place, the conference of York was organized for October 1568. A panel of English officials, headed by the Duke of Norfolk examined the evidence. Both Mary and the Earl of Moray were permitted to send commissioners. The commissioners for Lord James included himself and Lord Maitland; Mary's commissioners included John Leslie, Bishop of Ross, and Lords Boyd, Livingston and Herries, whom she instructed to convey her belief that the conference was only a formality convened to allow Elizabeth to restore Mary to her Scottish throne. The Queen of Scots' commissioners were further instructed to accomplish 'the reduction of our said disobedient subjects to their dutiful obedience to us'.

Opposite Bolton Castle in Yorkshire. Mary arrived at this 14th-century castle, the property of Lord Scrope, on 15 July 1568. The move increased the distance between the Queen and her supporters in Scotland, and excluded Mary from the political mainstream. While she was in Bolton, the Conferences of York and Westminster were held to determine whether or not she had been involved in Darnley's murder. Nothing was 'sufficiently' proven against Mary, but she remained a prisoner.

GEORGIVS TALBOTVS
COMES SALOPIÆ
AN ÆTATIS 58
S·H
1580

GEORGE TALBOT, 6th EARL OF SHREWSBURY

ELIZABETH HARDWICK, COUNTESS OF SHREWSBURY

As Mary awaited the outcome of the enquiry, she continued to listen with patience, if not genuine conviction, to Sir Francis Knollys's lectures on the merits of Protestantism, and under his tuition she began to learn to write English. The two were becoming friends, and when Sir Francis was absent from Bolton for a few days, Mary wrote to him, her first letter in English, which ends with friendly affection: 'Escus my ivel vreiten thes furst tym….' ('Excuse my evil writing this first time').

The conference at York which began in confusion was moved to Westminster where it reconvened on 25 November. Mary was not allowed to appear to defend herself. In doing so she would have undoubtedly denied the authenticity of the Casket Letters, and hence might not be convicted on their evidence. The aim of the English commissioners appears to have been an outcome that would save Mary's honour without exposing the rebel lords as forgers of the incriminating evidence. The conference at Westminster was officially ended by Elizabeth on 11 January 1569. It was decided that 'there has been nothing deduced against' the rebel lords 'that may impair their honour and allegiances'. Lord James (with an extra £5,000 in his pocket) and his friends were allowed to return to Scotland to resume their lives as before. With regard to Mary, 'there had been nothing sufficiently produced nor shown by them against the Queen their sovereign, whereby the Queen of England should conceive or take any evil opinion of the Queen her good sister for anything yet seen.' Nothing was proven either way, but, whereas the Earl of Moray was allowed to go free and resume his position as Regent, governing Scotland, Mary was to spend the remaining eighteen years and three months of her life in England as a prisoner.

Mary was placed in the custody of George Talbot, 6th Earl of Shrewsbury, a wealthy nobleman with estates in central England – Tutbury Castle, Sheffield Castle, Wingfield Manor, Worksop Hall and Chatsworth. Shrewsbury was a Protestant, and, although he had several Catholic relations, was unstintingly loyal to Elizabeth. Mary's long, tedious years of captivity were begun at Tutbury Castle in Staffordshire. It was there that she first met the redoubtable Countess of Shrewsbury, known to history as Bess of Hardwick. Mary and the Countess had in common a talent for needlework in which they were both keenly interested. In March 1569 Lord Shrewsbury noted: 'This Queen continueth daily to resort to my wife's chamber where with the Lady Lewiston [Livingston] and Mrs [Mary] Seton [two of the four Maries] she useth to sit working with the needle in which she much delighteth and in devising works.' The previous month when Mary was asked, by the English emissary Nicholas White, how she passed her time:

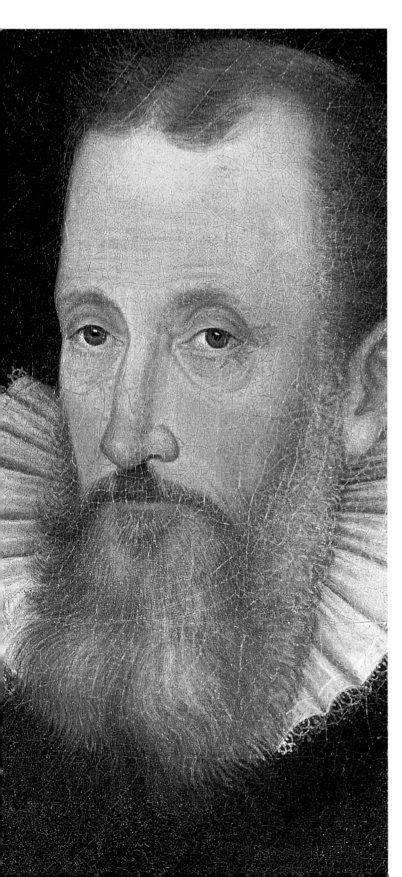

Opposite and left and above George Talbot, 6th Earl of Shrewsbury, by Rowland Lockey (copy of a portrait of 1580), and his wife, Bess of Hardwick, Countess of Shrewsbury, 16th century. Mary was over fourteen years in Shrewsbury's custody, and spent much time with Bess.

She said that all the day she wrought with her needle, and that the diversity of the colours made the work seem less tedious, and continued till very pain did make her to give over; and with that she laid her hand upon her left side and complained of an old grief newly increased there. Upon this occasion she entered on a pretty disputable comparison between carving, painting and work with the needle, affirming painting in her own opinion for the most considerable quality.

Above *Mary Queen of Scots*, miniature by Nicholas Hilliard, 1578. Mary was in her mid-thirties when this and an almost identical miniature were made. Many full-sized portraits, painted at the beginning of the 17th century, were based on these miniatures.
Opposite 'Phenix', a needlework panel believed to have been embroidered by Mary during her captivity. A phoenix rinsing from the flames had been the *impresa* of her mother, Mary of Guise.

During her captivity in England Mary had difficulty in obtaining paintings of herself to distribute to her most loyal supporters and friends. It seems she had to resort to having them manufactured in France, and smuggled back to her in England. To the Archbishop of Glasgow she wrote in 1575: 'There are some of my friends in the country who ask for my portrait. I pray you, have four of these made, which must be set in gold, and sent to me secretly, as soon as possible.'

Whether or not these portraits were made is uncertain. They were probably miniatures. In their book *The Queen's Image* (1987), art historians Dr Duncan Thomson and Helen Smailes write: 'The only portraits made directly from Mary herself during her captivity in England appear to have been miniatures.' Queen Elizabeth's renowned miniaturist, Nicholas Hilliard, painted two portraits of Mary. Another miniature of Mary was painted by an unknown artist; the portrait was later encompassed in a reliquary. In August 1577, Mary's secretary, Claude Nau, wrote to the Archbishop stating: 'I had hope to send with the present letter a portrait of her Majesty, but the painter was not able to bring it to perfection before this dispatch.' As Hilliard was in France when this letter was written, the 'painter' mentioned is unknown. The miniatures provided the source for several full-length portraits of the Queen of Scots, which were painted at the beginning of the seventeenth century, although they all bear the date 1578.

In 1569, Nicholas White, the recipient of Mary's views on art, engaged in their delightful conversation at Tutbury Castle while Mary was seated on a velvet-covered chair beneath a cloth of estate which she herself had probably embroidered with the motto: '*En Ma Fin Gît Mon Commencement*' (In the end lies my beginning), 'which is a riddle I understand not', said White. The riddle, for Mary, would become a prophecy. She had adopted the motto from Mary of Guise's *impresa* of a phoenix rising from flames. The Queen of Scots, still an anointed Queen, was allowed a certain amount of regalia – chairs of estate, cloths of estate, an assemblage of rooms with a presence chamber. She had her ambassadors to the courts of England and France, her master of household, her ladies of the bedchamber, and her secretary, treasurer, pages, apothecary, embroiderers and domestics including cooks and scullions – some thirty

to forty persons in all. But regard for her status was one thing, the foul-smelling surroundings of crumbling Tutbury Castle were something else, and quite unacceptable. The sprawling medieval fortress reeked with a noxious odour emanating from a nearby marsh. It was perpetually cold and damp, unrelieved by tapestries brought over from Sheffield Castle. Even Elizabeth sent furnishings to Tutbury to enliven Mary's apartments, but the overall gloom of the castle pertained, and Mary was much relieved the following April when she was moved to Wingfield Manor in Derbyshire. It was an elegant hilltop mansion, built in the fifteenth century around two courtyards. The Queen was lodged in the north-west tower with views across the valley through which flowed the River Amber.

Mary's chronic illnesses had been exacerbated by the discomforts of Tutbury. Lord Shrewsbury had noted that she suffered with 'grief of the spleen', which her doctors explained as '*obstructio splenis cum flatu hypochondriaco*', pains induced by 'windy matter ascending to the head'. At Wingfield a different malady plagued the Queen: swelling of the face, and again melancholia with long episodes of weeping which had begun soon after she received news of the unhappy fate of some of her supporters in Scotland. A move to Chatsworth caused little improvement, and throughout the rest of her life Mary would be tormented with bouts of illness – pains, stomach trouble with vomiting, hysteria and nervous collapse – followed by a rapid recovery, only to relapse again. It has been suggested that the Queen of Scots suffered from the recurring illness famously associated with King George III, porphyria. Towards the end of her life, lack of exercise would cause Mary to become lame with rheumatism. Her jailers sometimes suspected the Queen of exaggerating the violence of her symptoms in order to be whisked away for a cure at Buxton, the Derbyshire spa town celebrated even by the Romans for the therapeutic powers of its tepid mineral water. Shrewsbury built a small house next to the baths which she visited on four occasions. Her longest sojourn was in 1573, when she stayed for five weeks. Buxton was in vogue with the upper echelons of society, and frequented by members of Queen Elizabeth's court. It was just the sort of diversion Mary hungered for – the tantalizing possibility of seeing and being seen. Although Mary was entirely restricted from mingling, since this might win sympathy, the Queen of Scots did meet William Cecil and her former suitor Robert Dudley, Earl of Leicester. Leicester was also lavishly entertained with copious food and drink provided by the Earl of Shrewsbury at Chatsworth. During Mary's last visit to Buxton she reputedly wrote:

Opposite The ruins of Wingfield Manor in Derbyshire. It had once been an elegant hilltop mansion built around two courtyards and dating from the 15th century. Mary was lodged in the north-east tower with views across the valley.
Background An engraving of Tutbury Castle, a sprawling medieval fortress, perpetually cold and damp, and worse – it reeked with noxious odours emanating from a nearby marsh. Not surprisingly, Mary was ill and wretched during her stays here.

Buxtona, quae calida celibriris nomine Lymphae
Forte mihi post hac non adeunda, Vale.

Buxton, whose warm waters have made thy name famous,
perchance I shall visit thee no more – farewell.

Bess, Countess of Shrewsbury, four times married, had inherited Chatsworth from her second husband, Sir William Cavendish, with whom she had had eight children. She completed the construction of the mansion, arranged around a rectangular courtyard, and became so fond of the place that her third husband,

Sir William St Loo addressed her as the embodiment of the residence, 'my honest sweet Chatsworth'. Set amid the scenic moors and dales of Derbyshire, the mansion was close to the village of Edensor, and through its parkland a river flowed, and overflowed to be captured in a series of ponds. Mary was allowed to take air on the rugged moor, or in the park where Queen Mary's Bower, a small moated building, still commemorates the enclosed raised garden approached by a flight of steps where she is said to have taken exercise. Mary was confined with varying degrees of strictness, tending to be 'straitly' when funds or national security were a concern. When all was well she could enjoy riding and hawking. At one point Mary kept ten horses requiring three grooms and a farrier. She also kept a carriage. She continued to enjoy archery, and had obtained a greyhound with the hopes of training it to run at deer. The Queen also took endless delight in small dogs, not only reflected in the subject matter of her jewels, but also in her needlework. In 1574 she wrote to the Archbishop of Glasgow with instructions for their procurement:

If my uncle, the Cardinal of Guise, has gone to Lyons, I am sure he will send me a couple of pretty little dogs, and you will buy me as many more; for except in reading and working [needlework] my only pleasure is in all the little animals I can get. They must be sent in baskets, well stored, so as to keep them warm.

The Archbishop was also to send birds: 'some turtle-doves, and some Barbary fowls, to see if I can rear them in this country…. I shall take pleasure in bringing them up in a cage, as I do all the little birds that I am able to obtain. These are pastimes for a prisoner.' The prisoner also enjoyed lute playing and card games, and for the pleasure of her companions she secured a billiard table. Fashion remained a keen interest, though 'the new things', Mary admitted, she no longer wore – the colours of her wardrobe were now black, white, grey and violet, embroidered with black cord or trimmed with gold and silver braiding; lacy starched collars and ruffs framed Mary's face. Her tailor was an important member of the household, and was given instructions for creating the latest Paris fashions. Still, Mary wrote to her agent in France giving orders that an 'artificer' make her ' a couple of head-dresses, with a crown of gold and silver, such as they were formerly made for me'. And what were the latest styles in Italy, 'in head-dresses, and veils, and ribbons'? She liked to make gifts of such items to her ladies. For herself, Mary

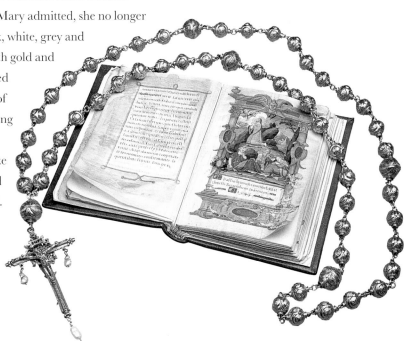

Opposite Chatsworth in Derbyshire, as it appeared in the 17th century. Mary was allowed to take exercise in the enclosed garden and on the surrounding moor. During her captivity in England, the Queen of Scots was confined with varying degrees of strictness. Sometimes she could enjoy riding and hawking, archery and other outdoor pursuits. But later she was restricted to a few rooms.

Below Mary's gold rosary and prayer book. The jewelry favoured by the Queen of Scots during her captivity were her crucifix and rosary. She continued to hear Mass in Protestant England, though her priest had to disguise himself in court attire: a brooch on his hat, silver buttons and clothes of 'all colours'. The Queen of Scots carried this rosary and prayer book to her execution.

Above and opposite

Mary Queen of Scots, perhaps
by Rowland Lockey. A full-
length version of Hilliard's
miniatures of Mary, it is
also dated 1578, but in fact
was painted early in the
17th century, when James
VI and I was rehabilitating
his mother's reputation.

took to wearing long diaphanous veils, and for jewelry favoured a crucifix and rosary beads. For all her seeming interest in Protestantism, the Queen of Scots continued to hear Mass, quietly, her priest disguised in the attire of some other profession. In 1584, Camille de Préau was her priest in disguise, 'in court-like suit, a brooch in his hat, silver buttons, his garments of all colours'. Mary's other jewels, apart from the symbols of her religion, were few in contrast to the magnificence of her collection in France and Scotland. These included a gold jewel made in the shape of a tree with a lady sitting in its branches; bracelets of agate; a looking-glass garnished with diamonds and containing miniatures of Mary and Elizabeth; a chest set with diamonds, rubies and pearl; a pin case of gold that dangled at the end of a waist chain. Nothing from Bothwell was among her jewels. Yet she preserved miniatures and portraits of Francis II and Darnley. Another jewel in the Queen's possession was an oval stone set in gold 'against melancholy'. And there were jewels against poison. 'I am not out of danger if my food is not closely watched,' wrote Mary to the Archbishop of Glasgow, adding: 'I beg you to send me some genuine *terra sigillata*, if it is to be had for money.' Brantôme provided a minute description of *terra sigillata*: 'They are [cups] made of earth of a tan-coloured red, and have this virtue, that when cold water is poured therein, your cup boils and foams over the brim in little bubbles, as if fire were within.' Thus, it was thought, neutralizing the effect of any poison which might be in the liquid. If the Archbishop had been unable to obtain the *terra sigillata*, Mary asked him to send 'a bit of fine unicorn's horn' – another antidote to poison – 'as I am in great want of it'.

Punctually at eleven o'clock each morning the great gates, entering upon the mansion or castle occupied by the Queen, were closed for an hour while the royal household had dinner. Some sixteen dishes were prepared for Mary who ate 'but little', it was reported in 1581, 'but drinks more', though 'not immoderately'. The food was served in gilt dishes and carried in procession to the Queen, then into each dish and each cup the 'bit' of unicorn's horn was ceremoniously thrust.

For solace, there was needlework; staggering quantities of fabric and thread in bold colours or in light-catching silver and gold were converted by Mary into art. Much of what exists today was created during the early years of her imprisonment working in the company of the Countess of Shrewsbury, Bess of Hardwick. Mary had a peculiar relationship with this woman, twenty years her senior. Bess's origins were humble, but through marriage and shrewd business practices she had amassed a fortune, 'a woman of masculine understanding…proud, furious, selfish and unfeeling'; to this add jealous – she was to accuse her husband of falling in love

Below Needlecase said to have belonged to the Queen of Scots, now at Traquair House.
Background 'The Monkfish', woodcut, from Pierre Belon's *La Nature et Diversité des Poissons*, Paris, 1555. Mary said that 'all day she wrought with her needle'. She and Bess, Countess of Shrewsbury often embroidered designs from this work, probably Mary's own copy.
Opposite background Cushion cover, probably by Mary, with the Scottish thistle, English rose and the white lily of France.
Top This panel of a ginger cat (Elizabeth's hair was red), wearing a crown and eyeing a mouse, is believed to be Mary's work.
Below A toucan, 'A Byrd of America', probably from naturalist Konrad von Gesner's illustrations.

and having an affair with the Queen of Scots, which led to a public scandal, and ultimately to the complete breakdown of their marriage. Early on, as the Countess and Mary sat working their pieces of embroidery, it was reported that they talked of 'indifferent trifling matters'. But the amiable chatter invariably turned to gossip, with Bess filling Mary's head with slanderous talk concerning the behaviour of the Queen of England – and what could have been more satisfying to one confined partly on account of her own moral turpitude? After some years, however, when Mary's friendship with the Countess of Shrewsbury turned sour, the Queen of Scots wrote to Elizabeth relaying all that had been confided to her; what had been meant to amuse their idle hours was in fact treason. Mary's letter accused the Countess of speaking 'licentiously' against Elizabeth, naming certain courtiers as the Queen of England's lovers; the Countess mocked her coquettishness, and then, triumphantly questioned her fitness to rule. The letter was intercepted by William Cecil, and exists today among the Burghley Papers. It was never received by Elizabeth; if it had been, the Countess of Shrewsbury would have been destroyed. But before the relationship became malicious, Mary presented her custodians with gifts. In 1577 she sent to France for a set of luxurious bedhangings and six 'grand chandeliers' for the Shrewsburys.

Mary's embroidery was not only a welcome and creative occupation for a prisoner, and a comfort, but like her letters and her compositions in verse, needlecraft became for the Queen a means of expressing the frustration of her plight in symbols and the double meanings of allegory. Designs were copied from emblem books such as *Devises héroïques* by Claud Paradin published in France in 1557, full of figures and Latin phrases – word tricks of complex significance – all the rage in England as they had been in France. Other designs of exotic birds and animals were taken from Mary's books of natural history published in France. It appears that Mary had studied the works of French naturalist Pierre Belon, whose woodcut illustrations of birds and fishes were published in Paris in the 1550s, and which she copied for her embroidery designs. She also fashioned embroidery patterns from the illustrations of Swiss physician and naturalist Konrad von Gesner (the copy she used was published in 1560). She embroidered a galaxy of creatures – the

Above Thomas Howard,
4th Duke of Norfolk,
engraving after a 16th-
century original. Mary
hoped to marry this
ambitious aristocrat, who,
after Queen Elizabeth, was
the highest-ranking person
in England, and was a
widower and a Protestant.
She never actually met
Norfolk but sent him
affectionate letters, and a
miniature set in gold in
return for his diamond
ring. After his execution
in 1572 for plotting against
Elizabeth, Mary took
an active interest in his
orphaned children.

mundane to the fantastic – including an ostrich, 'The Estriche'; a dolphin, 'Delphin'
(a pun on the word dauphin); an extraordinary beast – half-man, half-fish – 'A Sea
Moonke'; also a toucan which Mary calls a 'byrde of America' – 'the Beik of a fowle
of India or Brazile' belonged to the Queen's collection of curiosities left behind in
Scotland (under Henry II the French had set up colonies in Brazil, taking control
of Rio de Janeiro in 1555). What Mary dare not put into words, she embroidered –
works that were sometimes lighthearted, others that were cries of torment.
A woodcut of a domestic cat, becomes under Mary's needle a ginger cat – the
colour of Elizabeth's hair – wearing a crown and eyeing a mouse. From illustrations
in Gabriel Faerno's *Fables*, first published in Rome in 1563, Mary embroidered frogs
gazing into a well, uncertain whether they should jump, and a caged cat surrounded
by dancing mice. In other pieces, the Queen depicts her plight as a bird in a cage
with a hawk hovering above ready for the kill; a wheel of fortune rolling into a
menacing sea; a sun in eclipse. The designs for her needlework were first drawn on
canvas (occasionally on silk) by her embroiderer – Pierre Oudry or Charles Plouvart –
who might paint or suggest colours and work the outlines. Mary embroidered
a cushion with the arms of France, Scotland, England and Spain; another with
the Scottish thistle, the English rose and the white lily of France, highlighted with
a braid-stitch in gold and silver on a tent-stitch background worked with yellow silk.
Embroideries usually considered to be the work of the Queen of Scots bear her
cipher, which was included on the tapestry of Mary's emblem – the marigold turning
towards the sun – with the motto '*Non inferiora secutus*' ('not following lower things').

As early as October 1568 Mary had told Sir Francis Knollys, 'If I shall be holden
here perforce, you may be sure then, being as a desperate person, I will use any
attempts that may serve my purpose, either by myself or my friends.' This involved
an obsessive correspondence with France, Spain, the Pope, and her various agents,
building into a network of intrigue, plans for escape and dangerous plots. Before
the York conference in October 1568, it had been suggested that the Queen of
Scots' marriage to Bothwell could be annulled and that she should marry the Duke
of Norfolk. Thomas Howard, 4th Duke of Norfolk was thirty-three, a widower,
a Protestant, and, after Queen Elizabeth, the highest-ranking person in England.
While leading the enquiry into Mary's innocence, he read the Casket Letters and
reported to Elizabeth that one letter in particular contained 'foul matter…
abominable to be either thought of or to be written by a prince' – nevertheless
the Duke of Norfolk was ambitious, and agreed to make Mary his wife. He sent
Mary a diamond ring which she wore on a chain around her neck, unseen, 'until I
give it again to the owner of it and me'. In exchange for the ring Mary sent him

a miniature of herself set in gold, and countless letters. The Queen of Scots had never seen this prospective bridegroom, and had to form an estimate of his charms through conversations with Lady Scrope, his sister, whom she had met in Carlisle. In her letters Mary addressed him as 'my Norfolk', and wrote, 'You bid me command you, that would be beside my duty many ways, but pray you I will, that you counsel me not to take patiently my griefs'; then more affectionately, 'I trust none that shall say I ever mind to leave you.' Mary had come to believe that Elizabeth would approve the match. Meanwhile, Elizabeth's policies were becoming the source of increasing resentment amongst the powerful Catholic earls of northern England, nor did they trust her main adviser, William Cecil. When they learned of the proposed Norfolk marriage, they hoped the

Duke would use his influence to achieve their long-term objective of putting Mary on the English throne, and the restoration of Catholicism. But Mary's activities to obtain an annulment and negotiations for a marriage to Norfolk were discovered by Elizabeth's agents; the Duke was sent to the Tower of London, and Mary, under increased security, was moved back to Tutbury, then on to Coventry where she was briefly housed – first in the Black Bull Inn, then in a hall belonging to Trinity Guild, located in the town centre; her servants were reduced and she was prohibited from sending or receiving any communication with the outside world. With the arrest of Norfolk, the Catholic northern earls rebelled, and in November 1569 Elizabeth had to face the most serious uprising of her reign. When the rebellion was quashed, the Queen of England's vengeance (or that of her generals) towards the insurgents was extreme. During the uprising the rebels had offered to organize Mary's escape, but she refused (according to her envoy John Leslie, Bishop of Ross) and attempted to persuade them to abandon their revolt. It seems Norfolk had also discouraged an escape which

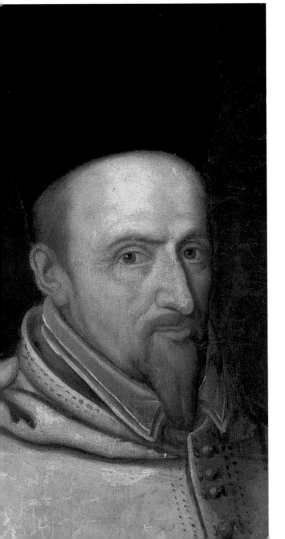

Above William Cecil, Lord Burghley, after 1585. Queen Elizabeth's Principal Secretary of State, he was also Master of the Court of Wards and Lord Treasurer. He was devoted to his Queen and his country, making his treatment of the Queen of Scots somewhat ruthless. **Left** John Leslie, Bishop of Ross, 18th-century copy of a 16th-century portrait. Leslie, a Catholic, asserted that 'feigned and forged reports' had maligned Mary. He had encouraged her proposed marriage to Norfolk, with whom he later plotted to depose Elizabeth. In prison, denied paper, he wrote his tributes to Mary between the lines of printed books.

would have destroyed any possibility of gaining Elizabeth's approval of the marriage – a delusion that Mary appears to have clung to even after the rebellion. In January 1570, she wrote to the Duke of Norfolk: 'Our fault were not shameful: you have promised to be mine and I yours; I believe the Queen of England and country should like of it.' Norfolk was released from the Tower in August 1570. Mary had been moved the previous January, from Coventry back to the dreaded Tutbury, but by May she was moved on to Chatsworth.

On 11 January 1570 Lord James, Earl of Moray, had been murdered as he rode through the streets of Linlithgow. Mary later arranged for his assassin, James Hamilton of Bothwellhaugh, who had fought for the Queen at Langside, to receive a pension. Love between Mary and her half-brother, if it ever truly existed, had long been extinguished. After the collapse of the Northern Rebellion in England, Moray wrote to Elizabeth that Mary was 'the ground and fountain from whom all these tumults flow', and that she should be put under his custody. Elizabeth responded by entering into discussions for Mary's return to Scotland, but these various plans and conditions over which Elizabeth prevaricated were finally dropped in March 1571. With Moray's death, the prospects of increased support for the Queen of Scots were soon dissipated. After six weeks of dispute amounting to civil war in Scotland, Mary's father-in-law, the Earl of Lennox, and her staunch enemy, became Regent.

In the summer Elizabeth promoted a plan for bringing Mary's son, four-year-old King James, to

England to be raised in the English court. Mary was thrilled with the prospect of having her child geographically closer, though she would have preferred him to be raised by the Guises in France. The Scots however would not agree, and it came to nothing. Mary pleaded to be allowed to correspond with her son, and was desperate for any scrap of news concerning his health and well-being. She wrote of her predicament as a desolate mother, 'whose solitary child has been torn from her arms'. Mary's love for James VI remained steadfast. She embroidered a set of child's reins, no doubt useful for keeping a lively toddler in safe harness in castle environments. The breast-piece of the reins, now at Arundel Castle, is worked in gold and silver thread with a crowned sceptre and harp in the centre, and flowers: rose, pink, pomegranate and thistle. On the red silk straps edged with a gold fringe, are the words '*Angelis suis Deus mandavit de te ut custodiant te in omnibus viis tuis*' ('God hath given his angels charge over thee: to keep thee in all thy ways'). The words are separated by figures surmounted with a crown: a sceptre, a lion, a swaddled infant and a heart. The King was raised as a Protestant, his education supervised by George Buchanan who would have inculcated the child with the belief that his mother was an adulteress and party to the murder of his father. When he was older, Mary embroidered a vest for him, which was promptly returned; the Queen had made the error of addressing her gift to the Prince of Scotland instead of King James VI; Mary refused to name her son 'King' throughout her captivity. She also sent him an enamelled gold jewel which she had designed and had made in France; whether or not he received it is unknown. Mary also composed a book of verse for her son, no longer in existence, though in 1616 it was recorded that: 'The Queen his Majesties Mother wrote a book of verses in French of the Institution of a Prince, all with her own hand, wrought a cover of it with a needle, and is now of his Majestie esteemed as a precious jewel.'

Opposite Portrait of James VI of Scotland as a child by Arnold Bronckorst. Above it are the leading reins and breast-piece, which Mary is said to have sewn for him.
Above Lady Arabella Stuart (Stewart), painted in 1577 when she was almost two. Mary, who was prevented from seeing her own son, always took delight in the company of children. While in the Shrewsburys' custody, she lavished attention on Arabella, Darnley's niece, who was also Bess of Hardwick's granddaughter.

Hanging, with embroidered panels – a square surrounded by octagons and cruciforms – on a green velvet background; many of the panels are believed to be the Queen of Scots' own work. The square panel is probably the cushion cover that Mary embroidered for the Duke of Norfolk. It shows a hand wielding a pruning hook and cutting withered branches from a vine, and the motto: '*Virescit Vulnere Virtus*' ('Virtue flourisheth by a wound'). It is probable that Mary had arranged for some of her embroideries to be sent to Norfolk's heirs. Eventually, through family inheritances, they were taken as hangings to Oxburgh Hall in Norfolk in 1761, where they can be seen today. Above the square is a panel with Mary's monogram beneath a crown, and thistles, her cipher, and the motto '*Sa Vertu Matire*' ('Her Virtue is Intrinsic').

Mary continued to take special delight in the company of children. She lavished attention on Lady Arabella Stuart, the Countess of Shrewsbury's granddaughter; Arabella, who lived with the Shrewsburys, was Darnley's niece, and had a potential claim to the English throne. Mary also stood as godmother to Bess Pierrepoint, another granddaughter of the Countess of Shrewsbury. Young Bess became a member of the Queen's household and remained in her service until 1586. In a letter to Bess Pierrepoint of 1583, Mary's fondness for this godchild is obvious:

To my well-beloved bed-fellow, Bess Pierpont

Darling, I have received your letter and pretty presents, for which I thank you. I am very glad that you are so well; remain with your father and mother freely this season, as they wish to keep you, for the climate and the season are so disagreeable here I am already very sensible of the change of the air of Worksop [another Shrewsbury residence where Mary stayed for a short period], where I had not gone again, but I am not suffered to command my legs. Remember me to your father and mother very kindly, and to your sister, and to all my acquaintances, if there are any there. I shall cause your black dress to be made and sent to you there, as soon as I have the trimming, for which I have written to London. This is all which I can write to you at present except to send you as many blessings as there are days in the year, praying God that this may be extended over you and yours forever.

In haste, this 13th September

Your very affectionate mistress and friend

Marie R

Within months of the collapse of the Northern Rebellion, a new plot was conceived for Mary's escape, and the overthrow of Elizabeth. During 1570 Pope Pius V issued a bull, *Regnans in Excelsis*, excommunicating Elizabeth and urging her Catholic subjects to anarchy: 'I take away Elizabeth's false claims to the throne, and English nobles and subjects are excused of all promises, loyalty or obedience to her. I forbid nobles and subjects to obey her orders or laws.' Soon after his release from the Tower, in August 1570, Norfolk entered into an intrigue with the Pope and the King of Spain for an English uprising to depose Elizabeth and place Mary on the English throne. Coded letters went back and forth for several months until April 1571, when a servant of Mary's envoy, John Leslie, Bishop of Ross, was apprehended carrying secret dispatches from Roberto Ridolfi, a Florentine banker, and also Norfolk's agent. The plot was revealed, John Leslie was arrested, and under torture

he claimed that Mary had been involved, and then went on to denigrate her character in lurid detail. Leslie wrote to Mary, righteously pointing out that the hand of providence had intervened to expose her scheming. Leslie, who had been encouraging the Queen of Scots for the past two years to marry Norfolk, was imprisoned for his involvement in what is known as the Ridolfi Plot. His confession may have saved his life; he was released in 1573. The Duke of Norfolk was captured and sent to the Tower of London. In January 1572 he was brought to trial, found guilty, and executed five months later. Mary had embroidered a cushion for the Duke of Norfolk depicting a hand wielding a pruning hook, cutting withered branches from a vine, with the motto: '*Virescit Vulnere Virtus*' ('Virtue flourisheth by a wound'). The message to Norfolk was clear: the unfruitful royal branch of the Tudors (Elizabeth) was to be cut down, so that the vital branch (Mary) would flourish. In his confession Leslie revealed that Mary had sent this cushion to Norfolk. After the Ridolfi debacle, the English Commons passed a bill depriving Mary of her right to succeed to the English throne, and declaring her liable to a trial by peers of the English realm should she be discovered plotting again.

The year 1572 also witnessed a bloodbath in France, the St Bartholomew's Day Massacre, in which some ten thousand Protestant men, women and children were brutally slain. This Catholic savagery was said to have been devised and initiated from the Guise mansion in Paris. Mary's cousin, Henry, the new Duke of Guise, who like his father also bore a scar across his cheek – another *le balafré* – reputedly led the slaughter with the agreement of Catherine de' Medici and her son Charles IX.

Anti-Catholic feeling in both England and Scotland was intense. In 1571 George Buchanan, full of Protestant zeal, had polished up his *Book of Articles* with more damning accusations against Mary, followed by a Scots version, *Ane Detection of the Doinges of Marie Quene of Scottis*, his so-called eyewitness account of Mary's lascivious behaviour during her marriage to Darnley; 'A woman raging without measure and modesty.' In the end he justifies the Queen of Scots' captivity by pointing out that 'we deprived [Mary] not of liberty, but of unbridled licentiousness of evil doing'. The work was popularly received and reprinted several times. John Leslie in turn repudiated attacks on the Queen from Knox and Buchanan and others in his *Defense of the Honour of the Right, High, Mighty and Noble Princess Marie Queen of Scotland*, declaring that her 'person…and the whole trade of her godly and virtuous life past, do far repel and drive away all…suspicion and conjectural presumptions'. The work was written in 1569, suppressed in England, and was eventually printed in France, from whence it was smuggled back into England, and reprinted with an abridged title in 1571. Leslie wrote several treatises – testimonials of Mary's virtue – between the late 1560s and the early 1580s including a history of Scotland published in 1578; Buchanan also wrote a history of Scotland, published in the same year. While in prison for his part in the Ridolfi plot, Leslie had composed *Piae Afflicti Animi Consolationes Divinique Remedia* ('Pious Consolations for the Afflicted Soul and a Divine Remedy'), intended to provide some comfort for Mary in her own imprisonment. Mary responded by composing a poem, exactly one hundred lines long, in which she attempts to reconcile Protestant and Catholic doctrines – which at the time was very much the subject of public debate. Her poem was published in 1574 in the first edition of the *Consolationes* by John Leslie. Upon the Bishop's release from prison Mary composed a short poem for Leslie entitled 'To the Bishop of Ross, After His Deliverance from Prison' originally in French; the second stanza reads:

Give thanks for his heavenly clemency
Which is the source and cause of all accord,
And with a humble heart pray to the Lord
That in my long ordeal he pity me.

The poem later appeared in a French edition of Leslie's works published in 1595. Mary's religious views in her first poem to Leslie show considerable tolerance, so unlike her implacable critic John Knox. He died after a lingering illness in November 1572, and, bitter to the end, he had urged Elizabeth 'to apply the axe to the root of evil', for 'until…the Scottish Queen was dead, neither her [Elizabeth's] crown nor her life would be in security'.

Above and opposite
George Buchanan, 1581, after a painting by Arnold Bronckorst. The multi-faceted Buchanan was a respected scholar, a poet, a leader in Scotland's Reformation and a historian. His verses written in France and Scotland had praised the Queen of Scots, before he fashioned his words into virulent accusations against her.

Events in Scotland continued to worsen with regard to Mary, and ultimately turned decisively against her. On 5 September 1571, the Earl of Lennox was murdered, and was succeeded as Regent by Lord Erskine, who had been made Earl of Mar after James Stewart had forfeited the title. Once a supporter of the Queen, he had entirely turned against her, believing that Mary's execution was 'the only salve for the cures of this commonwealth'. Mar died on 29 October 1572, and the Regency then passed to Mary's long-standing foe and persecutor of Catholics, the Earl of Morton. William Maitland, Mary's former adviser, who had transferred his allegiance from the Queen to Lord James, Earl of Moray, later abandoned Moray and switched back to Mary's cause. Together Maitland and Kirkcaldy of Grange (who had also abandoned then returned to Mary's side) held out for the Queen at Edinburgh Castle, thwarting attacks until they were at last overcome on 29 May 1573. Kirkcaldy was hung, and Maitland, who had long been gravely ill, was rumoured to have committed suicide. Shortly after his death the castle was surrendered. Shrewsbury had the task of telling Mary of Maitland's death. He later reported: 'She makes little show of grief, and yet it nips her near.'

Back in June 1570 Mary had made her first acquaintance with Sheffield Castle, the solid fortress tucked into a valley. It had been rebuilt in 1383, then altered and extended countless times before the Queen of Scots became an inmate. Occasionally, she was moved to the hunting lodge on the hill, about a mile's distance from the castle. The lodge, which had once housed Cardinal Wolsey, was expanded and made elegant enough to be called Sheffield Manor. The removal of Mary's household from one to the other generally occurred when the castle needed cleaning. At Sheffield, more than anywhere else, Mary and her little court were forced to endure long periods of the strictest confinement. No riding out, no hawking, no promenading in the park or gardens. The Queen was to remain in her chambers, taking air only along the leads (walkway) of the roof. Eventually, exercise was extended to a gentle perambulation around the great dining hall and then the courtyard. There were times when these conditions would become more relaxed, but then new political dramas would again tighten Mary's restrictions. News from France brought more distress, when Mary learned of her uncle, the Cardinal of Lorraine's death in 1574. From Sheffield she wrote:

Though I cannot, at the first moment, command my feelings, or prevent the tears that will flow, yet my long adversity has taught me to hope for consolation for all my afflictions in a better life. Alas! I am a prisoner, and God has bereft me of one of those persons whom I most loved; what shall I say more?

Other dramas were financial. Mary's revenues from France were not forthcoming, and the Earl of Shrewsbury, too, was feeling the burden of maintaining the Queen. Although he was a wealthy man, there were years when the cost of keeping his prisoner put his annual losses at nearly ten thousand pounds, an awesome sum. He wrote begging letters to Elizabeth, but she ignored his cries for money, or begrudgingly sent an inadequate amount.

Mary continued to resort to her needle for working out her frustrations. She would also make kind overtures to Elizabeth, possibly with the hope of obtaining some relaxation in her constrained captivity. One of her more ambitious projects, was a skirt of crimson satin, embroidered with vividly coloured lilies, roses, honeysuckle, pinks and daffodils, arranged to form triangular shapes, rising to points formed by thistles. Mary sent the skirt to Elizabeth 'as evidence of the honour I bear her, and the desire I have to employ myself in anything agreeable to her'. As a New Year's gift in 1575 Mary made for her cousin a piece of lacis (a design made by darning on net), which was presented to Elizabeth by the French Ambassador along with effusions of flattery. And to adorn the Queen of England's distinctive red-gold hair, Mary sent her three *coyfures de nuit* (nightcaps or head-dresses).

Norfolk's execution had caused the Queen of Scots many tears, also 'great contemplation, fasting and prayer'. Nevertheless another plan emerged for her marriage; this time the Pope suggested a union between the Queen of Scots and Philip of Spain's handsome illegitimate brother, Don John of Austria. The wedding was to be preceded by a Spanish-led invasion of England. But Mary's hopes were again dissolved when Don John died of typhoid in October 1578.

As the years of her confinement increased so too did devotion to her religion and acts of piety. One of Mary's most precious possessions was an *Agnus Dei* of rock crystal engraved with the Passion, which had been given to her by Francis before their marriage; a poignant reminder of happier times at the French court when she had been a triple Queen, and the most dazzling young woman in Europe. In prison, Mary began to compose verses in the margins of her Book of Hours, sometimes the handwriting is unsteady, at other times it is clear. In 1579 she wrote:

My Fame, unlike in former days,
No longer flies from coast to coast.
And what confines her wandering ways?
The very thing she loves the most.

But then, in prison the only fame or reputation she desired, was for piety.
In 1582 she writes:

To pray, weep, suffer, be a friend to everyone
Are the only cures for the many woes I see.

Twice each day Mary and her little Catholic flock gathered in the dining-room to hear sermons (and surreptitiously the Mass) in French, and occasionally in Latin — so Elizabeth's spies reported.

1583 was a complicated year for Mary. Poetry, that so liberally swathed every occasion, but also the pure speech of Mary's heart, for once failed the Queen. Her beloved tutor, mentor, friend Pierre de Ronsard, now old and in failing health, dedicated a volume of verse to the Queen of Scots and sent her a sonnet. In response she made several attempts to compose a work worthy of the man who had taught her the craft, but not satisfied with her efforts, she left the poem unfinished:

Ronsard, si ton bon coeur de gentille nature
Te ment pour le respect d'un peu de nourriture
Qu'en tes plus jeunes ans tu as reçue d'un roi
De ton roi allié et de sa même loi,

Je dirai non couard ni taché d'avarice
Mais digne à mon avis du nom du brave prince.
Hélas! Ne scrivez pas ses faits ni ses grandeurs
Mais qu'il a bien voulu empêcher des malheurs.

Ronsard, if your good, gentle-natured heart
Deceives you for some sustenance at court,
Which you received when young from a king's hand
In harmony with the royal command,

No stain of greed or cowardice shall I proclaim
But that you merit a brave prince's name.
Alas! Tell not of the heights to which he rose.
But that he'd fain be succoured in his woes.

In the place of her poem she sent Ronsard two thousand crowns and a silver vase which bore the device of Pegasus drinking at the fountain of Castalia on Mount Parnassus, inscribed *'A Ronsard – l'Apollo à la source des Muses'*.

In 1583 Mary also lost the companionship of Mary Seton, her faithful friend of thirty-five years, who alone among the four Maries had remained single. She was

Above and opposite
Sir Francis Walsingham, attributed to John de Critz the Elder, *c.* 1585. For over twenty years Walsingham served Queen Elizabeth most loyally. He helped unravel the Ridolfi plot, and was the mastermind of Elizabeth's secret service. A Protestant fanatic, Walsingham was convinced that England's safety depended on the removal of the Queen of Scots, whom he called 'the devilish woman'; he was ingenious in ensnaring her, and bringing about her downfall.

allowed to retire owing to ill-health, and spent the rest of her days in the convent of St-Pierre-les-Dames at Reims, of which Mary's aunt, Renée de Guise was abbess. On a happier note, King James's attitude towards his mother appeared to be softening, for he began, but never carried through, negotiations with the Duke of Guise and the Pope for Mary's release. The Regent Morton, after falling from power, had been executed in 1581 for his complicity in Darnley's murder. Ironically, the instrument of execution was the 'Maiden', an early form of the guillotine, which Morton had himself introduced into Scotland. The young King had, in 1578, nominally taken control of the government before he was twelve, and by 1583 the rule of the country was his. In the same year Mary proposed an association with her son whereby they would jointly rule Scotland. For a time James went along with the idea, but in 1586 he signed an Anglo-Scottish agreement in which Elizabeth would name James as her successor and grant him a pension, in exchange for peace between England and Scotland; a prospect that was considerably more attractive.

Mary continued with increasing fervour to seek an end to her captivity, and also support in reclaiming her throne, redoubling her pleas to the continent. More significantly she saw herself as the head of the Catholic cause in Britain, and in Europe she was becoming thought of as a living martyr for the 'true faith'. A network of intrigue spread out from the Queen, with agents and double agents, coded dispatches, and with brewers, pantrymen, glovers, a musician or a bookseller acting as couriers. Mary herself gave instructions on the preparation of invisible ink to be used on paper or cloth, and suggested that the best place for concealing secret messages was in the hollowed-out cork heel of a shoe.

In 1583 Henry, 3rd Duke of Guise, was involved in a plot to liberate Mary, which entailed invading England with foreign troops, supported by armies from Scotland and northern England. The messenger, Francis Throckmorton, cousin to English envoy Sir Nicholas Throckmorton, was betrayed by a double agent and arrested. Before his execution Throckmorton implicated Philip II of Spain and the Duke of Guise. This resulted in the expulsion from England of the Spanish Ambassador, Bernardino de Mendoza, and diplomatic relations between the two countries ceased. Throckmorton's confession also implicated Mary. She was taken to Wingfield Manor and placed under the charge of the elderly Sir Ralph Sadler; he had once admired the infant Queen Mary, 'as goodly a child' as he had ever seen. The change of custodian occurred in the wake of the Shrewsbury scandal in which the Earl was accused by his wife of having an affair with the Queen of Scots. Mary's stay at Wingfield was cut short, and she was moved to Tutbury Castle with its foul middens for the harshest regime of her captivity. Mary's jailer was now Sir Amyas Paulet,

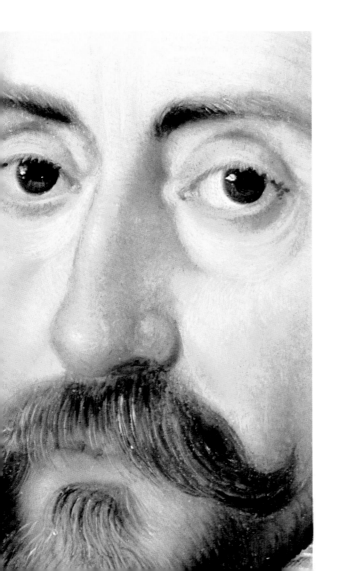

a dour fanatical Puritan who hated everything about the Queen of Scots, which he demonstrated by tearing down the royal cloth of estate beneath which she sat. Nor would he permit her to go outside, since giving alms to the poor she 'hath won the hearts of the people that habit about those places where she hath heretofore lain'. Here was one man immune to her charms, 'one of the strangest and most *farouche* [unsociable] men she had ever known'. Contact with the outside world was prohibited, but word of the Queen's conditions reached the French court, and Elizabeth was pressured into having Mary transferred to more tolerable surroundings. In December 1585 she was taken – quietly, under heavy guard, without fanfare – to Chartley Hall, a moated manor house some twelve miles from Tutbury. While she was still at Tutbury, Mary's health had again weakened, and soon after arriving at Chartley she lapsed into a decline. Her condition became so pitiable that even Paulet 'for charity's sake' was moved to comply with Mary's request to exchange her bed, 'stained and ill-flavoured' for a mattress of down. Mary's recovery was slow, her 'pain defluxions' persisting until the following spring.

Beyond the manor house, events edged the Queen of Scots ever closer to her destruction. Arising from the Throckmorton Plot, the English parliament passed the Act of Association whereby anyone implicated, even unknowingly, in a plot against Elizabeth would be put to death. In 1585 Mary avoided retribution by revealing to Elizabeth a plot against her involving one Dr Parry. However, Francis Walsingham, a mastermind of intrigue appointed to root out Catholic plotters, now became even more determined upon his particular quarry – Mary. He had laid the trap that ensnared Francis Throckmorton, and, while Mary lay physically and emotionally vulnerable at Chartley Hall, he devised a plan to bring her to the scaffold. On 16 January a brewer smuggled a packet of letters into Chartley Hall and into Mary's hands. The brewer then told her that by the same means, a leather pouch concealed in a beer-barrel, he could take Mary's dispatches out of Chartley. The Queen dictated letters to her French secretary, Claud Nau, and these, in cipher, were given to the brewer, who then passed them to Walsingham's agent. The dispatches were decoded, read, resealed and eventually sent to their original destination. Once this procedure was working satisfactorily, Walsingham eased into place an assassination plot. It centred upon Sir Anthony Babington, a Catholic who had been a page in Lord Shrewsbury's service. Babington believed that Mary had been unjustly imprisoned, a martyr to her faith, persecuted by Scottish and English Protestants alike. He became the leader of a group of young Catholic idealists with the aim of rescuing Mary and installing her on the throne of England. Walsingham, through his agents, learned of Babington's scheme and put together his own plan, adroitly interlocking the two. Mary learned of Babington's conspiracy in June 1586 and wrote to 'Master Anthony Babington' on 25 June. Her letter, via Walsingham, was received by Sir Anthony on 6 July. The young man foolishly responded by relaying every detail of the plot, including the fact that the assassination of Elizabeth was to be carried out by six of his closest comrades, whereupon one hundred able and loyal men would rescue Mary from Chartley. Mary received Babington's letter on 14 July, and was thus implicated in the plot. She then abandoned all caution, and, against the advice of Nau, her secretary, responded to Babington by endorsing the plot. The Queen of Scots had now put herself entirely in Walsingham's grasp. When Mary's letter, through the established mechanism, reached the English agent who deciphered it, he immediately understood what its outcome must be and drew a gallows on it before sending the letter on to Walsingham. As a final touch, a forged postcript was added asking Babington to supply the names of the six assassins. Two weeks later the bells of London rang out in jubilation – a conspiracy to murder the Queen of England had been defeated.

In August, too, Mary received an unexpected invitation from Sir Amyas Paulet to join him for deer hunting. She 'arrayed herself suitably, hoping to meet some pleasant company', as did her secretary Nau, 'who had not forgotten to adorn himself'. The Queen and her ladies, together with her secretary, were joined by Gilbert Curle, Mary's Scottish secretary, her physician Dominique Bourgoing, Bastien Pagéz who carried her cloak, her groom Hannibal Stewart who carried the Queen's bows and arrows, along with another attendant Andrew Melville. The day was perfect as the company rode out, and, when Mary noticed that her jailer, Paulet, was trailing behind, remembering that he had recently been unwell, she kindly slowed her pace. Then in the distance she saw a group of horsemen rapidly advancing in her direction, and her heart suddenly leapt with joy, for she believed that Babington had arrived to rescue her. But the group's leader Sir Thomas Gorges, emissary to Elizabeth, approached her, dismounted, and addressed the Queen of Scots in a brisk officious manner:

Madame, the Queen my mistress finds it very strange that you, contrary to the pact and engagement made between you, should have conspired against her and her state, a thing which she could not have believed, had she not seen proofs of it with her own eyes and known it for certain.

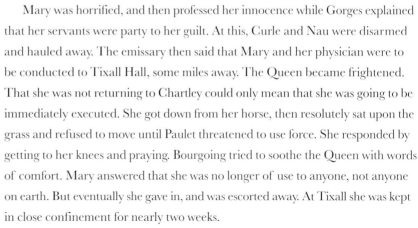

Mary was horrified, and then professed her innocence while Gorges explained that her servants were party to her guilt. At this, Curle and Nau were disarmed and hauled away. The emissary then said that Mary and her physician were to be conducted to Tixall Hall, some miles away. The Queen became frightened. That she was not returning to Chartley could only mean that she was going to be immediately executed. She got down from her horse, then resolutely sat upon the grass and refused to move until Paulet threatened to use force. She responded by getting to her knees and praying. Bourgoing tried to soothe the Queen with words of comfort. Mary answered that she was no longer of use to anyone, not anyone on earth. But eventually she gave in, and was escorted away. At Tixall she was kept in close confinement for nearly two weeks.

On 25 August Mary was returned to Chartley where she was distressed to discover that her personal effects had been ransacked, many of her valuables confiscated, including miniatures of the French royal family and of Francis II, though these were later returned. But there were two precious treasures that could never be taken from her, she proudly told Paulet – her royal blood, and her Catholic faith. During her absence from Chartley, Elizabeth Curle – her lady-in-waiting and wife of the Scottish secretary – had given birth to a daughter. Sir Amyas Paulet adamantly refused to allow the infant to be christened by a Catholic priest. Mary decided to baptize the child herself, and gave the baby the name Maria.

Babington, after four days of torture, confessed all, as did his friends. They were condemned and executed. Nau and Curle saved themselves by incriminating their mistress; Nau was eventually sent back to France with, according to some, £7,000 pounds in his pocket, while Curle had to remain in prison for a year. On 21 September Elizabeth's bold emissary Sir Thomas Gorges arrived at Chartley. Mary's servants were locked in their rooms while she was escorted away from the manor house. After four days' travel they arrived at the vast royal fortress, Fotheringhay Castle, near Peterborough, then used as a state prison. When told that the road leading up to the castle was called Perryho Lane, she cried, 'Perio! I perish!'

At Fotheringhay her mood became placid, at times almost cheerful, and more than ever she took great consolation in her religion. When Sir Amyas Paulet told Mary that the date for her trial had been fixed, she replied with decorum:

As a sinner I am truly conscious of having offended my Creator, and I beg Him to forgive me, but as Queen and Sovereign, I am aware of no fault or offence for which I have to render account to anyone below…. As therefore I could not offend; I do not wish for pardon. I do not seek it, nor would I accept it from anyone living.

When it had first been explained to Mary that she should appear at her trial, she refused; after all, it was most inappropriate:

I am myself a Queen, the daughter of a King, a stranger, and the true kinswoman of the Queen of England. I came to England on my cousin's promise of assistance against my enemies and rebel subjects and was at once imprisoned. I have thus remained for eighteen years, always ill-treated and suffering constant trials at the hands of Queen Elizabeth. I have several times offered to treat with the Queen with good and honest intentions and have often wished to speak with her. I have always been willing to do her service and give her pleasure, but I have always been prevented by my enemies. As an absolute Queen I cannot submit to orders, nor can I submit to the laws of the land without injury to myself, the King my son and all other Sovereign Princes.

Preceding pages, background

A grassy mound now marks the site of Fotheringhay Castle near Peterborough in Northamptonshire. When Mary's complicity in the Babington plot was discovered, she was brought to Fotheringhay (then used as a state prison) on 25 September 1586.

Opposite A contemporary sketch of the trial of Mary Queen of Scots, 15 and 16 October 1586, from an account by Robert Beale, Clerk to the Council. Mary is shown twice: entering the hall with two of her ladies; and then seated ('A'). The empty throne beneath the cloth-of-estate represented Queen Elizabeth. Mary protested that she had 'come into this kingdom under promise of…aid against my enemies, and not as a subject…instead of which I have been detained and imprisoned.'

But at length Mary realized that if she persisted in refusing to appear before them, her silence would be taken as proof of her guilt; she decided to answer to one charge alone, that she had plotted against the person of Elizabeth.

The trial of the Queen of Scots opened on 15 October 1586. At nine o'clock in the morning, Mary entered the Great Hall at Fotheringhay wearing a gown of black velvet, a white head-dress and white veil. One of her ladies, Renée de Beauregard, carried her train. The Queen leaned upon the arm of her physician, Dominique Bourgoing, for support – trouble with her legs had made her steps unsteady. Behind them walked Jacques Gervais, her surgeon; her apothecary Pierre Gorion; a page, Balthasar Huylly; and three more of her ladies, Gillis Mowbray, Elizabeth Curle and Jane Kennedy.

Years of ill health had prematurely aged Mary. There were times during the later years of her confinement when she was too lame to walk, and had to be moved in a litter, or carried to the edge of the garden pond (when she was permitted outdoors) to take pleasure in watching ducks skim across the water. She was no longer the lithe, delicate beauty of France, or the boyish adventurer who had fled from Scotland. At forty-three her waist had thickened, her face was fuller and double-chinned, but she still retained a commanding height and grace.

The Great Hall was packed with noble gentlemen all curious to see this legend in her own lifetime, and Mary looked them over in return, enquiring of a servant, who was this one, and what was the name of the gentleman over there, who was that who just spoke, and so on. Her former jailer, the Earl of Shrewsbury was there – reluctantly – among a commission of twenty-four peers and privy councillors, including William Cecil, Lord Burghley; Francis Walsingham; the Duke of Warwick, brother to one of Mary's former suitors, Robert Dudley, Earl of Leicester, who did

not attend the trial. Queen Elizabeth was represented in the Great Hall by a throne set upon a platform at the head of the room; over the throne hung the cloth of estate – a symbol of the Queen of England's sovereignty. 'I am a Queen by right of birth, and my place should be there!' Mary demanded. Instead she was escorted to a front corner of the hall and seated in a red velvet chair, without her cloth of estate; her feet rested on a red velvet cushion. 'I see ye have many lords and counsels but none for me', she said. Nor was she permitted witnesses, or secretaries, or even papers, and added to this she had difficulty with the language.

The Lord Chancellor opened by explaining the purpose of the proceedings. Mary replied as before that she had 'come into this kingdom under promise of assistance and aid, against my enemies, and not as a subject…instead of which I have been detained and imprisoned. I protest publicly that I am an independent sovereign….' The events leading up to Mary's arrest were put forward. The Queen calmly pointed out that she had never met Babington, had never 'trafficked' with him and knew nothing of the six men who had been his cohorts. She was shown copies of Babington's confession and the depositions of Curle and Nau. Mary would not concern herself with copies, and, as the originals could not be produced, the evidence for the prosecution lacked validity. She had emphatically not planned Elizabeth's death. 'Yes, I have earnestly wished for liberty', and have 'done my utmost to procure it for myself. In this I have acted from a very natural wish.' But can I be held 'responsible for the criminal projects of a few desperate men, which they planned without my knowledge or participation?' Mary knew full well that by the 1584 Act of Association she would be held responsible, a law that had also been framed to destroy her claims to the English throne. She gave a superb account of herself and used the assembly to speak to a wider audience delivering a heart-rending description of the travails and injustice of the past eighteen years of her life spent in captivity.

The questioning then moved on to old history. Mary pointed out that England had 'pretensions to suzerainty [lordship] over my predecessors the Kings of Scotland, I utterly deny and protest against them', nor 'will I fortify such a claim whereby I should dishonour those princes my ancestors as well as myself, and acknowledge them to have been traitors or rebels.' But as to her own power to rule: 'My advancing age and bodily weakness both prevent me from wishing to resume the reins of government.' She was then attacked for assuming the 'name and arms of England, and of having aspired to the Crown', as well as her failure to sign the Treaty of Edinburgh. Mary was prepared for this charge, and argued that while Elizabeth lived she had never intended to seize her throne, though to her mind there was never any 'scruple of conscience in desiring the second rank as being the legitimate and nearest heir'. At length she in turn put a charge to the prosecution, specifically, 'Monsieur de Walsingham' whom 'I am certain has tried to deprive me of my life and my son of his.' When Walsingham had an opportunity to protest, he insisted that his soul was 'free from malice', and made an eloquent denial of 'any secret dealings'. Mary was impressed, and 'she implored him to give no more credit to those who calumniated her than she gave to those who accused himself'.

There then ensued fresh discussions regarding secretaries Nau and Curle. The commissioners maintained that Mary had received 'certain letters' and had commanded her secretaries to reply to them. Mary replied:

If they have written concerning the enterprise, they have done it of themselves, and did not communicate it to me, and on this point I disavow them. Nau, as a servant of the King of France, may have undertaken things not according to my wishes…. As to Curle, if he has done anything suspicious, he has been compelled to do it by Nau…. And yet, I do not think either the one or the other would have forgotten himself so far.

There were further accusations, many of them trifling, amid increasing disorder and fury. The English commissioners attacked her like 'madmen', declaring the Queen to be guilty, while she remained, for the most part, composed.

The trial resumed the next day, and, as soon as the commissioners were seated and had removed their hats, Mary gave them a gentle upbraiding for their unruly behaviour. They then continued to go over old ground – Babington, Nau, Curle, and so on – 'The circumstances may be proved,' said Mary, 'but never the fact itself.' And the names Parry and Morgan were mentioned by the prosecution. Thomas Morgan

Above *Elizabeth I*, by or after Gower, 1588 (detail), known as the *Armada Portrait*. For Elizabeth, keeping Mary captive had been her best political option. Mary's execution, although it had become inevitable, was still a gamble, and Elizabeth signed the Queen of Scots' death warrant with great reluctance. However, after Mary's execution, and the weather-aided defeat of the Spanish Armada, sent by Philip II as a reprisal for Mary's death, the Queen of England enjoyed greater popularity and security than ever before.

was a double agent who had inveigled his way into Mary's service, and Dr Parry, indirectly employed by Mary, had worked as an *agent provocateur* for England, and was sacrificed in order to trap the Queen of Scots. The previous day Burghley had confronted Mary with the fact 'that Morgan professes to be your servant, and you have pensioned him, although you are well aware that he plotted the death of the Queen along with Parry'. Burghley now reiterated: 'At the very moment that the last treaty for your freedom was concluded, Parry, one of your servants, was secretly sent by Morgan to assassinate the Queen.' Mary was shocked that this should be hurled at her again; it was well known that when the Queen of Scots had learned of the Parry-Morgan plot in 1585 she had written to Elizabeth warning her of the danger. 'You are indeed my enemy,' Mary exclaimed. 'Yes, I am the enemy of the enemies of Queen Elizabeth,' responded Burghley. The examination then focused on Mary's letters to Spain. Burghley now accused Mary of negotiating to send her son to Spain, and of transferring to Philip II of Spain her 'pretended rights' to the English throne. 'I have no kingdom to confer, but I have a legal right in giving what belongs to me, and on this point I have to answer to no one, be it who it may.' When she was again reproached on her connection with Spain: 'It is not your affair to speak of matters concerning princes,' she replied. 'If the Spanish army had entered the country, could you have answered for the life of the Queen?' demanded Burghley. 'I do not know what were their intentions, nor am I bound to answer for them…. I desired nothing save my own deliverance.'

Her response continued in this vein, but, at the suggestion that she had instigated Catholic uprisings, Mary turned the discussion by pointing out that she had always been tolerant of Protestants:

[This] has been the cause of my ruin, for my subjects became proud and haughty, and abused my clemency; indeed, they now complain that they were never so well off as under my government…but for the Catholic cause and for God's quarrel I desire the deliverance of the first and the defence of the second. In short you will find that I have no other desire than the overthrow of Protestantism and the deliverance of myself and the afflicted Catholics for whom (as I have often said) I am ready to shed my blood.

Mary made a final request for a hearing before Elizabeth, and, before the proceedings were brought to a close, she added, 'I am ready and willing to give pleasure and do service to the Queen my good sister, and to employ myself for her and for the good of the kingdom in all that I can, as I love both.'

Then as Mary left the room, slowly passing the table where her accusers were seated, she paused, and addressed them: 'Gentlemen, you have shown little mercy in the exercise of your charge, and have treated me somewhat rudely, the more so

Below background

Mary's last letter was to her brother-in-law, Henry III of France: 'It is now almost twenty years since I…came to throw myself upon the mercy of this Queen, my cousin, where I have had my trials; and now…I am condemned to death by her and her government…. I despise death, and faithfully protest that I suffer it innocent of all crime even were I their subject….'

as I am one who has little knowledge of the laws of quibbling', and with a wry smile, 'but may God pardon you for it, and keep me from having to do with you all again.' With that, the Queen of Scots withdrew.

The assembly reconvened in the Star Chamber at Westminster where on 25 October they pronounced Mary guilty of 'compassing and imagining since June 1st diverse matters tending to the death and destruction of the Queen of England.'

Mary had to wait more than two months for the formal signing of her death warrant, yet the winter of 1586 and into 1587 was probably one of the most tranquil periods of her adult life. She filled her days with prayer, with reading history, enjoining the easily provoked Paulet in philosophical debates, and all the while administering cheer to her distraught household. Elizabeth finally signed the warrant on 1 February after much anguished soul-searching and gauging of the repercussions. She would later claim that she had signed the document by mistake.

During the following days Mary could hear the hammering of carpenters constructing her scaffold as she wrote her final letters. The Earl of Shrewsbury and two other commissioners arrived at Fotheringhay from London, and after dinner, accompanied by Paulet, they went to Mary and solemnly read out her death warrant. 'I thank you for such welcome news,' she said. 'You will do me a great good in withdrawing me from this world.' Mary then asked when she was to die. 'Tomorrow morning at eight o'clock,' replied Shrewsbury. Knowing that her death was inevitable, Mary had written earlier to Elizabeth with a final request — to be buried in France:

Because in Scotland the bodies of the Kings my ancestors have been insulted, and the churches pulled down and profaned, and because, suffering death in this country, I cannot have a place beside your predecessors who are also mine; and what is more important — because in our religion we much prize being buried in holy ground.

Mary's letter had not been answered, and she now anxiously inquired of Shrewsbury whether Elizabeth would permit her body to be buried in France. He replied that Elizabeth would not allow it. 'At least then', Mary continued, 'my requests in favour of my servants will be granted?' The commissioners had no instructions on that point, but anticipated that her wishes would be carried out.

In Mary's final correspondence she took great care to see that her friends and servants would be provided for, before dealing with larger issues. She urged Pope Sixtus V to be a 'true father' to her son, 'as St John the Evangelist was to the youth whom he withdrew from the company of robbers', to 'constrain him, and if it please you to call upon the Catholic King [Philip II] to assist you in what touches temporal matters, and especially that you two may together try to ally him in marriage'.

She was much 'indebted and obliged' to the Catholic King, 'being the only one who aided me with his money and advice in my needs'. To the Spanish Ambassador, Mendoza, Mary wrote:

As I have always known you to be zealous in God's cause, and interested in my welfare and my deliverance from captivity, I have likewise also always made you a sharer in all my intentions for the same cause, begging you to signify them to the King.... This bearer [Pierre Gorion] has promised me to relate to you how rigorously I have been treated by this people, and ill served by others, who I could wish had not so much shewn their fear of death in so just a quarrel – or their inordinate passions.... Nau has confessed all, Curle following his example; and all is thrown upon me. They threaten me if I do not ask for pardon, but I say, that as they have already destined me to death, they may proceed in their injustice.

To the Duke of Guise, 'whom I hold as dearest to me in the world', she bade '*adieu*':

All those of our house have been persecuted by this sect [Protestants]; for example, your good father, with whom I hope to be received by the mercy of the just Judge. I recommend to you then my poor servants, the discharge of my debts, and I beg you to have soon annual obit [memorial Mass] founded for my soul, not at your expense, but please make the necessary solicitations and give the orders which shall be required.

She then asked that he believe 'all that shall be said to you by a person who will give you a ruby ring from me'. Mary's last letter was written to the King of France, Henry III, on the eve of her death.

[They have] refused the desire I expressed that my body should, after my death, be removed to your kingdom, where I, your sister and former ally, had the honour to be Queen. Today after dinner it was announced to me that tomorrow, without fail, I must die like a criminal at seven o'clock in the morning [some copies of this letter say eight o'clock].... The bearer of this and his companions – chiefly subjects of yours – will testify to you of my deportment at this the last scene of my life. It remains only for me to implore you, as Most Christian King, my brother-in-law, friend and ally, who have done me so much honour as to love me and protest of your affection, that under this blow you show proof of your virtue in these matters by charitably aiding me in that which it is impossible for me to do without your assistance, namely, to reward my desolate attendants by giving them their salaries, and by having prayer made to God for a Queen who has been called Very Christian, and who dies a Catholic and destitute of all means.

When Shrewsbury, Paulet and the other commissioners left the room, Mary turned to her sorrowful attendants. 'Well, Jane Kennedy, did I not tell you this would

Opposite A portrait of James VI, dated 1586; artist unknown. At the time of his mother's execution he was twenty years of age, as depicted in this portrait. He had done nothing of significance to prevent Mary's death; his acceptance as Elizabeth I's heir for the English crown was dependent upon good relations with Queen Elizabeth. In Mary's will she left James elaborate bed hangings including a set in which she had embroidered her history, with devices of the house of Guise-Lorraine, the kings of France, and the symbols of her misfortune.

happen?… Is it not notorious that they have always feared that if I lived they would never be in safety regarding their religion?' She willingly accepted her fate and urged them to abandon their tears. Mary then spent some time in prayer with her ladies, after which she divided her money into several small purses to be delivered to her servants. After a hasty supper the Queen drank a toast to the welfare of her friends and attendants, and reminded them to remain constant to their faith. She repeated that Nau was the instigator of her death, and then forgave him. Mary then examined an inventory of her wardrobe and possessions, and distributed to her attendants what was left of her valuables, with instructions that certain other items be delivered to her son, to the King and Queen of France, Catherine de' Medici, her Guise cousins and other friends. To Bourgoing she gave 'two rings, two small silver boxes…two Lutes, her music-book bound in velvet, and the red hangings of her bed'. Elizabeth Curle received several items, including a gold and enamelled 'tablet' containing portraits of the Queen, Francis II and her son. Mary's maid, Renée Ralley, received a black velvet gown trimmed with ermine. Renée, it seems, was put in charge of the Queen's embroidery – scores of items, much of it left unfinished – and she received 'sowing silk and rawe silk of all colours'. Two of Mary's *tabourets*, or sewing cushions, were given to her apothecary, with 'all her confitures, succates, preserves, conserves and other medicinable drugges'. Jane Kennedy received 'furniture for a bed, of network and holland, not half finished', and was also to distribute 'at her discretion' all of Mary's linen: 'eight payre of sheets: 12 pilloberes: fyve dozen smockes, dyvers handkerchers, some wrought, some playne', along with coifs and veils, night rails and 'all her other pieces of common linen'. Other items that Mary had in her chambers at Fotheringhay included globes of the world, and what was, perhaps, her favourite tapestry – it depicted the victory gained by the French at Ravenna in 1512. But the most interesting of all her possessions was the set of bedhangings that she left to her twenty-year-old son, James VI, in which she had embroidered her history including the devices of the house of Guise and Lorraine, the kings of France, and the rest a tableau of her misfortune, rich with allegory, such as a cornucopia with the motto, '*Fortunae Comites*' – the companions of fortune – referring to the two Queens, Mary and Elizabeth. On another panel of the bedhangings Mary is depicted kneeling below a crucifix. In one of her last letters to Elizabeth, Mary wrote:

I implore you anew to permit me to send a jewel and a last adieu to my son, together with my blessing, of which he has been deprived, owing to what you informed me of his refusal to enter into a treaty in which I was included – by the unhappy advice of whom? This last point I leave to your conscience and favourable consideration.

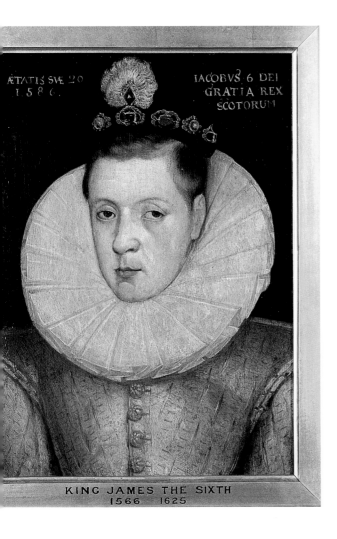

ÆTATIS SVÆ 20
1586.

IACOBVS 6 DEI
GRATIA REX
SCOTORUM

KING JAMES THE SIXTH
1566 – 1625

James did nothing to save his mother – his eyes were firmly fixed on the English crown, dependent on his good relations with Elizabeth.

Having distributed her belongings, Mary drew up her will, in which she ordered services for the repose of her soul at the cathedral of St Denis near Paris and at the church of St Pierre at Reims. Her debts were to be paid, and the remainder given to her servants. The principal executor of the Queen's will along with other important 'notes and papers' was Henry, 3rd Duke of Guise, the son of her beloved uncle, Francis. With her worldly affairs in order, she 'desired to employ the little time she had to live for the things of eternity'. It was two o'clock in the morning. 'In order to imitate our Lord, and to prepare for her last journey, the Queen had her feet washed.' Then she lay down on her bed, while her ladies, already clad in black mourning read to Mary from the pages of the lives of the saints. Mary asked Jane Kennedy, who was reading, to stop at the life of 'the good thief'. 'In truth, he was a great sinner,' said Mary, but 'not so great as I have been. I wish to take him for my patron.' Mary lay immovable for some hours seemingly in silent prayer. Jane Kennedy said that she appeared to be 'laughing with the angels'.

At six o'clock the Queen got up and dressed with great care in a skirt and bodice of black satin over a petticoat of russet-brown velvet. She wore a long mantle of black satin embroidered with gold and edged with fur. On her hair she wore a head-dress of white crape from which there flowed a long veil trimmed with lace. She then gave orders for her household to assemble, and distributed the little purses of money which she had put together the night before. Mary then embraced her friends and attendants, and, having made her good-byes, she passed into an antechamber, which had been arranged as an oratory, where, kneeling before the altar, she began to pray. Her physician, fearing for the Queen's strength, gave her a little bread and wine, and then she resumed her prayers until she was summoned.

Mary's servants 'took leave of her with cries and lamentations, some kissing her hands, some her feet, while others kissed her dress, and she, embracing them, was taken away'. Jane Kennedy and Elizabeth Curle were permitted to walk with her. The room chosen for the execution was the Great Hall where she had been tried, which was now hung entirely in black. At the upper end of the room a great fire blazed, and in front of the fire stood the scaffold, which was about twelve feet square and raised approximately two feet from the ground. The scaffold was covered in black serge, as were the stool and cushion that had been prepared for the Queen. On three sides of the scaffold was a balustrade, low enough so that the three hundred spectators crowding the room could get a good view. The fourth side of the scaffold was approached by two steps. The block itself was made of oak and covered in black

material. Next to the block stood the executioner and his assistant, they wore long gowns of black velvet with white aprons; black masks covered their faces. The executioner held a large axe, with a short handle 'like those with which they cut wood'. Stationed around the scaffold was a guard of halberdiers, while outside a large crowd surrounding the castle was kept under control by a troop of horsemen. When Mary arrived in the hall she held an ivory crucifix above her head, and advanced 'with great dignity'. At the scaffold she was unable to get up the steps without the assistance of Paulet. She thanked him, saying, 'This will be the last trouble I shall give you, and the most agreeable service you have ever rendered me'. Mary took her place on the stool, and asked for her Catholic Chaplain so that she could receive his last blessing; this was refused. The royal commission was read aloud, to which Mary listened 'attentively', but also as if her mind were elsewhere. At the conclusion of the reading of the sentence the hall reverberated with 'God save the Queen'. Lord Shrewsbury then approached Mary and said, 'Madame, you hear what we are commanded to do.'

'Do your duty,' said Mary steadily. She made the sign of the cross, and then, according to her servants' reports, spoke to the onlookers:

I was born a Queen, a sovereign princess, not subject to laws, a near relative of the Queen of England and her legitimate heir…wrongfully imprisoned…. I thank my God that He permitted that in this hour I die for my religion…. After my death it will be known and seen to what end those who are the authors of my being sent from this world have desired and procured my death. I accuse no one any more than I have done previously; my tongue shall do harm to no one.

The Protestant Dean of Peterborough, Dr Fletcher, now approached Mary and explained that 'he had come to her by his mistress's command in order to prepare her for death'. 'Peace, Mr Dean,' replied Mary calmly, 'I have nothing to do with you; I do not wish to hear you; you can be silent if you please, and go from hence.' Dr Fletcher sternly attempted to persuade her, but she would not have it. Lord Shrewsbury then 'proposed that as the Queen would not listen to the Dean's exhortation, they should all pray for her in common'. 'I thank you my lords,' said Mary, 'but I cannot pray with you, because we are not of the same religion. Pray if you wish, I will pray also.' The Queen then slid upon her knees and prayed aloud in Latin, now and then striking her breast with the crucifix during particularly fervent moments in her prayer. At length she rose and reseated herself. Lords Kent and Shrewsbury then approached the Queen, 'and asked her if she had no secret matter to reveal to them, but she replied that she had said enough, and was not

Opposite Contemporary sketch of the execution of the Queen of Scots in the Great Hall at Fotheringhay. Mary is shown three times: entering the room with Jane Kennedy and Elizabeth Curle; on the scaffold attended by the two ladies; and finally on the block. The Earls of Shrewsbury and Kent are seated on the platform, while the Protestant Dean of Peterborough (standing) attempts to prepare Mary for death. Seated on the far side of the scaffold is Sir Amyas Paulet, Mary's last jailer.

Background Thistles growing on the site of Fotheringhay Castle. They are sometimes called 'Queen Mary's tears'. Fotheringhay was eventually demolished on the orders of Mary's son, who became James I of England in 1603. Thistles are said to have been specially planted in the grassy fields there in the 18th and 19th centuries.

disposed to say more'. Then, instinctively knowing that the time had come, she rose, 'and prepared herself calmly and cheerfully for death'. The executioner advanced to assist Mary in removing her outer garments, but she gently moved his hand aside, smiling, 'Let me do this; I understand this business better than you; I never had such a groom of the chamber.' She then removed her head-dress and called for Jane Kennedy and Elizabeth Curle for their assistance. The two ladies 'wept bitterly… and crossed themselves, praying in Latin,' but Mary 'chid them tenderly', saying, 'Do not weep any more, I am very happy to go from this world.'

Then, laying her crucifix upon the stool, one of the executioners took from her neck the *Agnus Dei*, which she, laying hands on it, gave to one of her women, and told the executioners that they 'should be answered in money for it'. The Queen now wore only her russet-brown petticoat and black satin bodice with long sleeves. Then with 'smiling countenance' she turned to her menservants who were standing upon a bench near the scaffold, and making the sign of the cross she 'bade them farewell' and asked that they 'pray for her until the last hour'. Mary then embraced her ladies and made the sign of the cross upon their foreheads.

'*Adieu*, for the last time. *Adieu, au revoir.*' Jane Kennedy bandaged the Queen's eyes with a white Corpus Christi cloth (the linen cloth on which the Host is placed for Communion), after which Mary 'desired' both ladies 'to go down from the scaffold'. The executioners fell on their knees at the Queen's feet, begging her, as was the custom, to forgive them for what they were about to do. 'I forgive you with all my heart for in this hour I hope you will bring an end to all my troubles.' She was conducted to the block and assisted to kneel down with her head low upon the block. '*In manus tuas Domine commendo,*' were her last words. 'At the third blow' the Queen of Scots was dead.

All who witnessed the execution were astonished by her calmness and regal dignity – that was the sustained impression. The final disquieting details might have stung the consciences of the Queen of Scots' accusers, and there might still be a residue of shame. More important to Mary was the fact that at the moment of her most difficult challenge, she was, in every particle, a great Queen.

IACOBI MAGNÆ BRITANIÆ REGIS MATER, A SVIS OPPRESSA AN.º DNI 1568 AVXILII SPE ET OPINIONE A COGNATA ELIZABETHA IN ANGLIA REGNANTE PMISSI EÒ DESCENDIT, IBIQVE CONTRA IVS GENTIVM ET PROMISSI FIDEM CAPTIVA RETENTA, POST CAPTI VITATIS AN.ⁿ 19, RELIGIONIS ERGO, EIVSDEM ELIZ PERFIDIA ET SENATVS ANGLICI CRVDELITATE, HORRENDA CAPITIS LATA SENTENTIA NECI TRADITVR, AC 12 CAL. MARTII 1587 IN AVDITO EXEMPLO A SERVILI ET ABIEC TO CARNIFICE TETRV N MOREM CA PITE TRVNCATA EST. ANNO ÆTATIS REGNIQVE 45

AVLA FODRINGHAMII,

IOANNA KENNETHIE. | ELIZABETHA CVRLE.

REGINAM SERENISS.ᴹᴬ REGVM FILIAM, VXOREM ET MATREM, ASTANTIBVS COMMISSARIIS ET MINISTRIS R. ELIZABETHÆ CARIFEX SECVRI PERGVTIT ATQ VNO ET ALTERO ICTV TRVCVLENTER SAVCIATÆ TERTIO EI CAPVT ABSCINDIT,

PRIMA QVOAD VIXIT COL SCOT. PARENS ET FVND.

SIC FVNESTVM ASCENDIT TABVLATVM REGINA QVONDAM GALLIARV ET SCOTIÆ FLORENTIS.ᴹᴬ INVICTO SED PIO ANIMO TYRANNIDEM EXPROBRAT ET PERFIDIAM. FIDEM CATOLICAM PROFITETVR, ROMANÆ ECCLESIÆ

Opposite Mary's rosary, which she took to her execution. This and her prayer book she bequeathed to the wife of Norfolk's son, Philip Howard.

Left Mary Queen of Scots, *The Blairs Memorial Portrait*, early 17th century. This was probably commissioned by Elizabeth Curle who with Jane Kennedy had assisted the Queen on the scaffold. It is now in the Blair Museum in Aberdeen. The top inscription tells of Mary's plight in England. The inscription at the bottom refers to Mary on the scaffold, where she 'plainly professes that she always was, and is, a daughter of the Roman Church'. In the inscription below the scene of her execution on the left, Mary is described as 'the daughter, wife and mother of kings'. Mary's devoted ladies, Elizabeth Curle and Jane Kennedy, are shown on the right.

Below *The Martyred Queen of Scots*, engraving. Almost from the moment of her death Catholic apologists began to flood the continent with Marian martyrologies. The four crowns signify Scotland and France, and also England and Ireland which her supporters maintained Mary was entitled to rule.

Epilogue

The Wide Theatre of the World

No man ever saw her without love or will read her history without pity.

Brantôme, *Vie des Dames Illustres*, published in 1665.

Left *Francis II*, miniature by J. Simpson, *c.* 1850. As part of the cult of Mary Queen of Scots, artists painted events and people from her life.
Above *The Blairs Reliquary, c.* 1610–22, frames an earlier miniature done from life during Mary's captivity in England. Elizabeth Curle mentions in her will 'an ornament in gold containing a small portrait of Queen Mary of Scotland…given to me by her Majesty on the very morning that she was martyred'.

The story of Mary Stewart did not and does not end in the Great Hall at Fotheringhay on 8 February 1587. She had, in part, seen to that by urging her friends and servants to bear the message of her plight and the saintly fortitude with which she met her death. But even before they were able to deliver their eyewitness accounts, the Queen's supporters on the continent were hard at work producing rumoured and conjectured versions of all that had occurred at Fotheringhay. As long as Catholics battled to dominate Europe, and aspired to regain control of England and Scotland, Mary would remain the focus of propaganda. Her death was a blow to the Catholic/ Guise cause, making it all the more urgent for Mary's supporters to arouse sympathy for the Queen of Scots, anger towards Elizabeth and, ultimately, reprisals against England. The Queen of Scots was now heavily promoted as a martyr for her religion, and innocent of any involvement in plots against the English Queen. And after a period of mixed response in Europe, Philip II, with the aid of the Pope, sent the Spanish Armada to invade England in 1588. But the Armada was defeated, and Elizabeth came to enjoy greater security than ever.

Mary, however, would not be forgotten. After the political and religious issues became more settled, Mary continued – as she still does – to hold a prominent position in the world's imagination. The martyr becomes a tragedienne, a heroine and, later, the subject of romance. Not only in histories, novels and poetry, but also in drama, including Friedrich Schiller's tragedy *Maria Stuart* first produced in 1800; and in opera houses Donizetti's *Maria Stuarda* plays and replays. During the twentieth century the Queen of Scots graces the cinema screen, and in art Mary's image evolves from the mature martyred Queen to an ideal concept of beauty, while the events of her life are depicted in imaginative history paintings. Even portraits of individuals in Mary's life, such as Francis II, become the subject of artists trying

to capture, or recreate the Queen of Scots' era. Century upon century, the allure of Mary Stewart continued, and today – more than four hundred years after her death – she is still fascinating.

Of course Queen Elizabeth had foreseen that the execution of Mary would shock Europe, stimulating Catholics to view her as a martyr, if not more. And Mary herself had indicated something of the kind when she said to her judges in October 1586: 'Remember that the theatre of the world is wider than the realm of England.' Accordingly, everything stained with Mary's blood – the block, the scaffold, the black fabric, the floor of the Great Hall – everything was either scrubbed or burned so that nobody could dip a 'napkin' in the Queen's blood or snatch a scrap from the room to later treasure as a sacred relic. Shortly after the execution, Mary's weeping ladies and other attendants were taken from the Great Hall and locked in their rooms, while the castle gates were securely fastened. Every precaution was taken to prevent news from Fotheringhay reaching the outside world – with the exception of the official, English version of the proceedings.

Mary's body was put in the presence chamber and wrapped in the woollen cloth from her billiard table. At about four o'clock in the afternoon the body was stripped and dissected, whereupon it was discovered that the Queen, according to an English report, had actually been in reasonably good health in spite of her chronic ailments. The bodily organs, including the heart, were removed (again, for fear of creating relics) and buried secretly deep within Fotheringhay; the exact location was never revealed or discovered. Mary's body was then embalmed, wrapped in a waxed winding sheet, and, following Walsingham's instructions, encased in '900 weight' of lead. But Mary remained unburied for nearly six months, until – perhaps as an act of reparation – Elizabeth gave her victim a royal funeral in Peterborough Cathedral in Northamptonshire on 1 August 1587. Two days earlier, under cover of darkness, the Queen of Scots' body had been conducted by coach from

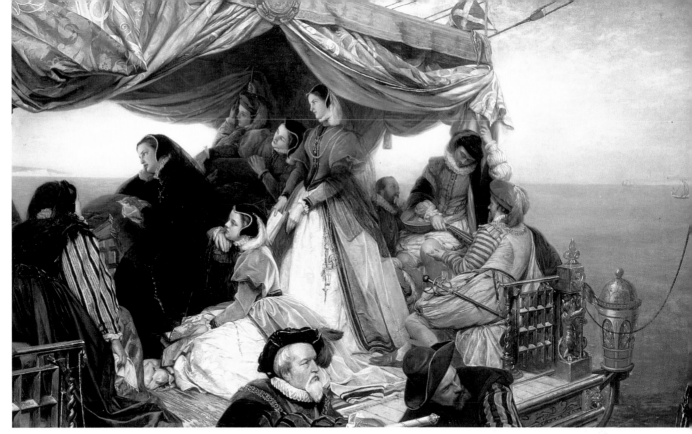

Mary Stuart's Farewell to France, by Henry Nelson O'Neil, 1862. In this painting, historical reality merges with romantic fiction. So eager were the artists – and writers – to respond to a market hungry for anything to do with Mary, that several versions of her departure from France appeared on canvas and in print. Even a poem, passed off as Mary's, but in fact the invention of an 18th-century journalist, was set to music by Béranger, a French song-writer: '*Adieu! te quitter c'est mourir*' ('In losing you I lose my life').

Fotheringhay, accompanied by Elizabeth's principal King of Arms, five heralds and forty horsemen. Behind the heralds walked Mary's servants, who were, with the exception of this excursion, kept imprisoned at Fotheringhay until the following October. The coach and its attendants reached Peterborough about two o'clock in the morning. At the door of the cathedral the body was received by the Bishop of Peterborough, 'and without bells or chanting', placed in a burial 'vault' in the south aisle, opposite the tomb of Henry VIII's first wife, Catherine of Aragon. Probably owing to its weight, the lead-encased coffin could not be carried through the cathedral during the funeral. The cathedral was draped with black 'six or seven yards high from the ground'. Every second pillar was similarly hung with black, and bore escutcheons displaying the arms of the Queen of Scots, or Francis II or Darnley impaled with the arms of Scotland; there was nothing connected with Bothwell.

At about eight o'clock in the morning on 1 August the designated chief mourner, the Countess of Bedford, 'bearing all the insignia' of Queen Elizabeth, whom she represented, entered the cathedral attended by earls from the neighbouring counties, and Lady St John carried the Countess's train. Next in the procession came the royal bier bearing an effigy in wax of the Queen of Scots. Escorting the bier was the Garter King of Arms followed by heralds, peers, peeresses, knights and ladies, all arrayed in 'deep mourning'. After these dignitaries came Mary's servants, visibly mourning. They were dressed as fittingly as possible, although all had stoutly refused

Above and opposite
*Mary Queen of Scots Being
Led to Execution*. This
painting by Laslett John
Pott was exhibited at the
Royal Academy in
London, when, according
to *The Art Journal* of 1 June
1871, 'Mr Pott, hitherto
all but unknown, vault[ed]
at one leap into fame.'
The work is perhaps the
most sensitive of the
history paintings associated
with the Queen of Scots:
here we see fear in Mary's
expression, but moreover,
dignity, while her gaze is
locked somewhere beyond
her immediate
surroundings. And Mary's
famous crucifix, quite
accurately depicted,
underscores
her martyrdom.

to wear the black mantles that Elizabeth had provided. The Queen of Scots' chaplain, De Préau, walked with the others, and it was observed – much to the discomfort of the English contingent – that he held aloft a crucifix. As the procession made its way down the main aisle the choir sang 'anthems', and, when the bier reached the place where the choristers stood, it was placed on a catafalque covered with black baize and decorated with the arms of Scotland and France, surmounted by a gilded imperial crown. The Protestant ceremony began with the Bishop of Lincoln preaching a sermon rejoicing the 'happy death of the high and mighty Princess Mary'; he side-stepped her tragic demise by adding, 'I have not much to say of her life or death, knowing little of the one, and not having assisted at the other.' Prayers followed, and 'at the offering, Lord Bedford advanced and placed before the altar the coat of mail, helm, sword, and shield which were afterwards hung over the grave'. At the conclusion of the funeral ceremony, the heralds in the usual tradition broke their staves of office and threw them into the 'grave'. Afterwards 'a most royal feast' was held in the Bishop's palace, with the English dignitaries seated in one room, and Mary's in another where they 'mingl[ed] many tears with their food and drink'.

Sixteen years later, after James VI of Scotland had ascended the English throne as James I, he sent to Peterborough an elaborate pall of velvet as a tribute to his mother, with the instructions that it was to be hung over her burial place. The general reaction of Scots to Mary's execution had been a mixture of horror and disgust, and Walsingham learned through his network of informers that placards had been raised in the streets of Edinburgh denouncing King James and England along with a broad clamouring for war; one agent sent Walsingham a twist of hemp in the form of a halter accompanied by the following anti-Elizabeth doggerel:

To Jezabel that English whore
Receive this Scottish chain
A presage of her great malheur
For murdering our Queen.

James himself was apparently stunned silent upon first receiving the news that his mother had been executed, although one courtier observed that in private James announced to his companions, 'Now I am sole King.'

In France the reaction to the death of their Dowager Queen was widespread sorrow, followed by rage, with crowds by the hundreds taking to the streets. More organized, but equally heartfelt, was the Requiem Mass held at the Cathedral of Notre Dame in Paris. The entire Valois court was present, including Henry III and Catherine de' Medici, along with the Guises young and old. The Archbishop of

Bourges delivered the sermon recalling another event, a glittering occasion that nearly thirty years earlier had also taken place in Notre Dame Cathedral – the marriage between the teenage Queen of Scots and Dauphin Francis:

Many of us saw in the place where we are now assembled to deplore her, this Queen on the day of her bridal, arrayed in her regal trappings, so covered in jewels that the sun himself shone not more brightly, so beautiful, so charming withal as never woman was. These walls were then hung with cloth of gold and precious tapestry; every space was filled with thrones and seats, crowded with princes and princesses, who came from all parts to share in the rejoicings. The place was overflowing with magnificence, splendid fêtes and masques; the streets with jousts and tournays. In short, it seemed as if our age had succeeded that day in surpassing the pomp of all past centuries combined. A little time has flowed on and it is all vanished like a cloud. Who would have believed that such a change could have befallen her who appeared then so triumphant, and that we should have seen her a prisoner who had restored prisoners to liberty; in poverty, who was accustomed to give so liberally to others; treated with contumely by those on whom she had conferred honours; and finally, the axe of a base executioner mangling the form of her who was doubly a Queen; that form which honoured the nuptial bed of a sovereign of France, falling dishonoured on a scaffold, and that beauty which had been one of the wonders of the world, faded in a dreary prison, and at last effaced by a piteous death? This place, where she was surrounded with splendour, is now hung with black for her. Instead of nuptial torches we have funeral tapers; in the place of songs of joy, we have sighs and groans; for clarions and hautboys, the tolling of the sad and dismal bell. Oh God, what a change! Oh vanity of human greatness, shall we never be convinced of your deceitfulness.... The marble, the bronze, the iron, are decomposed by the air or corroded by rust, but the remembrance of her bright example shall live eternally.

The Notre Dame funeral oration, originally in French, was widely circulated by Mary's supporters on the continent, and went into several printings. In 1725 it was reproduced in London in Samuel Jebb's documentary history, *De Vita et Rebus Gestis*, reappearing in the nineteenth century in Agnes Strickland's

Lives of the Queens of Scotland, and in *Marie Stuart: Son Procès et Son Exécution d'Après* by M. R. Chantelauze. During the twentieth century it reappears again in biographies, including Lady Antonia Fraser's highly successful *Mary Queen of Scots*. Chantelauze's work (1876) also included the 126-page journal, '*inédit*', of Mary's physician, Dominique Bourgoing. Though the journal, describing in detail the Queen's trial and execution, had been broadly distributed in manuscript form, it had not been previously published. In 1905 *The Tragedy of Fotheringhay* ,'founded' on Bourgoing's journal and other contemporary manuscripts, was published in Edinburgh; much of the previous chapter utilizes this work.

In 1612 King James had his mother's remains transferred from Peterborough to the burial place of English monarchs – Westminster Abbey – and entombed in a magnificent monument, the creation of Cornelius Cure, Master Mason of Works, and his son William. The edifice, carved in white marble, took six years to complete and is far more impressive than its neighbouring monument, that of Queen Elizabeth. The King's favourite, and brother of the ill-fated Duke of Norfolk, Henry Howard, Earl of Northampton, wrote a Latin inscription for the monument in which he extols Mary's virtues, deplores her misfortunes, and acknowledges her – while she lived – as the rightful heir to the crown of England. In early drafts of the epitaph Northampton had apparently intended to confirm the Queen's martyrdom and innocence. In the final inscription he praises Mary's courage and adherence to her faith. The Queen's unwarranted imprisonment – '*in custodia detenta fortiter et strenue (sed frustra)*' – is the result of evil slanders and harmful plots. The epitaph is signed '*H. N. Gemens*' (Henry Northampton, mourning).

Perhaps more interesting was the Latin inscription – or warning to all sovereigns – that Adam Blackwood, one of Mary's most energetic supporters, had written after the funeral of 1587 for the Queen's unmarked grave in Peterborough Cathedral:

Mary Queen of Scots, daughter of a king, widow of the King of France, cousin and next heir to the Queen of England, endowed with royal virtues and a royal mind (the right of Princes being oftentimes in vain implored) by barbarous and tyrannical cruelty, the ornament of our age, and truly Royal light is extinguished. By the same unrighteous judgment both Mary Queen of Scots with natural death, and all surviving kings (now made common persons) are punished with civil death. A strange and unusual kind of monument this is, wherein the living are included with the dead; for with the Sacred Ashes of the blessed Mary, know that the Majesty of all kings and princes lieth here violated and prostrated. And because regal secrecy doth enough and more admonish kings of their duty – traveller, I say no more.

ORAISON
FVNEBRE,
DE LA TRES-CHRE-
STIENNE, TRES-ILLVSTRE,
tres-constante, Marie Royne d'Escosse,
morte pour la Foy, le 18. Feburier, 1587.
par la cruauté des Anglois heretiques,
ennemys de Dieu.

*Sur le subiect & discours de celle mesme qui fut
faicte en Mars, à Nostre Dame de Paris, au
iour de ses obseques & seruice, & lors pronon-
cee par R. P. Messire Renauld de Beaulne,
Archeuesque de Bourges, Patriarche d' Aqui-
taine, Conseiller du Roy en son Conseil Priué,
& d'Estat.*

A PARIS,

Chez Guillaume Bichon, ruë S. Iacques,
à l'enseigne du Bichot.

M. D. LXXXVIII.

Opposite Portrait
of Mary on the joint
monument of Elizabeth
Curle and her sister-in-law,
Barbara Curle (born
Mowbray) who had also
been one of Mary's ladies-
in-waiting. The monument
was erected *c.* 1620 at the
Church of St Andrew, in
Antwerp, where they had
both ended their lives. This
round painting on copper,
was inserted in the top tier
of the monument. For
Elizabeth Curle, Barbara
Mowbray Curle, Jane
Kennedy and Mary's other
countless supporters and
admirers, the Queen of
Scots became canonized
in their hearts.
Left The funeral elegy
for the Queen of Scots,
Dowager Queen of France,
delivered by the Archbishop
of Bourges at the Cathedral
of Notre Dame in Paris,
printed in 1588. She is here
described as having 'died
for the Faith…by the cruel
hands of English heretics,
the enemies of God'.

FAMILY CONNECTIONS OF THE QUEEN OF SCOTS

Scotland

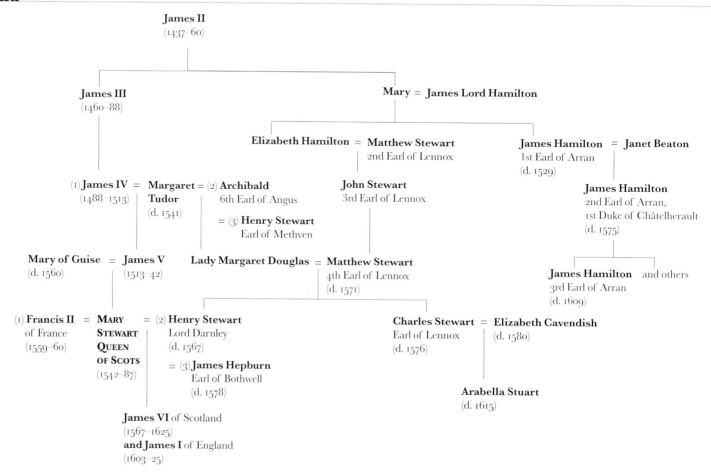

James II
(1437–60)

James III
(1460–88)

Mary = James Lord Hamilton

Elizabeth Hamilton = Matthew Stewart
2nd Earl of Lennox

James Hamilton = Janet Beaton
1st Earl of Arran
(d. 1529)

(1) James IV = Margaret = (2) Archibald
(1488–1513)   Tudor   6th Earl of Angus
              (d. 1541)
                         = (3) Henry Stewart
                               Earl of Methven

John Stewart
3rd Earl of Lennox

James Hamilton
2nd Earl of Arran,
1st Duke of Châtelherault
(d. 1575)

Mary of Guise = James V
(d. 1560)   (1513–42)

Lady Margaret Douglas = Matthew Stewart
                         4th Earl of Lennox
                         (d. 1571)

James Hamilton   and others
3rd Earl of Arran
(d. 1609)

(1) Francis II = MARY = (2) Henry Stewart
of France   STEWART   Lord Darnley
(1559–60)   QUEEN   (d. 1567)
                 OF SCOTS   = (3) James Hepburn
                 (1542–87)   Earl of Bothwell
                                  (d. 1578)

Charles Stewart = Elizabeth Cavendish
Earl of Lennox   (d. 1580)
(d. 1576)

Arabella Stuart
(d. 1615)

James VI of Scotland
(1567–1625)
and James I of England
(1603–25)

The House of Guise

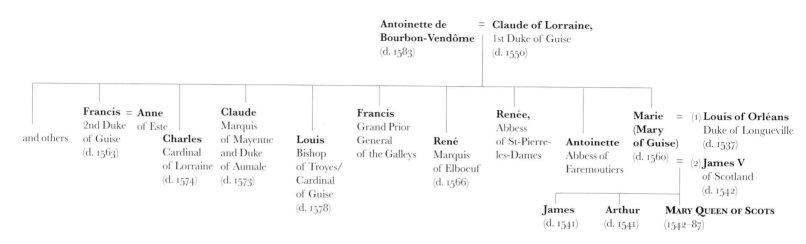

Antoinette de = Claude of Lorraine,
Bourbon-Vendôme   1st Duke of Guise
(d. 1583)   (d. 1550)

and others

Francis = Anne
2nd Duke of Este
of Guise
(d. 1563)

Charles
Cardinal
of Lorraine
(d. 1574)

Claude
Marquis
of Mayenne
and Duke
of Aumale
(d. 1573)

Louis
Bishop
of Troyes/
Cardinal
of Guise
(d. 1578)

Francis
Grand Prior
General
of the Galleys

René
Marquis
of Elboeuf
(d. 1566)

Renée,
Abbess
of St-Pierre-
les-Dames

Antoinette
Abbess of
Faremoutiers

Marie = (1) Louis of Orléans
(Mary   Duke of Longueville
of Guise)   (d. 1537)
(d. 1560)
      = (2) James V
            of Scotland
            (d. 1542)

James
(d. 1541)

Arthur
(d. 1541)

MARY QUEEN OF SCOTS
(1542–87)

England

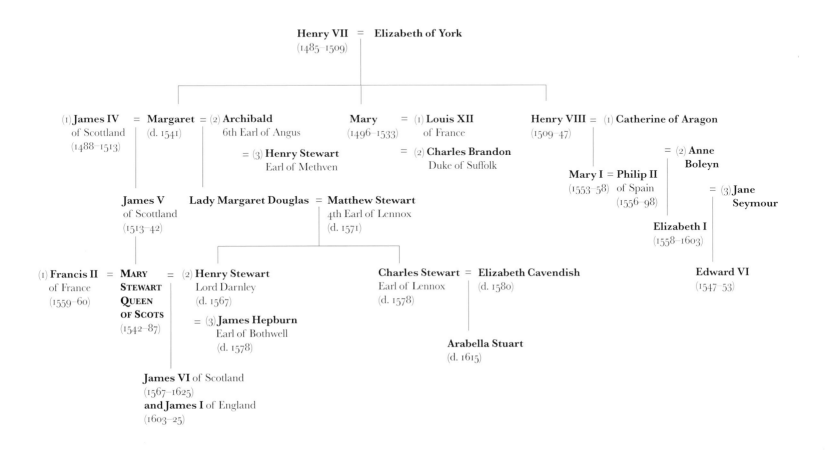

Henry VII = **Elizabeth of York**
(1485–1509)

(1) **James IV** = **Margaret** = (2) **Archibald**
of Scottland (d. 1541)   6th Earl of Angus
(1488–1513)

     = (3) **Henry Stewart**
     Earl of Methven

Mary = (1) **Louis XII**
(1496–1533)   of France

= (2) **Charles Brandon**
   Duke of Suffolk

Henry VIII = (1) **Catherine of Aragon**
(1509–47)

= (2) **Anne
Boleyn**

Mary I = **Philip II**
(1553–58)   of Spain
        (1556–98)

= (3) **Jane
Seymour**

James V
of Scottland
(1513–42)

Lady Margaret Douglas = **Matthew Stewart**
4th Earl of Lennox
(d. 1571)

Elizabeth I
(1558–1603)

(1) **Francis II** = **MARY**
of France   **STEWART**
(1559–60)   **QUEEN**
       OF SCOTS
       (1542–87)

= (2) **Henry Stewart**
Lord Darnley
(d. 1567)

= (3) **James Hepburn**
Earl of Bothwell
(d. 1578)

Charles Stewart = **Elizabeth Cavendish**
Earl of Lennox   (d. 1580)
(d. 1578)

Edward VI
(1547–53)

Arabella Stuart
(d. 1615)

James VI of Scotland
(1567–1625)
and James I of England
(1603–25)

France

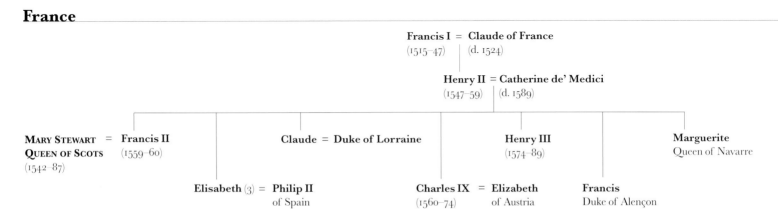

Francis I = **Claude of France**
(1515–47)   (d. 1524)

Henry II = **Catherine de' Medici**
(1547–59)   (d. 1589)

MARY STEWART = **Francis II**
QUEEN OF SCOTS   (1559–60)
(1542–87)

Claude = **Duke of Lorraine**

Henry III
(1574–89)

Marguerite
Queen of Navarre

Elisabeth (3) = **Philip II**
of Spain

Charles IX = **Elizabeth**
(1560–74)   of Austria

Francis
Duke of Alençon

Mary Queen of Scots: A Chronology

1503 Marriage of James Stewart, James IV of Scotland to Margaret Tudor, eldest daughter of Henry VII of England. Their marriage later gives Mary Stewart a claim to the English throne.

1538 Marriage of James Stewart, James V, the son of James IV and Margaret Tudor, to his second wife, Mary of Guise, the widowed Duchess of Longueville.

1542 8 December: Mary Stewart, daughter of James V and Mary of Guise, is born at Linlithgow.
14 December: James V dies and Mary Stewart becomes Queen of Scots.

1543 July: Treaties of Greenwich between Scotland and England, providing for the marriage of the young Queen of Scots to Prince Edward, son and heir of Henry VIII.
9 September: Coronation of the infant Mary Stewart at Stirling Castle.
15 December: Scotland and France reconfirm the Auld Alliance.

1544 19 January: Birth of the Dauphin, Francis, to Henry II and Catherine de' Medici of France. 'The Rough Wooing' continues with the English invasion of Scotland in retaliation for the Scots' alliance with France and their repudiation of the betrothal of Mary to Prince Edward.

1547 28 January: Henry VIII, King of England, dies and is succeeded by Edward VI.
31 March: Francis I, King of France, dies and is succeeded by Henry II.
10 September: The Battle of Pinkie Cleugh. The Scots are routed by the English.

1548 January: The Earl of Arran, Governor of Scotland, signs a contract with Henry II of France agreeing to summon the Scottish parliament in order to obtain its consent for the betrothal of Mary Queen of Scots to Henry II's son Francis, heir to the French throne. The terms were: Mary was to depart for France and strategic castles were to be handed over to the French. Parliament agreed to these conditions of French aid.
June: French troops recapture the strategically important town of Haddington.
7 July: Treaty of Haddington, providing formal agreement to the eventual marriage of the Queen of Scots to Dauphin Francis.
7 August: Five-year-old Mary Stewart sets sail for France, arriving on 15 August.

1550 Mary's mother, Mary of Guise, visits her seven-year-old daughter in France.

1553 6 July: Edward VI of England dies. He is succeeded by his half-sister Mary Tudor, a Catholic.

1554 Mary of Guise becomes Regent of Scotland.

1558 24 April: Mary Stewart and Francis are married. She is 15, he is 14.
17 November: Mary Tudor, Queen of England, dies and is succeeded by her half-sister, Elizabeth I, a Protestant. On the accession of Elizabeth, the Queen of Scots becomes heir-presumptive to the English throne. In France Mary is formally proclaimed Queen of England, Ireland and Scotland, and both Francis and Mary assume the royal arms of England in addition to those of France and Scotland.

1559 10 July: Henry II dies and is succeeded as King of France by Francis, Mary's husband, and Mary is now both Queen of Scots and Queen of France.

1560 27 February: Treaty of Berwick, by which English troops enter Scotland – a pact for Anglo-Scottish defence against France.
11 June: Death of Mary of Guise, Mary's mother and Regent of Scotland.
6 July: Treaty of Edinburgh, providing for the withdrawal of both English and French troops from Scotland. Mary and Francis are to give up the use of the English royal arms. Mary never ratified the Treaty which, in her view, meant renouncing her claim to the English throne.
August: In Scotland, the Lords of the Congregation, a group of powerful Protestant noblemen, succeed in pushing through parliament a series of Acts introducing a Protestant Confession of Faith. The authority of the Pope is abolished and the observances of Catholicism – including the Mass – are declared illegal.
5 December: Death of Francis II. Mary is a young widow, the Dowager Queen of France. Francis's brother becomes King Charles IX, with his mother Catherine de' Medici as Regent. Catherine now manoeuvres to remove power from the Guises.

1561 14 August: Mary Stewart leaves France for Scotland, arriving at Leith on 19 August.
4 September: The first of Mary Stewart's five confrontations with John Knox, in which they dispute over whether subjects should obey a monarch who is mistaken over religion.

1562 28 October: Mary Stewart's forces win the Battle of Corrichie against the rebel Earl of Huntly and his son Sir John Gordon.

1563 22 February: The execution of the young Frenchman and poet Pierre de Châtelard who had compromised the Queen.
15 March: Mary learns of the assassination of her uncle, Francis Duke of Guise, 'the Scarface'.

1564 Musician David Riccio is appointed French secretary to Mary.

1565 February: Henry Stewart, Lord Darnley, enters Scotland and joins Mary's court. A Catholic of the exiled Lennox family, Darnley, through his mother, also has a claim to the English throne.
29 July: Mary and Darnley are wed. She is 22 and he is 19. The Protestant nobles resent the marriage, particularly Mary's half-brother, Lord James, Earl of Moray, who is soon declared an outlaw.
August–October: 'The Chaseabout Raid' – Mary suppresses Lord James's rebellion.

1566 The Queen's relationship with Darnley deteriorates.
9 March: David Riccio is murdered in front of the Queen at Holyrood in Edinburgh. Darnley, with others, had signed a bond for the destruction of Riccio; Darnley's knife is used for the murder.
19 June: Mary gives birth to a son, Charles James, in Edinburgh Castle.
8–28 October: While staying in the Border town of Jedburgh for the assizes, Mary learns that the Earl of Bothwell lies wounded at Hermitage Castle. She rides 25 miles to visit him there, but on returning to Jedburgh falls dangerously ill.
November: Mary returns to Edinburgh via Craigmillar Castle, where she discusses the problem of Darnley with Bothwell and other advisers.
17 December: The baptism of Prince Charles James at Stirling Castle.

1567 10 February: Murder of Darnley at Kirk o' Field near the walls of Edinburgh.
February and March: Placards appear in Edinburgh charging Bothwell with Darnley's murder and implicating Mary.
April: About 6 miles from Edinburgh, Bothwell, with a small army, intercepts Mary and takes her to Dunbar Castle. It was later asserted that he raped her at Dunbar.
7 May: A document is issued from the Queen saying that she has neither been held captive nor raped.
15 May: Mary marries the Earl of Bothwell in a Protestant ceremony in Holyrood.
6 June: The couple flee to Borthwick Castle, then on to Dunbar where they raise an army to fight the lords who want to remove Mary from Bothwell's control.
15 June: Mary surrenders to her nobles at Carberry Hill and is taken to Edinburgh as a prisoner. Bothwell leaves Carberry unpursued and is outlawed.
17 June: Mary is imprisoned on the island of Lochleven.
June : The Queen's enemies seize the silver casket allegedly containing Mary's letters and sonnets to Bothwell. The 'Casket Letters' were later used to incriminate Mary in Darnley's murder.
24 July: The Queen of Scots is compelled to abdicate in favour of her infant son.

29 July: The coronation of the infant James VI takes place at Stirling.

12 August: Mary's half-brother, Lord James, is proclaimed Regent.

15 December: Lord James pushes through an Act of Parliament pronouncing that it is evident from Mary's letters and her marriage to Bothwell that she was party to the murder of Darnley.

1568 2 May: Mary escapes from Lochleven.

13 May: At Langside near Glasgow, Mary's supporters are defeated in battle and the Queen of Scots is forced to flee.

16 May: Mary embarks for the Cumbrian shore of England.

18 May: Mary is conducted to Carlisle Castle where she is received in protective custody.

15 July: Mary is moved to Bolton Castle in Yorkshire.

October: The Conference at York, an enquiry into Mary's guilt.

25 November: The enquiry is reconvened at Westminster. Mary is not allowed to appear. A proposal is made that Mary should wed the Duke of Norfolk. She embarks on an affectionate correspondence with him.

1569 January: Mary is transferred to the custody of George Talbot, Earl of Shrewsbury (a Protestant) at Tutbury Castle in Staffordshire. She is later moved to Shrewsbury's Wingfield Manor and Chatsworth in Derbyshire and Sheffield Castle in Yorkshire.

11 January: The enquiry into Mary's guilt ends with nothing proven, but Mary is kept a prisoner of the Queen of England.

The proposed union between the Queen of Scots and the Duke of Norfolk is backed by the Catholic Earls of northern England, and has the support of Spain. It is the northern earls' plan that this marriage should restore Catholicism in England, after which Elizabeth would be deposed. Mary disapproves of the rebellion. Norfolk is imprisoned in the Tower of London, and Mary is taken, temporarily, to Coventry.

November: The Northern Rebellion is quashed.

1570 August: Norfolk is released from the Tower.

1571 April: The Ridolfi Plot is uncovered. The intrigue involves Norfolk and others in an English uprising (with Mary's approval) to depose Elizabeth and place Mary on the English throne. Norfolk is re-arrested.

1572 January: Norfolk's trial.
June: Norfolk is executed.
November: John Knox dies.

1574 Charles IX dies and is succeeded as King of France by his brother, King Henry III.

1578 Bothwell dies in a Danish prison.

1583 November: The Throckmorton plot is uncovered – a plot for the invasion of England and Scotland

by Guise-led forces with the support of English and Scottish Catholics. Mary is implicated.

1584 November: The Act of Association is passed. Anyone implicated, even unknowingly, in a plot against Queen Elizabeth is to be put to death.

1586 14 July: The Babington Plot – Mary is implicated in this plot to murder Queen Elizabeth.

15 & 16 October: The Queen of Scots is tried for conspiracy to murder Elizabeth.

25 October: Mary is pronounced guilty in the Star Chamber at Westminster.

1587 1 February: Queen Elizabeth signs the warrant for Mary's death.

8 February: Mary Queen of Scots, aged 44, is executed at Fotheringhay Castle, Northamptonshire.

1 August: The funeral and interment of the Queen of Scots is held at Peterborough Cathedral.

October: Mary's attendants, including Dominique Bourgoing, Elizabeth Curle and Jane Kennedy, arrive in Paris.

1603 March: The death of Queen Elizabeth and the accession of Mary's son, James VI of Scotland, as James I of England.

1612 The Queen of Scots' remains are transferred to Westminster Abbey and honoured by a stately monument erected at King James's expense.

Select Bibliography and Sources

Bain, J., et al., (eds), *Calendar of State Papers 1547–1603*, Vols I–X, Edinburgh, 1898–1969

Bax, Clifford, (ed.), *The Silver Casket*, London, 1946

Bell, Robin, (trans. and ed.), *Bittersweet Within My Heart*, London, 1992

Bertière, Simone, *Les Reines de France au Temps des Valois*, Paris, 1994

Bingham, Madeleine, *Scotland under Mary Stuart, an Account of Everyday Life*, London, 1971

Blanchemain, Prosper, (ed.), *The Works of Ronsard*, Paris, 1857

Blunt, Anthony, *Art and Architecture in France 1500 to 1700*, Baltimore, and London, 1953

Bourdeille, Pierre de, Seigneur de Brantôme, *Vies des Femmes Illustres*, Paris, 1665

Bourdeille, Pierre de, Seigneur de Brantôme, (trans. H.M.), *The Lives of Gallant Ladies*, Vols I & II, 1924

Breslow, Marvin A., (ed.), *The Political Writings of John Knox*, London and Washington, 1985

Breeze, David, *A Queen's Progress*, HMSO, Edinburgh, 1987

Bryce, W. M., 'Voyage of Mary Queen of Scots in 1548', *English Historical Review*, Vol. XXII, 1907

Cameron, Euan, (ed.), *Early Modern Europe*, Oxford, 1999

Cave, Terence, *Ronsard the Poet*, London, 1973

Chatelauze, M. R., *Marie Stuart: Son Procès et Son Exécution d'après*, Paris, 1876

Cloulas, Ivan, *Cathérine de Médicis*, Paris, 1979

Cloulas, Ivan, *Diane de Poitiers*, Paris, 1997

—, *Henri II*, Paris, 1985

Cust, Lionel, *Authentic Portraits of Mary Queen of Scots*, Glasgow, 1906

Donaldson, Gordon, *All The Queen's Men*, London, 1983

Fawcett, Richard, *Stirling Castle*, Edinburgh, 1983

Fraser, Lady Antonia, *Mary Queen of Scots*, London, 1969

French Connections: Scotland and the Arts of France, HMSO, London 1985

Gatherer, W. A., (trans. and ed.), *The Tyrannous Reign of Mary Stewart by George Buchanan*, Edinburgh, 1958

Glendinning, Miles, et al., *A History of Scottish Architecture*, Edinburgh, 1996

Haynes, Alan, *Invisible Power: The Elizabethan Secret Services 1570–1603*, Stroud, 1992

Hume Brown, P., *Early Travellers in Scotland*, Edinburgh, 1981

Ireland, William, *Effusions of Love from Chatelar to Mary Queen of Scotland*, London, 1805

Jebb, Samuel, *De Vita & Rebus Gestis, Serenissimae Principis, Marie Scotorum Reginae Franciae Dotoriae*, 2 vols, London, 1725

Knecht, R. J., *Catherine de' Medici*, London and New York, 1998

—, *Renaissance Warrior and Patron: The Reign of Francis I*, Cambridge, 1994

Labanoff, Prince Alexander (trans. William Turnbull), *Letters of Mary Stewart*, London, 1845

—, *Lettres, Instructions et Mémoires de Marie Stuart*, London, 1844

Laclotte, Michel, et al., *L'École de Fontainebleau*, Paris, 1972

Ladurie, Emmanuel Le Roy, *The Royal French State 1460–1610*, Oxford, 1994

Lewis, Jane Elizabeth, *Mary Queen of Scots: Romance and Nation*, London and New York, 1998

—, *The Trial of Mary Queen of Scots*, Boston and New York, 1999

Lindsay, Maurice, *The Castles of Scotland*, London, 1986

Lynch, Michael, *Mary Stewart, Queen in Three Kingdoms*, Oxford, 1988

—, 'Queen Mary's Triumph: The Baptismal Celebrations at Stirling in December 1566', *The Scottish Historical Review*, Vol. LXIX, No. 187, April 1990

—, *Scotland: A New History*, London, 1991

McFarlane, I.D., *The Entry of Henry II into Paris, 16 June 1549*, Binghampton, N. Y., 1982

MacKay, James, *In My End is My Beginning: A Life of Mary Queen of Scots*, Edinburgh, 1999

The Maitland Club, *Adam Blackwood's History of Mary Queen of Scots …*, Glasgow, 1834

Mapstone, Sally, and Juliette Wood, (eds), *The Rose and the Thistle*, East Linton, 1998

Marshall, Rosalind K., *Mary of Guise*, London, 1977

—, *Mary Queen of Scots*, Edinburgh, 1986

Maxwell-Scott, Hon. Mrs, *The Tragedy of Fotheringhay, Founded on the Journal of D. Bourgoing… and an Unpublished MS Document*, Edinburgh, 1905

Melchior-Bonnet, Sabine, *L'Art de vivre au temps de Diane de Poitiers*, Paris, 1998

Merval, S. and L., *L'Entrée de Henri II Roi de France à Rouen…*, Rouen, 1868

Michel, Pierre, *La Renaissance*, Paris, 1989

Miller, Joyce, *A Wee Guide to Mary Queen of Scots*, Edinburgh, 1996

Neale, J. E., *Queen Elizabeth*, London, 1934

Phillips, James Emerson, *Images of a Queen: Mary Stuart in Sixteenth-Century Literature*, Berkeley and Los Angeles, 1964

Pitti, A. G., 'Richard Verstegan and Catholic Martyrologies of the Later Elizabethan Period', *Recusant History*, V, 1959–1960

Potié, Philippe, *Philibert de L'Orme*, Paris, 1996

Robertson, Joseph, (ed.), *Inventaires de la Royne Descosse, Douairière de France*, Bonnatyne Club, Edinburgh, 1863

—, *Inventories of the Jewels and Dresses of the Queen of Scots*, Edinburgh, 1843

Routh, C. R. N., (ed.), *Who's Who in Tudor England*, London, 1990

Seward, Desmond, *Prince of the Renaissance: The Life of François I*, London, 1973

Smailes, Helen, and Duncan Thomson, *The Queen's Image*, Edinburgh, 1987

Smout, T. C., (ed.), *Scotland and Europe*, Edinburgh, 1986

Stoddart, Jane T., *The Girlhood of Mary Queen of Scots*, London, 1908

Strickland, Agnes, *Life of Mary Queen of Scots*, Vols I & II, London, 1873

Strong, Sir Roy, *Art and Power: Renaissance Festivals 1450–1650*, Woodbridge, 1984

—, and Julia Trevelyan Oman, *Mary Queen of Scots*, London, 1972

Swain, Margaret, *The Needlework of Mary Queen of Scots*, London and New York, 1973

Teulet, A., (ed.), *Lettres de Marie Stuart*, Paris, 1859

Wallis, Alfred, (ed.), *The Works of François Rabelais*, Books I & II, London, 1891

Whyte, Ian D., *Scotland before the Industrial Revolution*, London and New York, 1995

Williams, Jane Hadley, (ed.), *Stewart Style 1513–1542*, East Linton, 1996

Wood, Marguerite, (ed.), 'Foreign Correspondence with Marie de Lorraine Queen of Scotland', *Balcarres Papers*, Vols I & II; *Scottish History Society*, 3rd series. Edinburgh, 1923 and 1925

Wormald, Jenny, *Court, Kirk and Community: Scotland 1470–1625*, London, 1981

—, *Mary Queen of Scots: A Study in Failure*, London, 1988

List of Places

A selection of the castles and galleries connected with the Queen of Scots and open to the public:

France

Château d'Amboise
BP 371
37403 Amboise
02 47 57 00 98

Château d'Anet
28260 Anet
02 37 41 90 07

Château de Blois
41000 Blois
02 54 90 33 33

Château de Chambord
41250 Chambord
02 54 50 40 00

Château de Chenonceau
37150 Chenonceaux
02 47 23 90 07

Château de Fontainebleau
77300 Fontainebleau
01 60 71 50 70

Château de Saint-Germain-en-Laye
78103 Saint-Germain-en-Laye
01 34 51 53 65

Musée du Louvre
75001 Paris
01 40 20 51 51

Scotland

Edinburgh Castle
Edinburgh
EH1 2NG
0131 225 9846

Falkland Palace
Falkland
Fife
KY15 7BU
01337 857397

The Palace of Holyroodhouse
Canongate
Edinburgh
EH8 8DX
0131 556 7371

Linlithgow Palace
Linlithgow
Lothian
EH49 7AL
01506 842896

Stirling Castle and Palace
Upper Castle Hill
Stirling
FK8 1EJ
01786 431316

Traquair House
Innerleithen
Peeblesshire
EH44 6PW
01896 830323

The Museum of Scotland
Chamber Street
Edinburgh
EH1 1JF
0131 225 7534

National Gallery of Scotland
The Mound
Edinburgh
EH2 2EL
0131 556 8921

Scottish National Portrait Gallery
Queen Street
Edinburgh
EH2 1JD
0131 556 8921

England

Carlisle Castle
Castle Way
Carlisle
Cumbria
CA3 8UR
01228 591922

Acknowledgments

Grateful ackowledgment is made to Robin Bell for his permission to use his translations from *Bittersweet Within My Heart*, Pavilion Books, London, 1992, (now sadly out of print), for the lines of poetry quoted on pages 118, 146, 147, 148, 188, 190 and 191. Grateful acknowledgment, too, to Gordon Donaldson, *Scottish Historical Documents*, 1970, for the translation of the Declaration of Arbroath, quoted on page 8.

I would like to pay tribute to my dear friend, Dr Elizabeth Jacobs, a great scholar and artist, and, though she is deeply missed, her views will always continue to guide me. I would also like to thank Ros Osinki and Lynne Sharpe for their ever-willing assistance; Dr Rosalind Marshall for kindly reading the text and offering suggestions; Dr Duncan Thomson for kindly reading the text, offering advice and suggestions; Professor Guy Aimé Patard for making the time to read the text, and for offering a French perspective as well as translations (particularly for the verse on page 117); Lady Scott, who has a magical ability to make things happen, and for her translations; Richard Scott and his team for their enthusiastic translations; Christine Grimaud and Brendon McKay, and Clarissa Cairns and Cecilia Brucciani for their translations. I would also like to thank François Avril, Conservateur en Chef of the Department of Manuscripts at the Bibliothèque Nationale, for his invaluable help and kindness in allowing me to read Mary's Latin exercises and other documents; the archivists of the National Library of Scotland; the archivists of the British Library; and the staff of the London Library. Special thanks also to Françoise Portelance and staff at the Ecole des Beaux-Arts; Catherine Maxwell Stuart for her kindness in allowing us to photograph at Traquair House; Lt Col. David Anderson and the staff of the Palace of Holyrood House for allowing us to photograph; Jean de Yturbe for his hospitality and kindness in allowing us to photograph at Anet; Bernard Voisin and the staff at Chenonceau; the staff of the Office Municipal in Villers-Cotterêts; also English Heritage; Historic Scotland; the National Trust for Scotland; and, as always, Alyce Nash for her guidance and advice.

Most of all, immeasurable gratitude to my husband, Sid, and to our family.

Illustration Credits

Bibliothèque Nationale de France, Paris: 26, 36, 36 background, 38, 40, 40–41 background, 41, 44 ,46–47 background, 62 background, 70, 72, 76, 77 background, 79 both, 105, 126, 208. Bibliothèque de Reims: 86, 87. Reproduced by permission of the Blairs Museum Trust: 207, 209 above right. By permission of the British Library, London: 24–25, 63, 197, 204. Château et Musées de Blois: 52. By kind permission of the Trustees of the Chatsworth Settlement © 1995 Chatsworth Photo Library: 176. Conseil Général de la Haute-Marne, Archives Départementales: 45. Photo Diatotale, Paris: 53 above. Crown Copyright: Reproduced Courtesy of Historic Scotland: 16. The Royal Collection, © 2001 Her Majesty Queen Elizabeth II: photo Stephen Chapman 20 & 21, 71 above, photo Stephen Chapman 82 & 83, photo Antonia Reeve 94, photo Antonia Reeve 107 bottom, 181 top. Photo Giraudon: 54. © Courtesy of the Duke of Hamilton, Lennoxlove House: 167. Photo Vanessa Harwood: 209 below. Reproduced by kind permission of the Baroness Herries: 184 above. Copyright IRPA–KIK, Bruxelles, Institut Royal du Patrimoine Artistique: 2, 214.

Kunsthistorisches Museum, Vienna: 51 bottom right. Kunstmuseum, Basel, photo Artothek/Hans Hinz: 61 left. Musée des Beaux-Arts de Rouen: photo Didier Tragin/Catherine Lancien: 80–81. © Photothèque des Musées de la Ville de Paris: photo Toumazet 33 left, photo R. Briant 77. © National Gallery, London: 51 centre left. National Gallery of Scotland, Edinburgh/The Bridgeman Art Library: 128–29. National Library of Scotland, Edinburgh: 37 left, 89, 97, 180 background, 200 & 201, 215. © The Trustees of the National Museums of Scotland 2001: 95, 103, 106 above, 106 centre above and below, 106 right, 107 centre, 107 top, 125. By courtesy of the National Portrait Gallery, London: 9, 104, 119, 160, 183 above right, 192 & 193, 199. National Trust for Scotland © NTS Photo Library: 110. National Trust Photographic Library: photo Hardwick Hall 122–23, 170 above & 171 left, photo Hawkley Studios 170 below & 171 right, photo Angelo Hornak 181 background, photo John Hammond 185, photo John Hammond 187. Reproduced by kind permission of His Grace the Duke of Norfolk: 106 (bottom). Reproduced by kind permission of His Grace the Duke of Norfolk and the Baroness Herries: 177, 206. Photo Nottingham Castle Museum/The Bridgeman Art Library: 212 & 213. The Ossolinski National Institute – The Lubomirski Museum in Wroclaw. Photo Andrzej Niedźwiecki: 32 left. Photo Phillips, International Fine Art Auctioneers/ Bridgeman Art Library: 210 & 211. Public Record Office Image Library, London: 142–43, 144, 152, 153. Photo Rotherham Arts Centre: 4–5. © Photo RMN: Gérard Blot 28 & 29 , 30, C. Jean 42 & 43, Michèle Bellot 46, Caroline Rose 48, Peter Willi 49 top, Lagiewski 49 centre, Gérard Blot 49 bottom, Lagiewski 50, 50 background, Jean Schorman 51 top left, Michèle Bellot 51 top right, C. Jean 51 centre right, J. G. Berizzi 51 bottom left, Caroline Rose 68, C. Jean/J. Schorman 69. Scottish National Portrait Gallery, Edinburgh: 84 & 85, 98, 99, 100 & 101, 120 & 121, 135, 178 & 179, 182, 183 below left, 184 below, 188 & 189. V&A Picture Library: 1, 37, 172, 173, 181 bottom. Courtesy of the Trustees of The William Salt Library, Stafford: 174–75 background. ©Worcester Art Museum, Worcester, Massachusetts, Museum Purchase: 61 right.

Index

Subheadings are broadly chronological, followed by more general topics in alphabetical order. The page numbers of illustrations are in italic.